THE CAREER ADVENTURER'S FIELDBOOK

Copyright © Stephen Coomber, Stuart Crainer & Des Dearlove, 2002

The right of Stephen Coomber, Stuart Crainer & Des Dearlove to be identified as the authors of this work has been asserted in accordance with the Copyright, Designs and Patents Act 1988

First published 2002 by
Capstone Publishing Limited (A Wiley Company)
8 Newtec Place
Magdalen Road
Oxford OX4 1RE
United Kingdom
www.capstoneideas.com

CIP catalogue records for this book are available from the British Library and the US Library of Congress

ISBN 1-84112-044-8

Designed and typeset by Baseline, Oxford, UK
Printed and bound by TJ International Ltd
This book is printed on acid-free paper

Substantial discounts on bulk quantities of Capstone books are available to corporations, professional associations and other organisations.

Please contact Capstone for more details on +44 (0)1865 798 623 or (fax) +44 (0)1865 240 941
or (e-mail) info@wiley-capstone.co.uk

"It is only in adventure that some people succeed in knowing themselves – in finding themselves."

André Gide

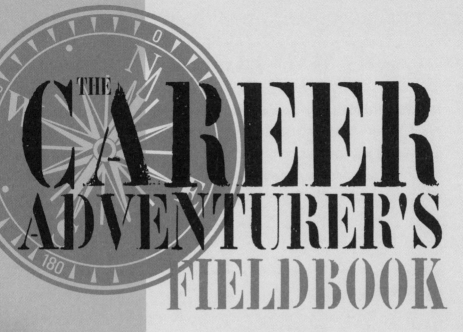

THE CAREER ADVENTURER'S FIELDBOOK

YOUR GUIDE TO CAREER SUCCESS

Stephen Coomber

Stuart Crainer

Des Dearlove

CAPSTONE

ACKNOWLEDGEMENTS

No book is a solo effort, least of all this one. We would like to thank the many people who helped us along the way. A huge thanks to: all those we interviewed who gave us both their time and a valuable insight into their own career adventures; to Steve Fitzgerald for rounding up a wonderful selection of interviewees Stateside; to Robert Sharrock and Jonathan Hill for giving us a psychologist's perspective; and of course to Mark, Richard and the gang at Capstone without whom this book would not have been possible.

INTERVIEWEES

LESLIE L. KOSSOFF

Title/Position: Chief Executive Officer
Company: Menton Productions LLC

SERENA WILSON

Title/Position: Middle Eastern belly dancing instructor; company owner
Company: Serena Studios, Serena's Closet
Location: New York
Website: www.serenastudios.com

JOHN BROOKS

Title/Position: Senior VP and Manager – Media Practice
Company: Silicon Valley Bank
Industry: Commercial Banking

JOYCE E. BARRIE

Title/Position: Founder, President, CFO – Chief Fun Officer
Company: Joymarc Enterprises, Inc.
Industries: Consulting/Coaching, Professional Speaker, Seminar Leader, TV & Radio Personality

BETTY BIANCONI

Title/Position: Food Stylist, Recipe Developer, and Food Editor
Company: In Good Taste… Creative Food Services
Location: Plainfield, New Jersey

Dr. PETER NEVILLE
Title/Position: Animal Behaviorist
Location: Salisbury, Wiltshire, UK
Website: www.pets.f9.co.uk

DONNA MARTIN
Title/Position: Senior Vice President, Human Resources
Company: Faulding Pharmaceuticals
Industry: Pharmaceuticals

JOHN REESE
Title/Position: Business Services Visionary

FIONA BAILEY
Title/Position: Director of Culture
Company: Safeway plc
Industries: Retail

FRANCO SAMA
Title/Position: Producer/Consultant
Company: Samaco Productions
Industry: Entertainment
Location: West Hollywood, CA

JEAN-FRANCOIS LOUMEAU
Title/Position: Director Business Development
Company: Faulding Pharmaceuticals Plc
Location: United Kingdom

KENNY ENDO
Title/Position: Taiko Artist
Company: Kendo Music
Industry: Music

FRANZ LANDSBERGER
Title/Position: VP Human Resources, Bioscience Division
Company: Baxter, Europe
Industry: Pharmaceuticals

JONATHAN HILL

Dr Jonathan Hill works both in his own psychology business, and at the Centre for Applied Psychology, at Leicester University in the UK, where he investigates employment interviewing policy and practice. Before that he was Research Director in the London office of the Gallup Organization.

MARK FASICK

Title/Position: Captain
Company: Pasadena City Fire Department, Pasadena, CA
Industry: City Services

JOHN BROOKS

Title/Position: Senior VP and Manager – Media Practice
Company: Silicon Valley Bank
Industry: Commercial Banking

ELAINE SOLOWAY

Title/Position: Owner
Company: Elaine Soloway Public Relations
Industry: Public Relations

JOHN HUDDY

Title/Position: Owner
Company: The Illustration Cupboard
Location: London
Website: www.illustrationcupboard.com

SUSI RICHARDS

Title/Position: Product Developer
Company: Safeway
Location: UK

HOWARD AND MARIKA STONE

Position/Title: Founders
Company: 2 Young 2 Retire
Location: Weehawken, NJ
Website: www.2young2retire.com

CONTENTS

Like life, a career is a journey.
Think of this book as your route map.

INTRODUCTION

Work has changed.

Employment has changed.

Careers have changed.

Consider this:

■

On average most people have been with their current employer for just 3.5 years.

■

Between the ages of 18 and 32, the average worker in the US has 8.6 different jobs.

■

In a recent survey 40 percent of interviewees said they would change their career straight away given the chance.

■

50 percent of Americans will be self-employed by the year 2010.

What do these statistics say to you? They tell us that the world of work and how we understand our role within it is undergoing a major shift. A typical career is no longer a long hard slog through the ranks of a single organization. It is a series of career adventures: a journey towards career enlightenment. It is a search for the perfect fit between you and your work.

The Career Adventurer's Fieldbook will help you navigate from one adventure to the next. Jammed full of tips, advice and information from experts and fellow adventurers will help you get the best out of your career journey.

Whatever point you have reached in your life, regardless of age or achievement, this book will help you fashion an uplifting, motivating and meaningful career. But before we get down to business, let's explore your motivation.

Why are you reading this? Yes, you. Why are you reading this book? Idle curiosity, perhaps? It was there with some other career books and you just sort of picked it up. Right? Wrong. You picked it up for a reason. You know you deserve more from your work.

The book shelves are full of career advice. *The Career Adventurer's Fieldbook* is different. Your eye was drawn to the title. The combination of the two words 'career' and 'adventure' struck a chord with you.

Deep down you'd like your career to be an adventure. This book can help you make it happen. But only if you are prepared to work at it.

> **Adventure**: An unusual and exciting experience. A daring enterprise; a hazardous activity. Enterprise (the spirit of adventure). A commercial speculation.
>
> **Adventurer/ adventuress**: A person who seeks adventure, esp. for personal gain or enjoyment. A financial speculator.

The fact that you have picked up this book indicates that something is lacking in your working life. There's something missing. You may be at the start of a career and want to accelerate through the early learning curves. Or perhaps you're bored with your current job and are ready for a new challenge. Maybe you want to make a clean break with the past and set off in a new career direction altogether. Or you may be approaching retirement age and want to do some of the things you have never quite got around to, while there's still time. Whatever your situation, you've come to the right place.

You see, what is odd, sad or downright weird, depending on your point of view, is that most people spend very little time thinking about what they really want from their working lives. They carry on doing what they are doing with hardly a second thought for what they could be doing. If they do think about it, they regard it as day-dreaming. You can't give up the day job, they reason. For most people, financial responsibilities mean this is true. But that doesn't mean you can't make the day job and the day-dream coincide, or at least overlap.

What do you want from your work? Money. OK, that's a given. Status, perhaps? A sense that you perform a useful role in society and enjoy a modicum of respect among your peers? It's not unreasonable. It is achievable.

The Career Adventurer's Fieldbook is exactly what its name suggests: a practical manual for people who see their career as an adventure. It is packed with information, techniques and advice from people who have dared to pursue their career aspirations. Some of them have reached the summit of those aspirations, while others are still striving. But what unites them all is their conviction that there should be more to working life than brain-numbing, soul-withering tedium.

If that's not you, then now is the time to stop reading. If you're not prepared to make your career into an adventure then please put this book down.

However if you are, then read on, because whether you are just starting out, changing direction or winding down; whether you are happy in your work or loathe every minute; whether you are a wage slave or a free agent; *The Career Adventurer's Fieldbook* can help you find the road to your vocational Valhalla.

Like life, a career is a journey. Think of this book as your route map. We can help you discover new career vistas, point out some of the obstacles, and help you overcome them. We can help you navigate through the changing landscape of work. But what we can't do is tell you what will constitute a satisfying career for you. No book can tell you that. You have to supply your own career compass. That's the deal.

BEFORE YOU START: SOME NOTES FOR THE CAREER ADVENTURER

Note 1. A career is not a job.

A 'career' is more than 'a job'. A job is an increasingly transient phenomenon. Most of us will do several different jobs during our lifetime. Some of us will do many jobs, not all necessarily in the same field. A career is the collective experience of a working life. A job is a part: a career is the sum of the parts.

There's a big distinction between having a job and having a career. As one career adventurer told us: "A job is where you look at the clock, leave promptly at five, and report to other people. A career is one where you fully own your responsibilities. Even though you may have other people that you answer to, you are clearly responsible for the results that you produce in your own niche in the organization. I never went after a job; I always went after a career."

Note 2. A career implies purpose.

If a boat drifts aimlessly on the seas before coming to rest can it be said to have undertaken a journey? If a person shifts from one job to the next without thought, consideration or planning, are they enjoying a career? Asked to describe his career, consultant and business author Fons Trompenaars told us: "It was muddling through with a purpose".

Trompenaars is typical of those who get on. The vast majority of the people doing the kind of job you want to do got there not by accident or luck, but by having a sense of purpose. They had a design, albeit an abstract design. They may say it was down to a lucky break, but that is like saying you fluked the US Masters golf championship with a hole in one. You have to be in it to win it.

Note 3. A career is an adventure.

Some careers are pure adventure. Consider the escapades of one famous leader. Born in 1874 he served as an officer in the 4th Hussars, saw military action in Cuba as reporter for *The Daily Graphic*, fought at Omudrman in the Sudan under Field Marshall Kitchener, resigned his commission and covered the South African war for *The Morning Post.* In South Africa he was captured and imprisoned by the Boers, escaped and made his way back to England. All before the age of 30.

The best was yet to come. Elected to Parliament in 1900 as a Conservative, he switched to the Liberal Party became President of the Board of Trade, Home Secretary and then First Lord of the Admiralty. During the First World War he fought on the front line in France and served as Secretary of State for War and for Air.

In and out of office and favour between the wars, in 1940 at the outset of the Second World War he became Prime Minister at the age of 66. During the War he inspired the allies to victory and helped negotiate the post-war structure of Europe at the Yalta Conference with President Roosevelt and Stalin, the Soviet Leader.

After the War the British people showed their gratitude by voting him out of office in the 1946 general election. He returned as Prime Minister for the final time from 1951 to his resignation in 1955. With his political career he combined a prestigious literary career that encompassed works such as *The Story of the Malakand Field Force* (1898), *The River War* (1899), *The World Crisis* (1923 - 29) and the ambitious *A History of the English-speaking Peoples* (4 vols, 1956 -58); work that was recognized by the award of the Nobel Prize for literature in 1953.

An extraordinary life. An extraordinary career. An extraordinary adventure.

You may have already guessed the identity of the man; it is of course Sir Winston Churchill. Not everyone's life can be as rich and rewarding as Churchill's. He was a career adventurer extraordinaire. But we can try.

We are all career adventurers.

What kind of adventure is down to you.

Note 4. Career adventurers need a career compass.

As the nature of work and careers change, so too do the practicalities. Even the things that stay the same are different. Now, if that's not confusing. Take resumes, they are still an integral part of the job application process, but now we send them electronically over the Internet. Where once people were grateful just to be employed, now they market themselves aggressively to prospective employers, confident that the balance of power lies with them rather than the employer.

In these changing times where does the career adventurer turn for guidance? How do the adventurers negotiate the stormy corporate seas, survive the storms of redundancy, cross the becalmed seas of career doubt and despondency, and navigate their way to the safe haven of retirement?

Use this book as your career compass to guide you. Wherever you are in your career, starting out, coasting to a halt, changing, you will find something of value here; a word of comfort, helpful advice, reassurance that you are not the only one struggling to find your way.

Note 5. It's up to you

So when you next cast an envious glance at someone who seems to have it all - the dream career, work-life balance, personal fulfillment - remember the chances are they made it happen for them.

You can too.

CAREER ADVENTURERS: THE AUTHORS

You are what you eat or in this case we are what we write. In the course of writing this book we, understandably, reflected on our own career adventures. What we discovered was a route map that was less a roman road, but more akin to crazy paving. We're still pursuing our personal career adventures, and who knows what destinations lie ahead, but here is a selection of some of the stops we've made along the way:

Mill worker (in a felt mill)

Research assistant

English teacher

Pig-farm labourer

Short-order line cook

Roadsweeper

Company history writer

Insurance underwriter

Supermarket shelf-stacker

Gas station attendant

Construction worker

Editorial assistant

Commissioning editor

Company director

Chairman

Chief editorial officer

Tree surgeon

Painter & decorator

Web designer

Person who fills in the holes that racehorses leave on a racetrack

Timeshare salesman

Model

Solicitor's assistant

Salesman at Burberry

Supermarket trolley collector

Researcher

Golf caddy

Author

Do you see a pattern emerging? No, nor do we. But, that's all part of the adventure.

Who in the world am I? Ah, that's the great puzzle.

Lewis Carroll, *Alice's Adventures in Wonderland*

ONE

THE GREAT ADVENTURE

WHY IT STARTS WITH YOU

Understanding and managing your career begins with self-knowledge:

Who are you?

How would you describe yourself?

What are you good at?

What do you value?

What do you love to do?

1. FIRST, THINK

So, here you are, poised to start the great adventure. The road lies gleaming before you and can take you anywhere. The only limit is your own imagination. It's your first day and you are understandably keen to get on. You want to make a start, to begin to make your career dream a reality. You want to get out there and start applying for jobs, knocking on recruiters' doors, networking and the like. Of course, you do. It's only natural. But wait. Relax. The first stage of the journey is a reflective one. The adventure begins inside your head.

Your career adventure starts with some simple questions. Three, in fact: Who am I? What am I good at? And what do I really want to do with my life?   This may seem an obvious starting point. So obvious that you may be tempted to miss them out altogether. But that would be a mistake. Many people, the vast majority, never really confront these issues. Even seemingly successful people, if you ask them, will tell you that they didn't think about what they really wanted from their careers. The world is full of chief executives who harbor secret ambitions to be soccer players; hairdressers who want to be brain surgeons; and accountants who yearn to be pilots, ballerinas, lumberjacks or something other than what they are.

This does not mean that they are unhappy with the way things have turned out, or that they are in the wrong careers. What it probably means is that they didn't explore the possibilities fully, or that they limited their own career horizons. Perhaps you are one of them. Perhaps that's why you are here, standing on this spot today. Maybe you are dissatisfied with your earlier career choices and want to change the road you are on. Or maybe you are just starting on your first career and don't want to make the same mistakes your parents made. Whatever your reasons, you have an opportunity to take stock. And take stock you must. It is only through reflection that you will identify the right road to take. The time you invest now will save you a lot of time and heartache later. This is where you will take your first compass reading.

This is not a one-off exercise. You will return to this place many times in the course of your career adventure. You will come here to get your bearings. Your priorities will change. You will still be you, but you will be a different you, changed by your experiences and circumstances. This is a special place. Somewhere you can come to think. Somewhere you can always return to and begin again. The most successful career adventurers come here often. They come to check their coordinates, to plan their next moves, to take stock of how far they have traveled. You, too, should never be afraid to return to this place.

Buy a drum

The first rules for the career adventurer:

- *Career adventurers listen to their own inner voice, march to their own drum beat.*

- *Career adventurers are flexible enough to change direction. They are not afraid of change.*

Know thyself and you will experience adventure. Ask Charles Handy. A former oil executive turned academic, Handy is now enjoying a glorious third career as a populist social philosopher. His own life experiences have provided many of the insights contained in his books and thinking about the world of work.

It took Handy many years to figure out what he really wanted to do. He worked for the oil company Shell International until 1972 when he left to teach at the London Business School. He wrote a number of best-selling textbooks, but first came to public attention with his 1987 book, *The Future of Work.* In this he set out the idea that companies would become 'cloverleaf' organizations (later called shamrock organizations), with a small core at the center of a system of 'leaves' made up of outsourced work, contractors, consultants and temporary workers. Revolutionary at the time, it turned out to be an accurate prediction of the future. Handy also coined the term 'portfolio career'.

"I spent the early part of my life trying hard to be someone else. At school I wanted to be a great athlete, at university an admired socialite, afterwards a businessman and, later, the head of a great institution. It did not take me long to discover that I was not destined to be successful in any of these guises, but that did not prevent me from trying, and being perpetually disappointed with myself. The problem was that in trying to be someone else I neglected to concentrate on the person I could be. That idea was too frightening to contemplate at the time. I was happier going along with the conventions of the time, measuring success in terms of money and position, climbing ladders which others placed in my way, collecting things and contacts rather than giving expression to my own beliefs and personality."

Handy sums up the way many people feel. Even those with successful careers can feel oddly ill at ease with themselves. Deep down they know that their professional persona is at odds with who they really are. Handy had the courage and the talents to do something about it. You can, too.

Handy's career is an inspiration for adventurers everywhere. It provides two lessons. The first lesson is that you have to be honest with yourself about what you really want to do. The second lesson is that it's never too late to change careers.

So why don't more people pursue their true career ambitions? There are three main reasons. First, most people don't actually know what they want to do. Like Handy, they either take the path that is laid before them, or follow the received wisdom of those around them. Second, those who do have an inkling of their true vocation don't know how to go about making it a reality. They don't do the work required to put it to the test. They may make a token effort in their youth, but they don't apply any serious discipline to matching their aspirations with their talents. So, although they may continue to harbor some lingering aspiration, most people settle for something else. It's all part of growing up, they reason. Or, they believe there's no future in it. Both points may be valid, but you owe it to yourself to consider all the possibilities.

This is linked to the third reason: fear of failure. Many people don't pursue their true career aspiration in case they fail. Rather than chase their dream, they settle for something that seems more attainable. Subconsciously they apply a perverse logic. It is better to fail at something that isn't what I really want, they reason, than to fail at something I really care about. This, of course, is nonsense. But, if they are really honest with themselves, a lot of people apply this sort of odd logic to their careers.

Honesty can be incredibly liberating. It is a necessary first step to a truly great career adventure. If you are really candid with yourself about what you hope to achieve then you can start to make it happen. You can begin to assemble the necessary tools and skills to make your journey. Some people may think, ah yes, but I've left it too late. They are wrong. It may be easier to dismiss their ambitions than to pack up their career kit bags and trek off into the unknown. No one said it would be easy. If it was, it wouldn't be an adventure.

It's never too late

For a career adventurer there is no such thing as too late.

History is littered with the stories of individuals who had a eureka moment that enabled them to change the career path they were on and to achieve their true ambition. A career adventurer may change direction many times.

Take the advertising executive David Ogilvy. Ogilvy eventually found the career in which he excelled. But he took a circuitous route. After Oxford University, the young Ogilvy made his way to Paris. There he worked in the kitchens of the Hotel Majestic. When he grew tired of France, he returned to England and pursued a career as an Aga cooker salesman. He dallied briefly with advertising at the agency Mather & Crowther, before heading for the United States. In the US, a job as a pollster for Dr George Gallup was followed by an improbable spell as a tobacco farmer with the Amish community in Lancaster County, Pennsylvania. Finally, in 1948 Ogilvy started his own advertising agency. With a flair for memorable copywriting, he was soon acknowledged by competitors and clients alike as one of the most brilliant advertising executives of his generation. He retired in 1975 after building Ogilvy & Mather into a business with annual billings of $800 million.

Ray Kroc was another late starter. He was heading for a comfortable retirement after a successful, if not earth-shattering, career as a milkshake mixer salesman. That all changed when he walked into a small hamburger restaurant in San Bernardino, California, owned by the McDonald brothers. His visit, in 1954, was the catalyst for a global food revolution. Kroc's vision extended a lot further than San Bernardino. He cut a deal with the McDonald brothers, and drawing up a set of rules governing the operation of new McDonald's restaurants, set about creating a franchise network.

In 1961, he bought out the brothers for a bargain $2.1 million. By 1963 the company had notched up the sale of 1 billion burgers, and opened restaurant number 500. The company went public in 1965. By the 1970s Kroc had turned a $2.1 million investment into a $500 million fortune. By the time of his death in 1984, the McDonald's golden arches were recognized the world over as a symbol for convenient and cheap fast food.

Sam Walton, the founder of the Wal-Mart empire, was another who started late. He did not open his first Wal-Mart store until he was 44 years old. After a hard upbringing in the depression-ridden Midwest he worked for JC Penney until, with $25,000 borrowed from his father-in-law, he obtained a franchise on a Ben Franklin store in Newport, Arkansas. When he lost his lease on his first store he merely opened another, and then another. Soon he had a small collection of retail outlets. To keep tight control of them he would fly himself from one to the other in an ageing aircraft. Walton opened the first Wal-Mart in 1962 and the second in 1964. By 1987 there were over 1000. At the time of his death in 1992, Walton had made millions of dollars and established one of the greatest retail store empires the world has ever seen.

Of course, not everyone will turn out to have the entrepreneurial spark of a David Ogilvy, a Ray Kroc or a Sam Walton. But these examples underline the point that it's not when you start but how you finish that defines a career adventure.

CAREER ADVENTURER

Leslie L. Kosoff
Title/Position: Chief Executive Officer
Company: Menton Productions LLC

Whatever you do, don't think in terms of the next big thing. Don't move into trendy areas just because they are trendy. As you look toward your career future, first look inside yourself. Think about what you really want to do – what kind of job, in what kind of environment, with what kind of people. Identify those things that give you the greatest satisfaction and know why that is the case.

Develop a dream for yourself and your career and make that dream the guiding force in every decision you make. Sometimes the decisions will seem lateral - or even backwards. Don't worry about that. As long as every step you take is pointing you toward your career goal – and that goal is representative of the best that you have to offer – you will succeed.

THE FUTURE OF CAREERS

We asked some management gurus, all experts in their respective fields, some crucial career questions: What will happen to the concept of the career in the future? What career advice would you offer tomorrow's managers?

While there was little consensus among our gurus, their answers were certainly thought provoking.

Sumantra Ghoshal :
The career advice follows from the idea of the volunteer investor. Some people Charles Handy among others have talked about the portfolio career. People will move from job to job and so on. I think there is a lot of truth to it but that it is also exaggerated. It does not recognize how important the company and the workplace are to the life of individuals.

In the past people had three places: work where they made money; the family; and traditionally there was a third place the pub in the UK or the teashop in India or whatever. Gradually, with global mobility, and the nature of jobs with a variety of sociological factors the third place is becoming harder and harder to find. For a lot of people the company is also the place of affiliations. Therefore constantly moving from job to job except for the lucky and the elite few I don't think is going to take root.

People will want to continue in the same place for their affiliation needs. What will emerge is a new relationship between the individual and the organization, where this paternalistic idea of the company that will develop you and do what is good for you and align you to the company needs will give way to one where the company will make choices available. It will offer a whole portfolio in terms of development choices, it will be your portfolio. You are the boss. You are the investor, it is your choice.

You will choose from this portfolio to meet your requirements. When you are 27 the things you want from a job will be different to the things you want when you are 47. We won't have 'one size fits all'. Companies will create this choice, so that the individual's need to develop his or her own human capital will not necessarily translate in continuous hopping from company to company. There will be enough variety within companies, enough autonomy, and enough choice so that we'll gradually come to a broad continuity of relationship that is very different to the old idea of job security for obedience and loyalty contract. We'll move to a contract based on continuous development based on availability of choice within the company for enhancement of human capital based on different projects and different kinds of jobs. So the concept of career is not dead and everyone is not going to become a mercenary. But nevertheless it will take a very different form to what we have seen in the past. Internal labor markets will become much more effective. There will be much more of an open marketplace inside as the traditional barriers to mobility come down.

Individuals will become much more central. The democratization of the careers. We have seen the triumph of democracy at societal level, just about the last bastion where individuals still don't have autonomy is the democratization of the workplace. You are seeing the democratization of the workplace. The basic principles of democracy, individuals being able to choose the nature of their occupation, the redefinition of autonomy and authority are being used to construct a very different sort of organization.

Henry Mintzberg

I don't know because I'm not sure I can say anything intelligent about current trends and whether people will work more or less independently. My hope is that there will be more of an appreciation of the bond between individuals and organizations. I don't believe this easy-come easy-go culture makes a lot of sense. That people are just hired labor, contracted to do some things and then they leave, I think you need to develop bonds and long-term relationships to build a strong organization. So I hope there will be a swing back to that. I mean a social infrastructure and a long-term commitment between individuals and their organizations, instead of this idea that staff sit on two months notice and could be gone tomorrow. Anyway, that's a very American phenomenon. It's not a common phenomenon in Europe outside of the UK at least. It's not a French or German attitude, or a Japanese one for sure.

Patty Seybold

Peoples' careers will be a progression of sequential projects, moving both within companies and from company to company. For each project, there will be new learnings, new accomplishments, and the ability to educate others. Tomorrow's managers should hone their ability to manage structural tension: formulating and keeping a clear vision and setting up measurement and monitoring systems to provide them an accurate view of current reality. They also need to develop both pattern sensing and recognition skills in order to contribute to tomorrow's sense-and-respond organizations.

2. WHO ARE YOU?

So, what sort of career adventure are you looking for? Just as importantly, what sort of person are you?

When we make consumer choices we buy according to our preferences. Nervous drivers don't tend to buy Ferraris. Given a choice, lovers of peace and quiet prefer not to live in the hurly burly of the city. When it comes to holidays, thrill seekers will choose skydiving over lying on a beach in the

Caribbean, bungee jumping over a golfing vacation. That is not to say that you can't have an adventure on a golf course. It's a matter of personal taste.

The starting point for any career adventure is self-awareness. Having a thorough knowledge of your likes and dislikes, strengths and weaknesses, values and other character traits is essential for selecting the right career adventure for you. The more you understand yourself the easier it becomes to make career choices, and the better chance you have of matching those choices with your capabilities.

> 'Self-knowledge is extremely important,' says Joyce E. Barrie, career coach and founder and chief fun officer (yes, really) of Joymarc Enterprises. "You have to really know yourself, your strengths and weaknesses, and be able to reinvent yourself on a dime, literally, to be able to advance in life. The world is moving so quickly that it's not a matter of just catching up, but of being in the forefront given all of the competition.'

Back in the 1960s, the Beatles memorably sought enlightenment from an Eastern mystic, Maharishi Mahesh Yogi. Whether he provided them with career direction or spiritual clarity is unclear. The career adventurer has no such luxury. He or she must look within for guidance. No one can do your thinking for you. There is no hirsute guru with all the answers. Only one person can provide the key to career happiness.

You.

Ask and you will find

Ask yourself searching questions. It is better to find out now that salary is the most important factor in choosing a career than when you're stuck in a company that pays you peanuts. It's best to discover you hate being responsible for others in advance, rather than when your boss tells you that you're in charge of hundreds of co-workers. If you are a down-to-earth, rational, logical-thinking person you will be miserable when it turns out that your chosen career requires a creative dreamer.

So how do you go about finding out about yourself? You might think that sitting quietly on your own and having a good think will be sufficient, but this is unlikely to reveal the real you. On your own it's difficult to separate out the how you would like to be self from the how you really are self. Labels can also get in the way.

A publisher found himself out of a job and asked a career advisor friend for help. 'Well, what are you good at?' His friend asked him. 'I'm a very good publisher', the man replied. 'Yes, but what skills do you possess?' the career adviser asked. 'Publishing skills', the publisher replied. The conversation went round in circles for a while until the career advisor said he would help the publisher but only if he would agree to a simple condition. The publisher had to ask people who knew him - friends and professional contacts - what he was good at, and come back in a week.

A week later, he duly appeared and reported that he had done as asked. 'And what did these people say?' his friend enquired. 'The funny thing is', he observed, 'no one mentioned publishing.'

The publisher reeled off a list of useful attributes. He was a good communicator, who could talk to anyone; he had a knack of summarizing the main points of an argument without going into too much detail; he was good at persuading other people to do what he wanted them to do; and was skilled at mirroring the views of the people he was with to make them feel comfortable. Beyond this he was skilled at manipulating and massaging words.

'Ah', said the career advisor, 'that is interesting. Have you considered a career in politics?'

The point of the story is simple. You are not defined by your job, your industry or your preconceptions.

Adventure 1

Other people can often see what you cannot. Try asking your family, friends and acquaintances to list your talents and you may be surprised. Record what they say as a reminder. Then consider whether and how you utilize that talent in your current life and work.

MY TALENTS	WHEN UTILIZED

CAREER ADVENTURER

Serena Wilson

Title/Position: Middle Eastern belly dancing instructor; company owner
Company: Serena Studios, Serena's Closet
Location: New York
Website: www.serenastudios.com

'I own a dance studio that specializes in the Serena Technique of Belly Dancing, which I devised many years ago (we documented it in a book published by Simon and Schuster, now out of print). As a result of my study of other dance forms, including ballet, jazz and modern dance, I realized that Middle Eastern dance would have to be broken down into its most basic body positions. Those body positions become building blocks that students can use to learn this dance form. They can also be combined into more complex arrangements. My technique gives people a genuine foundation for the dance.

I've been a dancer all of my adult life. I've also painted, sculpted and written poetry. I've dabbled in all of the arts, but this is the one that I've been able to base my entire career on. My parents were in show business, so I think performing was something that came very naturally to me. When I was 7 years old, my mother took me to study with a legendary dancer named Ruth St. Denis (she must be in all of the dance history books). She did a lot of mystical dance that was very influenced by Hindu and Indian movement. She taught me arm and hand movements when I was seven.

But when I actually started doing this dance, it was a different kind of a circumstance. I met a young man who had a Dixieland band, and we were going together for a while. I was 17 at that time. He had a big event that he was playing for, and he asked me to do an Oriental dance. I'm not sure why he wanted it for his Dixieland show, but that's what I gave him. That was my first experience of performing, and it was really just my own idea of what the dance might be. I probably got that idea from movies.

I married the boy with the Dixieland Band. My husband was in the Coast Guard and stationed in New Orleans. We had a baby at the time and needed some extra money. So I got a job on Bourbon Street as a "fake" oriental dancer. I only stayed there one week. It was not a very nice place. I didn't dance again for a long time.

When I came back to New York, I began to dance again with an Armenian band. This Armenian band kind of adopted me, and I became their dancer. Wherever they went, I went along, and they had a lot of jobs. They called themselves "The Orientals". This was in the late 1960s.

I worked with them for a while, and then met another Armenian musician who said that if I really wanted to perfect my dancing, I should get a job in one of the Greek clubs in "Greek Town" along 8th Avenue in New York City. Every one of the clubs employed at least four Middle Eastern dancers. Most of the dancers were Turkish, and they were good. The rule of the club was that we had to sit up on the stage with the musicians until we danced. While sitting there I had the opportunity to watch the other dancers perform, and play the Oriental drum for them.

I began to develop my own style. Unlike the Turkish dancers that I worked with, I brought into the dance those graceful hand and arm movements that I'd learned as a child with Ruth St. Denis. And that's how I developed my style of dance. And I think the graceful hands and arms made the dance sensual rather than sexual. Women began to respond to the dance and it became very graceful. It had not always been known for that gracefulness.

Over the years I've also taken dancers and other interested people to Turkey and especially Egypt. I began to import costumes and other dance accessories as part of my studio. I have a separate boutique called Serena's Closet. When I was still a teenager I majored in fashion design at the Fashion Institute of Technology. I use some of that expertise when I receive these costumes; I sometimes redesign them. My third business is booking dancers on shows. Fourth, I choreographed the show for a very lavish Egyptian club here in New York City using dancers that I have trained. It was quite a lavish production. That went on for four years. Now I'm also on the faculty of the Harkness Dance Center at the 92nd Street YMHA in New York. I started in fall of 2001. They have a very broad spectrum of dance programs.'

The appliance of science

Not convinced that self-discovery is a matter of self-help? OK, then maybe you'd prefer something more scientific. When it comes to self-awareness what the career adventurer requires is unbiased, objective help. And there's a whole industry out there waiting to provide you with it. There are a plethora of tools and techniques to help you understand the sorts of roles you are best suited to.

Many of these tests were developed by psychologists. They cover four main areas – Personality, Skills, Values and Interests – and provide an objective assessment of each of these aspects (each is explored in more detail below).

Some of these tests have been used for over fifty years and are recognized by many employers. Most of the tests, or inventories as the psychologists prefer to call them, cost money. (Costs can range from just under $15 for a full report on the online Keirsey Temperament Sorter II to about $100 for a comprehensive Myers-Briggs inventory report.)

If you are still not persuaded, weigh the cost of the test against a lifetime working in a career for which you are ill suited, and which consequently makes you unhappy. Working in an unsuitable job can make you miserable, worse, it can make you ill. There's plenty of research to support the link between dissatisfaction at work and ill health.[1]

When it comes to personality tests most roads lead back to the Swiss psychologist Carl Jung (1875 - 1961) who developed a theory of personality based on eight personality types: extroverts, introverts, thinking, feeling, sensing, intuitive, judging and perceptive. (Jung was something of a career adventurer. His eclectic interests encompassed occultism and Eastern religions as well as mythology. Today's New Age philosophies owe Jung a great debt.)

Jung believed that individuals use two basic kinds of function: how they perceive things or take in information and how they make decisions. These categories were further divided in two. Individuals perceive things via their senses or intuitively. Individuals make decisions objectively or subjectively. Although Jung believed people use all four functions, he also believed they do so to different degrees. One function would be dominant. These functions in turn could be "extraverted" or "introverted". (Jung considered himself an introvert.)[2]

Jung ended up with eight personality types:
1. Extraverted Sensing
2. Introverted Sensing
3. Extraverted Intuition
4. Introverted Intuition
5. Extraverted Thinking
6. Introverted Thinking
7. Extraverted Feeling
8. Introverted Feeling

Many personality tests used in career planning are based on Jung's personality types. The most popular of these are the Myers-Briggs Type Indicator and the Keirsey Temperament Sorter.

Myers-Brigg Type Indicator (MBTI)

The MBTI is the mother of all personality inventories. It is used by over 3 million people annually. The groundwork for the inventory was conducted by Katherine C. Briggs around the time of the First World War. Her work built on Jung's theories of personality and was further developed by her daughter, Isabel Briggs Myers, who created the Myers-Briggs Type Indicator in the 1970s.

Briggs Myers concluded that each of us has a principal way of operation with respect to:
◆ Our flow of energy
◆ How we take in
◆ How we make
◆ The every day lifestyle we lead

Within each of these categories we prefer to be:
1. **E**xtraverted or **I**ntroverted
2. **S**ensing or i**N**tuitive
3. **T**hinking or **F**eeling
4. **J**udging or **P**erceiving

Individuals are naturally more comfortable with one or other of these modes of operating.

◆ Our flow of energy - how we receive our stimulation — either internally or externally.

◆ How we take in information — how do we absorb information — by trusting our senses to take it in or by trusting to our intuition?

◆ How we make decisions — do we make decisions by utilizing objectivity and thought or do we trust our personal subjective value systems?

◆ The every day lifestyle we lead — on a day-to-day basis do we prefer to be structured and organized (judging) or laid back, relaxed and open (perceiving)?

◆ Taking the test will result in a score indicated by the four letters denoting the individual's preferences — ESFJ, for example, denotes an extraverted, sensing, feeling, judging individual. Numbers next to the letters indicate their weighting. The MBTI instrument is regularly updated to reflect the latest research in type theory. Data for over 4,000 research studies provides a robust empirical foundation for the test.

RESOURCES

On the web

Given MBTI's long history, extensive resources are available. One helpful site is the US-based Personality Pathways (www.personalitypathways.com), which offers an introduction to the MBTI and a free self-scoring personality test that purportedly approximates one's MBTI type, along with links to other resources. A fascinating application of MBTI to team development may be explored at the UK-based Team Technology (www.teamtechnology.co.uk). Here you may click on "dynamic" descriptions of the 16 Myers-Briggs psychological types, take a self-assessment, and learn about the various roles that people contribute to teams (e.g. Crusader, Explorer, Innovator, Sculptor, Scientist, Coach). In addition there is useful information to be found at the publishers of the MBTI (www.cpp-db.com), as well as at www.mbtypeguide.com/Type and www.knowyourtype.com, where you can take the inventory online.

Bibliography

Briggs Myers, Isobel & Mc Caulley, Mary H *Manual: A Guide to the Development and Use of the Myers-Briggs Type Indicator* (Consulting Psychologists Press, 1992).
Briggs Myers, Isobel *Gifts Differing* (Consulting Psychologists Press, 1972).
Krebs Hirsh Consulting, *Using the Myers-Briggs Type Indicator in Organizations.* (Psychologists Press, 1991).

CAREER ADVENTURER

JOHN BROOKS on the Myers-Briggs

Title/Position: Senior VP and Manager – Media Practice
Company: Silicon Valley Bank
Industry: Commercial Banking

'We're probably one of the few banking organizations where everyone must take the Myers- Briggs Type Inventory. It's a useful management tool, another way to find out what makes people tick and what the best ways are to relate to them. It helps in understanding their behaviors. My boss is really into it.

I had taken it twice before – about 20 years ago when I'd just gotten out of college, and again about 3 or 4 years ago during my period of unemployment (I'm an ISFJ). I find it helpful because my big challenge is managing people. I haven't had a lot of experience managing people, and I now have a staff of four. Some of them have performance issues, and the MBTI helps me better understand why people are the way they are. It helps me conduct more positive performance reviews. For example, in a review with one staff member, we both pulled out our MBTI results and acknowledged that we were polar opposites of each other, which is probably why we get on each other's nerves.'

Keirsey Temperament Sorter

The Keirsey Temperament Sorter is another popular indicator of personality type. The test, now over 20 years old, was devised and developed by the American clinical psychologist David West Keirsey. It is now available online (www.keirsey.com). The sorter is intended to indicate temperament. Individuals complete the test and according to their answers are categorized as Artisans, Guardians, Idealists or Rationales.

According to Keirsey, **Guardians** are "concrete in communicating, operative in implementing goals and highly skilled in logistics". They tend to be reliable, respectable and do good deeds. Guardians comprise up to 45 percent of the population. Famous guardians include Mother Theresa, George Washington, F. W. Woolworth and Thomas Hardy.

Artisans are "concrete in communicating, utilitarian in implementing goals and can become highly skilled in tactical variation". They can be daring, adaptable, and graceful in action. Artisans comprise up to 40 percent of the population. Famous artisans include Barbra Streisand, Elvis Presley, Ernest Hemingway and Winston Churchill.

Idealists are "abstract in communicating and cooperative in implementing goals, and can become highly skilled in diplomatic integration". Benevolent, empathetic and authentic, Idealists make up only about 10 percent of population. Famous idealists include Plato, Gandhi, James Joyce and Lenin.

Rationales are "abstract in communicating and utilitarian in implementing goals, and can become highly skilled in strategic analysis". Rationals tend to be competent, autonomous, and strong-willed. Famous rationals include Abraham Lincoln, Albert Einstein, Walt Disney and Bill Gates.

RESOURCES

On the web
www.advisorteam.com/user/ktsintro.asp

The Keirsey Temperament Sorter II: Take David Keirsey's 70-question personality assessment online to learn which of the four "temperament" types (an extension of the sixteen Myers-Briggs personality types) you are. Find out if you're an Artisan, Guardian, Rational or Idealist. You get a free description of your temperament, and can purchase a ten-page report with more information on your type. Keirsey's test is used in career development programs at Fortune 500 companies as well as in counseling and career placement centers at major universities.

Bibliography
Keirsey, D., *Please Understand Me II* (Prometheus Nemesis Book Co, 1998).
Bates, M & Keirsey, D., *Please Understand Me* (Prometheus Nemesis Book Co, 1984).

Adventure 2

For a less researched but more immediate take on personality and attitude try the following. Ring the personality traits and characteristics that are most applicable to you. Then write down the ten that are your strongest and justify with examples from past behavior.

academic	cooperative	imaginative	poised	strong
accurate	courageous	independent	polite	strong-minded
active	creative	individualistic	practical	supportive
adaptable	curious	informal	precise	sympathetic
adventurous	deliberate	intellectual	progressive	tactful
affectionate	determined	intelligent	prudent	teachable
aggressive	diplomatic	inventive	punctual	tenacious
alert	discreet	kind	purposeful	thorough
ambitious	dominant	leisurely	quick	thoughtful
analytical	eager	likeable	quiet	tolerant
articulate	easy-going	logical	rational	tough
artistic	efficient	loyal	realistic	trusting
assertive	emotional	mature	reflective	trustworthy
bold	empathetic	methodical	relaxed	unaffected
businesslike	energetic	meticulous	reliable	unassuming
calm	enthusiastic	mild	reserved	understanding
capable	fair-minded	moderate	resourceful	unexcitable
careful	farsighted	modest	responsible	uninhibited
caring	firm	motivated	retiring	verbal
cautious	flexible	natural	risk-averse	versatile
charming	forceful	obliging	risk-taking	volatile
cheerful	formal	open-minded	robust	warm
clear-thinking	frank	opportunistic	self-confident	wholesome
clever	friendly	optimistic	self-controlled	wise
competent	generous	organized	sensible	witty
competitive	gentle	original	sensitive	
confident	good-natured	outgoing	serious	
conscientious	healthy	painstaking	sincere	
conservative	helpful	patient	sociable	
considerate	honest	persevering	spontaneous	
consistent	humorous	persuasive	stable	
cool	idealistic	pleasant	steady	

CAREER ADVENTURER

JOYCE E. BARRIE's career tips

Title/Position: Founder, President, CFO (Chief Fun Officer)
Company: Joymarc Enterprises, Inc.
Industries: Consulting/Coaching, Professional Speaker, Seminar Leader, TV
& Radio Personality

Joyce is Founder and President of Joymarc Enterprises, Inc., a company which offers comprehensive seminar programs, and personal and professional consulting services to individuals and corporations. The New York Times called her work "Chutzpah Therapy" and Joyce has appeared on a number of US television shows including Sally Jessy Raphael, Phil Donahue and Joe Franklin.

Joyce's career tips

If you're going into a new career:

1. Make a list of all of your assets and liabilities, so that you can make sure you're going to best utilize what works for you.

2. Make a list of everything you like to do or want to do in the position you seek, vs. everything you really don't want to do. This helps you find something that best matches your natural inclinations.

3. Decide whether location is a factor. Are you willing to move out of town to get the career you really want?

4. Is money a factor? Are you willing to start this new career in an entry level position vs. something more advanced based on your current level of experience?

5. Last but not least, how much do you want it? To put it another way, are you willing to do whatever it takes to get it? For example, sometimes you may have to go through a long series of interviews. Today they really put you through the mill to get a job, even to get an interview!

3. SKILLS SORTING

Having contemplated who you are, now we turn to what you are good at.

You may have spent your whole life harboring a secret desire to be pilot. But if your hand-eye coordination is so bad you have trouble hitting a tennis ball; if your math barely runs to working out your tax; if you have difficulty navigating your way to the local supermarket; then flying is probably not for you.

A skill is the ability to do something. More than that it is the ability to do something well. For every thousand-bedroom guitarists, competent and incompetent strummers, there are one or two highly skilled musicians, an Eric Clapton or an Andrés Segovia. For all of the fumbling students in the biology dissection class there will be one person who renders the whole messy process effortless - the next Christian Barnaard? But skills aren't the sole preserve of the supremely gifted. Even the most humble individual has a skill or two tucked away even though they may not realize it.

Understanding skills

Skills can be loosely divided into **work** or **job specific skills** and **transferable skills.**

Job specific skills are skills such as the ability to perform complex surgery or read music; strip an engine or program a computer; to navigate a cargo ship or tailor a suit. These are the skills that are essential for performing your work. You may acquire them during education, learn them on the job, train yourself or pick them up on life's journey. As you learn what is easy to do and what is difficult, what you enjoy and what you dislike, so you refine your own personal suite of work specific skills.

Transferable skills are something different. These are non-work specific skills, which can be carried from one job to the next, many of which we use in everyday life. Problem solving, the ability to communicate, to organize your time, research information, these are all transferable skills. (See Chapter 3 for a list of skills in the resume writing section).

Skills assessment enables you to determine what skills you possess and what skills you are good at. It is also worth considering what skills you enjoy doing. If job satisfaction is important to you, as it tends to be for most people, then a lifetime of performing a skill you detest, regardless of how you good you are at it, is not a recipe for fulfillment. You may be a gifted mathematician, but that doesn't mean that you want to spend your working life crunching numbers.

Some skills, too, are more useful than others in a work situation. In the US in 1990 the then Secretary of Labor Lynn Martin set up the Secretary's Commission on Achieving Necessary Skills (SCANS). Its goal was to "define critical skills that everyone needs in order to succeed in the workplace". The commission defined the skills it thought necessary in a high performance economy and published them in its report *A SCANS Report for America 2000*. In the high-performance workplace envisaged by SCANS, basic skills such as computation and literacy form a foundation. On top of this workers need more advanced soft skills such as complex problem solving and the ability to apply this knowledge.

If you are a person who can do all or most of the following then you are well equipped for work in the new millennium. If not then it is time to think about acquiring some of these must have skills as indicated by SCANS.

SCANS SKILLS

Workplace Competencies

Resources
C1 Allocates Time
C2 Allocates Money
C3 Allocates Material and Facility
    Resources
C4 Allocates Human Resources

Information
C5 Acquires and Evaluates Information
C6 Organizes and Maintains Information
C7 Interprets and Communicates
    Information
C8 Uses Computers to Process
    Information

Interpersonal
C9 Participates as a Member of a Team
C10 Teaches others
C11 Serves Clients/Customers
C12 Exercises Leadership
C13 Negotiates to Arrive at a Decision
C14 Works with Cultural Diversity

Systems
C15 Understands Systems
C16 Monitors and Corrects Performance

Technology
C17 Improves and Designs Systems
C18 Selects Technology
C19 Applies Technology to Task
C20 Maintains and Troubleshoots
    Technology

Foundation Skills

Basic Skills
F1 Reading
F2 Writing
F3 Arithmetic
F4 Mathematics
F5 Listening
F6 Speaking

Thinking Skills
F7 Creative Thinking
F8 Decision Making
F9 Problem Solving
F10 Seeing Things in the Mind's Eye
F11 Knowing How to Learn
F12 Reasoning

Personal Qualities
F13 Responsibility
F14 Self-Esteem
F15 Sociability
F16 Self-Management
F17 Integrity/Honesty

For full details on the competencies
and skills go to: www.scans.jhu.edu

Adventure 3

List what you consider to be your key skills under the two headings: job specific and transferable. Then think about what you would have written five years ago. Have your skills changed? What would you like to write in five years time?

MY JOB SPECIFIC SKILLS	MY TRANSFERABLE SKILLS

4. WHAT DO YOU VALUE?

What are values? It's a difficult question to answer simply, but one way of understanding the concept of values is to consider them as priorities that relate to an individual's behavior. They are priorities that motivate a person's course of action. Values can be divided into two categories — intrinsic and extrinsic:

◆ Intrinsic values are about the work you are doing and how it relates to society.
◆ Extrinsic values are related to external factors such as salary, location and work environment.

Making sense of values

Various approaches have been developed to better understand and make sense of values.

Hall Tonna Inventory of Values

Psychologist Brian Hall and sociologist Benjamin Tonna conducted research into the nature of values over a twenty-year period. They identified 125 cross-disciplinary and cross-cultural values that played a fundamental part in the personal growth and development of an individual.

The conclusions they drew from their research were that:
◆ Values are an expression of concepts (i.e. personal constructs) that represent dynamic clusters of energy.
◆ Values are described by those words in a language that convey significant personal meaning. This meaning carries with it a certain psychological energy that activates a persons' behavior.
◆ Values are learned and can be measured.

From the research findings Hall and Tonna developed the **Hall Tonna Inventory of Values** built on four premises:

1. Values are an important component of human existence and can be identified and measured.
2. Values are described through words.
3. Values are learned and developed through assimilation.
4. Values are modified and shaped by our world-view.

What does this mean for the career adventurer? A values inventory such as that devised by Hall and Tonna allows you to assess what values are important to you. From this you can ensure that any job and career you pursue encompasses those values. So if helping others is important to you, a career in public service is likely to be more satisfying than a career in the money markets.

The Minnesota Importance Questionnaire (MIQ)

The Minnesota Importance Questionnaire (MIQ) is another tool that looks at vocational needs and values. It aims to measure six vocational values (altruism, comfort, safety, autonomy, status and achievement) and 20 vocational needs derived from those values.

A paper-and-pencil inventory of vocational values and needs. The MIQ comes in two forms:

In the paired form pairs of vocational needs statements are listed. The person taking the test selects the most important needs from each pair. The test takes roughly 30 minutes.

In the ranked form vocational needs statements are grouped in batches of five. The person taking the test ranks each set of five, according to their importance. The ranked form MIQ is quicker to complete than the paired form taking roughly 15 to 20 minutes.

Survey of Interpersonal Values (SIV)

The Survey of Interpersonal Values measures six critical values regarding an individual's relationship with others. Those values are:

◆ **Benevolence**: Doing things for others.

◆ **Conformity**: Being accepted. Doing what is socially correct.

◆ **Independence**: Making decisions, getting your own way.

◆ **Leadership**: Being in charge; having power and authority.

◆ **Recognition**: Being highly regarded and admired; having status, being important.

◆ **Support**: Being treated with understanding and consideration.

Organizational values

It's not just about finding out your own values either. Values are important to organizations. In their book *Built to Last*, authors James C. Collins and Jerry I. Porras discovered that one quality of enduring companies is that they establish and cherish a set of corporate values. These values are important for determining whether you are likely to feel comfortable within a particular organization.

Take General Electric for example. Under its former CEO Jack Welch, GE explicitly linked the performance of its managers to the company's values. (These include: setting stretching goals; using speed for competitive advantage; being anti-bureaucracy, and avoiding complexity.) Some 5,000 GE employees took part in the debate about the company's values over a three-year period. In 1989, an early draft of the values statement urged staff to embrace the GE values. Those who did not, Welch suggested, might fare better elsewhere. 'Individuals whose values do not coincide with these expressed preferences will more likely flourish better outside the General Electric Company', the statement read. It became known as the 'flourish off' statement, and caused such an outcry that it was dropped from the final values statement.

During his time at GE Welch carried a laminated card in his pocket bearing the GE values. Failure to live those values was grounds for dismissal. At one meeting Welch surprised his audience saying: 'Look around you: there are five fewer officers here than there were last year. One was fired for the numbers, four were fired for [lack of] values.'

RESOURCES

On the web

http://www.valuestech.com – *website of pioneering researcher into values Dr Brian Hall.*

www.careerinnovation.com/panel/values – *try taking the online values test*

www.cedarcreek.org – *another online values test and other values information.*

http://www.minessence.net/html/aboutavi.htm – *another good values inventory and background information.*

Bibliography

Bougle, C., *The Evolution of Values Studies in Sociology* (Kelley, 1970).

Rokeach, M., *The Nature of Human Values* (Free Press, 1973).

Rokeach, M. (ed.), *Individual and Societal* (Free Press, 1979).

Mercer Curtler, H. & Sharpe, M.E., *Rediscovering Values: Coming to Terms with Postmodernism* (Armonk, 1997).

Adventure 4

Values tests usually come in the form of values inventories. They ask questions such as: How important is a high salary to you? Do you want other people to be impressed by your job? How important is making a contribution to society to you? They ask you to select values from a list.

Select the three to five values from the list below which are most important to you.

VALUES	EXPLANATION
Achievement	Rising to the top of your field, career advancement, promotion
Adventure	Challenge, risk-taking
Altruism	Serving others, doing good for others and society
Authority	Being in charge of others
Challenge	Being challenged by your work
Competition	Competition with others in work
Creativity	Being imaginative and innovative
Flexible working hours	The ability to choose working hours to suit your needs
Harmony	Work in a non-conflict environment
Helping others	Directly dealing with other peoples problems
High salary	Big bucks
Independence	Autonomy, you choose what you do and how you do it
Influence	Opinion former, you influence the actions, decisions of others
Intellectual stimulation	Work that taxes your brainpower
Leadership	You're in charge, showing others the way
Manual work	Working with your hands
Moral values	Your personal ethics
Numerical work	Working with numbers
Outside work	Working outdoors
Persuading	You convince others of a course of action
Physical work	Manual work that involves a degree of physical challenge
Stability	Predictable work timetable and duties
Prestige and status	Work that accords respect from the public
Recognition	Work that gets you noticed
Seasonal work	Spring, summer, fall, and winter
Security	A degree of protection from redundancy
Social welfare	Doing something that has meaning for others, working for society or another person's benefit
Teamwork	Working with co-workers in teams or close contact
Travel	Work requiring lots of travel
Variety	Constantly changing duties
Work Mastery	Become expert in your field
Work Under Pressure	Work in situations where time pressure is common

5. WHAT DO YOU LOVE TO DO?

No one ever truly succeeded doing something they didn't love.

Tiger Woods loves to play golf. Tiger Woods plays golf for a living. Tiger Woods makes a lot of money playing golf. Martha Stewart developed an interest in cooking, gardening and homemaking as a young girl. Today she runs a million dollar lifestyle business. People who make a career out of their interests or hobbies seem to have it made, especially when the money is good. But before you can turn an interest into a career, you have to find out what your interests are. For the single-minded this task will be a lot easier than for the more eclectic natured among us. But while we aren't all as focused as Tiger Woods or Martha Stewart, by increasing the match between work and interests we can fashion a completely fulfilling career from a barely satisfying one.

Making sense of what you love

As with values, tests of interest usually come in the form of inventories asking questions designed to elicit your interests:

Strong Interest Inventory (SII)

Developed by celebrated psychologist E K Strong at Stanford University in 1927 "the Strong", as it is known, is the most powerful and widely used interest inventory. Since its inception it has been revised and upgraded.

The Strong consists of a questionnaire with 317 items – words or phrases covering a wide range of hobbies, activities, and occupations. The respondent expresses a preference for three response categories for each item. The responses are scored by computer and detailed in a report – usually called a profile.

The information from the test is broken down into five categories. Preferences for work in general are indicated by the scores on the six General Occupational Themes. Next come scores on 25 Basic Interest Scales; these indicate interests or aversions in 25 specific areas. Occupational Scales, 211 in total, demonstrate a similarity or otherwise between the respondent and men and women representing 109 different occupations. Style scales measure a person's preferences for the style in which they like to work, learn and take risks. Lastly, three administrative indexes weed out unusual or invalid responses.

The Strong assumes that there is a correlation between a particular job and the interests of people in that particular job. By assessing an individual's interests and comparing them to the interests of people in various occupations it seeks to determine the type of occupation most suitable for an individual.

Holland's Self-Directed Search

Another widely used interest inventory is Dr John Holland's Self-Directed Search. Over 20 million people worldwide have used it in their quest for self-awareness. The search is supported by over 500 research studies and translated into 25 different languages.

Holland developed a theory of personality that categorized individuals into one of six types: Realistic, Investigative, Artistic, Social, Enterprising, and Conventional. Furthermore, Holland found that occupations and work environments could be similarly categorized. This is a result of the tendency of similar types to associate together and create an atmosphere conducive to that type of person.

People are happiest and most likely to be successful in environments that they feel comfortable in. These environments are likely to be found where there are people of a similar type. So an artistic person is more likely to achieve success in an artistic environment such as a theater or dance studio than in a chemical research laboratory, or an accounting firm.

Handy's intelligence profiles

In his book *The Hungry Spirit,* Charles Handy outlines eleven different intelligence profiles, any of which can stimulate self-respect and subsequently become the foundation of a fulfilling career. Consider the following in light of your own life and learning experiences:

- ◆ **Factual Intelligence** – encyclopedic knowledge
- ◆ **Analytic Intelligence** – reasoning and conceptualizing
- ◆ **Numerate Intelligence** – mathematical skill
- ◆ **Linguistic Intelligence** – verbal and communication skills
- ◆ **Spatial Intelligence** – an ability to see patterns in things
- ◆ **Athletic Intelligence** – physical coordination
- ◆ **Intuitive Intelligence** – aptitude for sensing and seeing what is hidden from most others
- ◆ **Emotional Intelligence** – self-awareness, self-control, persistence, zeal, and self-motivation
- ◆ **Practical Intelligence** – common sense
- ◆ **Interpersonal Intelligence** – social and leadership skills
- ◆ **Musical Intelligence** – the creation, production or performance of music

'What matters most,' says Handy, 'is the message behind the list: these many and varied intelligences or abilities are all resources that we can use to contribute to the world, to earn a living, and to make a difference.'

RESOURCES

On the web
www.self-directed-search.com – *the main self-directed search website.*
www.ksu.edu/acic/career/holland/holland.html – *a brief explanation of Holland's personality types.*

Bibliography
Holland, J.L., *Exploring Career Options* (Psychological Assessment Resources, 1990).

Adventure 5

Try this: simply write down 20 things you love to do. Then consider why you don't do them more often?

WHAT I LOVE TO DO	WHEN I LAST DID IT

Retracing your steps

"No one has ever learned fully to know themselves" said the poet, novelist, playwright, courtier, natural philosopher and all-round career adventurer Johann Wolfgang von Goethe.

"The final mystery is oneself," concurred dramatist Oscar Wilde[3]. If you have tried any of the exercises above or followed up the web links and taken one of the many personality, interests, skills or values tests or inventories available you may sympathize with these sentiments. At least you will be a step on the way to discovering the answer to the question posed by Alice to the White Rabbit: "Who in the world am I?"

Armed with this knowledge you should be able to identify the areas in which you think you might be suited to working. Only then will you be ready to take the next step; ready to track down the next destination on your career adventure, the organization where you want to work.

But remember before you leave, self-assessment is an ongoing process. What is right for a teenager setting out from college is not necessarily right for the same person twenty years later, even a year later. You can return to the tests and inventories in this section at regular intervals along your career journey. That way you can make sure you stay on track. But most importantly, even if you don't use any of the tests, remember to take time to reflect on who you are, what you really want from your career journey. The inner journey is the most important adventure of all, and lasts a lifetime.

Adventure 6

The case for thinking first is persuasively put by the business psychologist Robert Sharrock of YSC, 'In considering their careers, people very rarely generate a range of options from which to make decisions. This is in contrast to more mundane decisions like buying a washing machine where decision-making is normally much more rational!'

This occurs for a number of reasons. First, there is the simple cost of time and effort that is involved. Secondly, at a more psychological level, individuals dislike the ambiguity that a broad range of options brings. In order to cope, they narrow down their choices and then rationalize why a particular career is uniquely suitable. Third, some individuals in work rationalize away their dissatisfaction rather than confront the painful reality that the work is not meeting their needs. Such individuals are prone to drifting in their careers and often receive a painful jolt when overtaken by organizational change, at which time they often think for the first time about their needs and aspirations.

Limiting the range of options in a career sense can be fatal. To put it another way, one or two false starts early, or even mid-career, can ultimately give rise to much greater levels of job success and satisfaction.

Individuals are best advised to create a number of options and, in addition, be mindful of the need to keep open later options. However, how can the range of options best be evaluated once the need to make a career shift is recognized?

One technique that is helpful is to list your, say, five key skills and five key needs on a matrix. In the columns, the possible options can be tabulated, starting with current role and then listing possible alternatives. Each role can then be evaluated against the criteria of whether it plays to an individual's strengths and meets their needs.

A rating between 1 and 5 is suggested - 5 being fully plays to my strengths or meets my needs, 3 being neutral and 1 being does not play to my strengths or meet my needs.

A simplified example follows.

	Current Role	Possible Role A	Possible Role B
Key Skills			
Problem Solving	3	2	4
Marketing	4	3	4
Inspiring Others	2	2	5
Driving Change	5	3	3
Key Needs			
Fun - Variety	3	3	3
Passion about the business	3	4	4
Financial	2	4	3
Will create later General Management roles	2	2	4
Total	**24**	**23**	**31**

This application of so-called Multi-Attribute Decision-Making Theory can help individuals think rationally about roles and minimize the extent of their irrationality. In the case of the above example, it is fairly clear that the individual should take Possible Role B. This approach can be made more sophisticated by adding weightings to each of the skills and needs.

Although this method increases objectivity, care should be taken not to adopt a 'the grass is always greener' syndrome in which too rosy a view of new possibilities is arrived at.

For more information about YSC see www.yscltd.co.uk

CAREER ADVENTURER'S RESOURCES

Personality Assessment and Self-Awareness Tools

Activate.co.uk This excellent recruitment site is geared toward UK college students, but it may be equally helpful to those further along in their careers. After registering on this free site, take advantage of the behavior profiling service. It uses the DISC system commonly used in UK business. Thus, while learning about yourself you can also see the type of information that prospective employers would receive in a report on the results of your pre-employment DISC test. There is also some good basic information on various types of interviews and general career paths (e.g. management consultant), and resources on job search and graduate programs, primarily for undergraduate students.
www.activate.co.uk

The Career Key Professor Lawrence Jones at North Carolina State University authored this free site as a resource for college students, parents, career counselors, teachers and other adults. Here you can take the 24-item Career Key personality assessment, which is based on John Holland's theory of vocational choice (the best known and most widely researched theory on this topic). The site offers basic information on Holland's six personality types and six corresponding work environments: Realistic, Investigative, Artistic, Social, Enterprising and Conventional. Once you complete the Career Key, you can learn about jobs that may best fit your personality type. A welcome feature of this site is the anonymity it provides. You don't need to provide your name, mother's name, email address etc., and so will not end up on any e-marketing lists.
www.ncsu.edu/careerkey

International Enneagram Association The Enneagram of Personality has become a hot approach to understanding and working more effectively with others. For example, a quick search on Amazon.com for "enneagram" yields 158 books on the topic, 16 of which are related to business and investing (e.g. *The Enneagram for Managers: Nine Different Perspectives on Managing People*, Oscar David, 2001). The Enneagram itself is an ancient 9-pointed symbol that is now used as a psycho-spiritual tool for personal development. Nine distinct personality 'types' are associated with the points in the symbol. The International Enneagram Association is a not-for-profit organization that promotes the highest

human values through the insights of the Enneagram. The association's website offers helpful background information on the enneagram, including detailed analyses of the nine personality types, an extensive bibliography and links to teachers and training resources.
www.intl-enneagram-assn.org

The Personality Page For just US $5 per person, you can obtain relatively reliable personality profiles on the Internet using a test that's been validated with over 100,000 users. Answer 60 questions, and find which of 16 types – based on the work of Carl Jung, Isabel Myers, and Katherine Briggs – you are. Great for do-it-your-self Career Adventurers, as well as for companies without the budget for expensive tests and associated consulting fees (though these can be very helpful). Then explore the pages with information on personality types and careers, relationships, and personal growth. There's also a library with links to books and informational materials on personality.
www.personalitypage.com/home.html

Reed This UK base recruitment agency offers a number of online career profiling and personality assessments (www.reed.co.uk/assessments.asp). Visitors to the site can test their commitment, reliability and interpersonal style as well as a detailed online personality questionnaire.

Notes

1. Warr, Peter, *Read Well-Being and the Workplace,* Chapter 20 in *Well Being: The Foundations of Hedonic Psychology* (Russell Sage Foundation, 1999).

2. McLynn, Frank, *Carl Gustav Jung* (St Martin's Press, New York, 1997).

3. Holland, Vyvyan, *De Profundis: The Complete Text by Oscar Wilde* (Philosophical Library, 1950).

" A commander's correct dispositions stem from his correct decisions, his correct decisions stem from his correct judgements, and his correct judgements stem from a thorough and necessary reconnaissance and from pondering on and piecing together the data of various kinds gathered through reconnaissance."

Mao Tse Tung

"You don't run twenty-six miles at five minutes a mile on good looks and a secret recipe."

Frank Shorter

TWO
RECONNAISSANCE & RESEARCH
MAPPING UNCHARTED TERRITORY

In this chapter you will learn how to:

Identify potential job targets

Research companies and industries

Use networking to build human bridges

Narrow your job search to a few key targets

1. STRIKING OUT FOR BASE CAMP

At about 11.30 am on 29 May 1953 Tenzing Norgay was having his picture taken. He probably didn't look his best, but then he probably didn't care. He was cold, tired and not a little exhilarated, as was the photographer. The photographer's name was Edmund Hillary, the location 29,028 feet above sea level. The occasion; the first ascent of Mount Everest, Chomolungma as it is known to the locals, the highest mountain on earth.

Hillary and Norgay were the first people to reach the top. But they weren't the first people to climb the mountain. Their success was the culmination of a process that stretched right back to 1913 when the Englishman Captain John Noel traveled illegally into Tibet, disguised as a Mohammedan from India. The purpose of Noel's journey was to scout possible approaches to the mountain named after Sir George Everest, the British surveyor general of India from 1830 to 1843.

In 1921 Colonel C.K. Howard-Bury, an Irish aristocrat, led an expedition to explore access from the north. His party was the first to set foot on the mountain. Further expeditions followed in 1922 and 1924. In 1922 George Ingle Finch and Geoffrey Bruce reached 27,000 feet, still a mile short of the summit. In 1924, British mountaineers Norton and Somervell climbed to 28,128 feet on the North Face without artificial oxygen while, George Mallory and Andrew Irvine made it even further but died in the attempt, although there is still speculation about whether they reached the summit (the consensus of opinion is that they did not). Mallory's body was discovered in 2000.

Following Mallory's ill-fated expedition, a period of several years passed during which access to the mountain was impossible for political reasons. Then, in 1951, a party set off to explore approaches to the mountain from the south side, through Nepal. The reconnaissance expedition party, led by Eric Shipton, also included a young New Zealander, Edmund Hillary, and a local Sherpa, Tenzing Norgay. They discovered what they thought was a climbable route to the summit on the south side but were forced to turn back due to poor weather. In 1952 a Swiss expedition accompanied by Tenzing Norgay made it to 28,210 feet but, without cooking equipment, were unable to eat or drink enough, and failed to reach the summit because of lack of strength. Another Swiss expedition also failed to make it to the summit in the autumn of 1952.

In 1953 the British, fearful that someone else would beat them to it, launched a determined bid for the summit under the leadership of Colonel John Hunt. It was an exceptionally strong party that included Edmund Hillary, Tenzing Norgay, Tom Bourdillon and Charles Evans. After lengthy and meticulous planning the expedition approached the mountain in March. On 26 May Bourdillon and Evans made a bid for the summit. They made it to 28,750 feet, less than 300 feet from the summit, only to turn back when one of their oxygen sets malfunctioned. Then, on 29th of May, Hillary and Tenzing set out to conquer the world's highest peak.

Plan then plan again

What has any of this to do with careers? (Other than the fact that Hillary switched from a career as a beekeeper to being a full-time mountaineer and explorer.) The point is that Hillary and Tenzing didn't just turn up at the Himalayas in 1953 and then stroll up the mountain. Their achievement was the end result of a lengthy and extended planning process that drew not only on their own experiences of the mountain from an earlier expedition, but also the experiences of the intrepid but unsuccessful mountain climbers who had tested the ground before them.

When you set out on your own personal career adventure you need to prepare as carefully and meticulously as Hillary and Norgay did. In their case their lives were at stake. In your case it is not quite as melodramatic. Nonetheless, neglect planning and your future happiness is at risk.

The aim of this section is to help with that planning; in particular to help with the process of identifying your career equivalent of Mount Everest, your next employer, scouting your approach and plotting the route to the summit.

Don't rule anything out

At this stage, keep an open mind. Everest could be where you least expect it. Did you ever visit your career advisor at school or at college? Most of us have had this experience at some point. Did the conversation go something like this?

'Ah Smith, I gather you are a fairly gregarious person, with good people skills, and an interest in the media. I suggest a career in the film and television industry making artificial snow. The biggest, and possibly the only company in the field, is a company called Snow Business, I just happen to know someone who works there....'

Or, 'Taylor I understand that you are an excellent driver with a special talent for driving at high speeds and fortunately you are under 6 feet in height. I would say you are perfectly suited for a career racing cars. The hours are good, and although the occupation is a little risky, the pay prospects are outstanding.'

If it did, you had an exceptional career advisor. A more probable conversational tack is:

'Ah Jones, more education? Or a nice administrative job in banking or insurance. Or how about something secretarial?'

Yes, hundreds of thousands of people do administrative and secretarial jobs and are very happy but there is more to the world than this type of work.

From pet-food taster to mountain guide, from tea buyer to wig maker, from bookbinder to belly-dance instructor there are hundreds of jobs out there that you have probably never heard of.

Not researching the different occupations available is bit like someone in the Middle Ages setting out for the holiday of a lifetime. Consulting a map of the known world during the planning stage of the journey, the intrepid adventurer would have discovered a fairly restricted choice of destinations. Hawaii beach holidays and white water rafting in New Zealand were out of the question – neither Australasia or the Americas were on the map. In fact, there was nothing on the map except three separate blank areas representing Africa, Europe and Asia. But had our early traveler managed to acquire an Ancient Roman or Greek map they would have discovered that the world's geography was a great deal more varied than the Church led them to believe and consequently their choice of destinations considerably expanded.

So it is with occupations. Don't be satisfied with the obvious. Don't limit your career horizons unnecessarily. Explore the possibilities until you have found the career that feels right.

For a start it is worth checking out Canada's National Occupation Classification 2001 (http://cnp2001noc.worklogic.com/e/groups/index.shtml); the US Labor Department's online Occupational Outlook Handbook, 2002-03 Edition (www.bls.gov/oco/home.htm) or the UK government's list of occupational descriptions (www.worktrain.gov.uk).

In addition, there is plenty of inspiration to be found in *Occupational Outlook Handbook 2000-01 Edition,* US Department of Labor; *Careers for Nonconformists: A Practical Guide to Finding and Developing a Career Outside the Mainstream,* Sandra Gurvis (Marlowe & Co, 1999); *100 Best Careers for the 21st Century,* Shelly Field (IDG Books Worldwide, 2000); *America's Top Jobs for People Without a Four-Year Degree: Jobs In All Major Occupation And Industries,*J. Michael Farr (Jist Works, 1998).

CAREER ADVENTURER

BETTY BIANCONI
Title/Position: Food Stylist, Recipe Developer, and Food Editor
Company: In Good Taste Creative Food Services
Location: Plainfield, New Jersey
Email: betscooking@home.com

'As a food stylist, it's my job to prepare and arrange the food for food pictures in magazines, ads, commercials and infomercials. I make it look absolutely ravishingly gorgeous for the photographer who snaps the picture. I even did a shoot that involved toothpaste, and styled the toothpaste on the toothbrush. I also develop recipes to go with the magazine articles and ad campaigns for clients' food products. I'm like a food architect: I translate my clients' concepts into form and make them concrete. For example, let's say a client wants to show that you can make a gourmet meal with mayonnaise. I come up with the ideas, whatever that gourmet meal might be from appetizer to dessert. Then I go into the kitchen with the concept, put ingredients together, cook it, and then write it up as a finished recipe. In my career I've done thousands. For chicken alone, I did about 250 recipes for Country Pride at once that showed up on all of their packaging.

As food editor I'm responsible for being the liaison between the magazine's editor and the people of the food department that work under my direction. I generate ideas for articles, and then make sure that the idea gets put into physical form. At Woman's World magazine, I supervise my department in recipe development, bring the ideas together, arrange for the prop stylists, photographer (if it's going to be photographed) and tasting, do the recipe editing, fit it into whatever space is allowed in the magazine, and pull it all together with photography and text. I'm the person who signs off to make sure that all of the t's are crossed, the i's are dotted, and nothing is misspelled or wrong. If it's for a cookbook my job involves taking the recipes I'm given, making sure the can sizes are right, the products are still available, the recipes are appropriate for the book and the chapters, etc.

My background is in nutrition and dietetics. I'm a registered dietician. While in college I did an internship in a leading Harvard-affiliated hospital in Boston. I worked in every aspect a dietician could work in, planning menus, speaking about nutrition to local groups, having food thrown in my face, that wasn't fun. At the hospital the one thing that patients can complain about in their care is the food. I decided that my life was not about handling complaints about hospital food.

How did you get to be a food stylist?

'How did I get this unique path? I was going to give up on dietetics. I didn't know about the openings in food companies and publishing. I answered an ad as a home economist for Good Housekeeping magazine. I was overqualified for that job, but the department that did the 'You and Your Diet' section had just lost their dietician and had an opening. Like one of those synchronistic moments in life, they just handed over my resume and I ended up where I was supposed to be. It was the first job that I applied for. So I fell into the perfect job given my qualifications and desires and the rest is history. That was first job out of college, working for Good Housekeeping in a test kitchen and writing the 'You and Your Diet' column for this national magazine. I thrived on the creativity and had a great time doing it.

Unfortunately, Good Housekeeping was among the companies that pioneered reductions in their workforce. One Friday afternoon after almost working there seven years they let about 24 people go, including me. So I so started freelancing for a little while. One of the places that I freelanced was Woman's Day Magazine. A home economist on their staff was leaving, so a position opened up. I said "I like it here, how about letting me stay as permanent." They said "Fine." I was there for about seven years. It was there that I added the art of food styling to my list of skills. Food styling is my way of being an artist without the frustration of trying to put paint on paper.

I chose motherhood over test kitchen/home economist. I left when I had my daughter. Kids grow too fast, and that's when I started freelancing again, so that I could pick and choose my days and hours and be with my daughter most of the time. Then things got a little bit tight financially, and it was time for mom to pitch in more with the family finances. Someone told me about a job as food editor in charge of the whole food department at Woman's World magazine. They had been interviewing candidates for three months. In another of those synchronistic moments, in less than two weeks I had two interviews and the food editor's position.

I worked there for about two years before a new editor-in-chief came in who brought in all of her own people, so I was back in the freelance business again and very happy about it. I have worked in corporate settings with time constraints and deadlines. I did the daily traveling, the hour commute on the Jersey Turnpike. Been there, done that, OVER!"

2. FINDING YOUR EVEREST

Meet newbie career adventurer Fay. Fay, who lives in Dallas, has carried out a comprehensive, self-assessment exercise as suggested in Section One. She has also consulted a career advisor. The results of the various tests she has taken suggest she is an outgoing, sociable and fun-loving individual who likes to help people and would prefer a job where she can travel, where no day is really the same and where she isn't working a straight 9 to 5.

After sifting through lists of jobs suggested by the self-assessment tests, checking out occupation descriptions at websites and listening to her career advisor, Fay decides that a career in the airline industry, possibly as a flight attendant, is perfect for her. The question is which airline?

An organization fit for you

Once you have decided what kind of adventure suits you best, what kind of industry you want to work in, the next step is choosing your first destination. There are many factors to consider when deciding which organization to make the first stop on your career journey. When considering an organization think about:

◆ What kind of shape is the company in financially?
◆ Is the company/industry expanding or contracting?
◆ Organizational structure e.g. flat or hierarchical?
◆ Company culture, values, vision, mission

◆ Locations

◆ What career paths are available?

◆ The range of business activities, products and services.

◆ How many employees are there?

◆ Promotion policy – based on ability or length of service?

◆ Standard working hours – fixed or flexible?

◆ Is remote working available?

◆ Who are the major competitors?

◆ Is the company technologically switched on?

◆ What is the work-life balance like?

◆ The attitude towards and provision of training.

◆ How do pay and benefits compare to the industry average?

This is just a start. Knowledge really is power. Just as knowledge confers a competitive advantage on companies, so knowledge will shift the odds of attaining a satisfying career in the career adventurer's favor. Company research is essential: firstly, to decide which company to apply to; secondly, to plan your approach strategy. However you decide to apply for a job, whether it is replying to job adverts or a more proactive approach (more on these later), thorough company research is a must.

Uncovering what you need to know

The first challenge, therefore, is to find the information.

The good news is that, for the majority of companies, there are plenty of resources available for researching the essential facts. The Internet is the best place to start. Basic information that can be gleaned online ranges from recent press coverage to in-depth financials and details of a company's product range.

Most companies now have their own websites, but general sources are a good place to start. Succinct corporate information is available in a format commonly known as company capsules or snapshots. Probably the best-known online source of corporate information presented in this format is Hoovers Online (www.hoovers.com). There you will find a treasure trove of

ONLINE COMPANY RESEARCH RESOURCES

http://home.sprintmail.com/~debflanagan
A business research tutorial that presents a "step-by-step process for finding free company and industry information on the World Wide Web".

http://www.jobreviews.com
Potentially an excellent resource with on-the-ground reports on companies from employees and interviewees. It has information on what jobs actually involve, on salary and on interviewing (see Section Three). Unfortunately the database wasn't working when we delved a little deeper so we are unable to attest to the depth of information available.

http://www.bondra.com/comptraining.htm
According to the website it is a guide intended to "help the user research information on both public and private companies using just the Internet. It is not meant to be all-inclusive but is a selected list of sources". It may not be all-inclusive but it is comprehensive enough to meet the needs of most people who need to analyze a company.

information on listed companies including: a summary of the company's activities, a link to recent news and articles about the company, details of executive officers, detailed financials, employee numbers, links to annual reports and lots more.

Another particularly good source of information is the financial section at Yahoo.com (http://finance.yahoo.com). Look up a company's stock ticker symbol, input it and then click on the Profile link. This will take you to an excellent snapshot of the company with text summaries and a range of historical financial data.

Corporate websites are another key resource. They can be particularly useful for finding more out about private companies that are not required by law to file detailed financials. Visiting the website of a company can also provide an excellent introduction to the culture.

Large corporations, Fortune 500 companies for example, put a wealth of information on their company websites. Take IBM for example. At www.ibm.com not only will you find comprehensive information about IBM's products and services but also a section titled 'Reasons to work for IBM'. There is also detailed financial information available, press releases and one of the best sections on corporate history you will find on any corporate website.

Logging off, there are a number of hard-copy publications, which also provide useful information on companies.

The local press is unlikely to be a great source of information on the Microsofts and Boeings of this world (unless you're reading *The Seattle Times*). But for local companies the local press, trade press and publicly filed accounts will provide your best chance of finding out whether a local company is financially robust and thriving, or teetering on the edge of bankruptcy.

For larger, better-known companies, the business press can give a good feel for whether a company's fortunes are waxing or waning. Try broadsheets such as the *Financial Times*, and the *Wall Street Journal*, as well as business magazines like *Fortune, Wired, Fast Company, BusinessWeek* and *Red Herring*.

Don't forget the specialized trade press. These publications will often provide a more detailed view of companies within a particular industry as is evident from titles such as *Corrections Technology & Management Magazine, Packaging News UK, Stitches Magazine* and *National Hog Farmer*. To track down magazines such as these try websites such as Primedia's (www.industryclick.com/ icmagazines.asp), TechExpo's scientific magazines (www.techexpo.com/toc/ tech_mag.html) and Yahoo's listings of trade magazines (http://dir.yahoo.com/business_and_Economy/Business_to_ Business/News_and_Media/Magazines/Trade_Magazines)

Good financial coverage is also available on many satellite and cable television channels. Bloomberg and CNBC, for example, provide detailed information, including broker and analyst opinions, on a range of companies.

Adventure 7

What are you looking for in an employer? Do you have great expectations or has your optimism been sucked dry by experience? Make a short list of the essentials you expect:

CAREER ADVENTURER

Dr PETER NEVILLE

Title/Position:	Animal Behaviorist
Location:	Salisbury, Wiltshire, UK
Email:	peter@pets.f9.co.uk
Website:	www.pets.f9.co.uk

Peter Neville is a companion-animal behavior therapist. He has been in practice for the referral and treatment of behavior problems in cats and dogs for more than 12 years.

He has a degree in biology from the University of Lancaster and a doctorate from the Etologisk Institute in Denmark for studies on feline behavior and the development of treatment for pet behavior problems. After completing his postgraduate studies he established the first companion-animal behavior referral clinic at a UK veterinary school at the Department of Medicine, University of Bristol, in 1990.

Peter, what drew you to this field?

'Accident. My father is 88; he paid for my education. He's still waiting for me to get a proper job. In my father's day, and I think right up to thirty years ago, companion animals were considered disposable. If your dog bit you or someone else, you'd get rid of it and get a new one. In fact, that was the way people were before the Second World War. For at least the past ten thousand years, dogs were selected for their ability to do a job. Nobody really asked them to be nice.

About a hundred years ago, perhaps more, people started to keep dogs just because they were nice to have around. At some point they started to live in peoples' homes instead of outside in kennels. And that's when the problems started.

Some people became even more attached emotionally to their animals. That became important as Western society's wealth grew and people could afford to have companion animals as friends. If something went wrong with their animal, they were also emotionally attached to them, and less likely to just throw them away. Of course the poor old dog and cat were increasingly expected to fulfill different demands to those they had been bred to do.

I started out as a biologist working in Kenya. I was looking at the predation of birds by small cats. When I came back to the UK people asked me to give talks about the behavior and ecology of small cats. And the next thing you know I've got veterinarians phoning me up asking "What do we do about this cat that does this or that in a domestic setting?" The professor of the medicine department at the Veterinary School at Bristol said, "Why don't you come in and run a clinic?" That's where it started.

I realized this was a big need among pet owners. It began in California, where these sorts of things generally begin. The veterinary approach tends to be based on medication rather than asking how animals learn and how we help them learn to cope better with the demands and frustrations of human life. A lot of what we call animal "behavior problems" are things that human beings find difficult to live with, but they're not really abnormal behaviors for the animal.

I think I was very lucky. I just happened to be in the right place when this was taking off. It was charm. Really all we were doing was applying what we knew of ancestral wild species' behavior to human companion animals. By and large, it was effective enough to prove that behavior therapy for animals could be effective. So we began to fill a need.

The whole idea of pets on the psychiatrist's couch is so media worthy, that as soon as I poked my head over the parapet, media people and pet food companies surrounded me. It had its own life very quickly. But as a biologist I studied various mammals such as cats, seals, and moles in terms of behavior. When I came back from Africa I got to know some very prime-moving, forward-thinking dog people. We formed a little association of pet shrinks (we're not pretentious here). We think of behavior as a "living room floor" subject.

I guess in the end I'm always thinking that I'll go back to being a biologist again, but that was twenty years ago. This just won't let go of me; it's such a huge subject now.

Occasionally I get asked to do lectures for big commercial interests, especially banks, about what animal behavior has to teach us in terms of corporate structure and institutional behavior. In the end, social animals are competitive. You look at the motivations and strategies that they use to advance themselves within social systems.

Good corporate managers have to be aware of how to get the best out of people. I work with wolves a lot. So we begin by looking at the way that wolf social behavior is socialized. They think it's a nice easy afternoon, until I start to point out the types. That's when they get the uncomfortable feeling that their identity in the corporate system has been identified. I point out that one of the behavioral purposes of testosterone is to protect males against the anxiety of physical competition. I'm there to make people realize that social systems are just as applicable on the African Savanna as they are in the corporate boardroom, and that can be a lot of fun.

How do people respond when you tell them what you do?

'Usually they look at me for a second, and then they start to tell me about their dog or cat. Ten years ago the first thing I'd get was a sort of stifled laugh, but if I kept a straight face they'd realize that they shouldn't laugh, and I'd be slightly on the defensive trying to defend what I do. But that's changed a lot in ten years. We've had endless television programs about pet psychology. So I think it's well enough established now that people say, "Oh you do that, do you." I'm no longer embarrassed about it.

In social situations I tend to not say what I do, because you know what's coming. People can't help telling me about their animal. Most of the time people seem genuinely interested, because after all, if someone tells you they are a civil engineer, what do you ask a civil engineer at a party? You tend to drop right off, don't you?"

3. ARE YOU FITTING COMFORTABLY?

As you seek out information on your potential employers, keep your eyes and ears open for information about a number of issues.

Pay

Comparative pay information is essential for successful career adventuring. Without knowing your own value in the market you will have no way of gauging what salary you should ask for. Don't be tempted to be guided solely by your existing salary; it may be way out of line with the rest of the market.

The following sites all contain information about occupational salaries. See what you could or should be earning:

http://stats.bls.gov/news.release/ocwage.toc.htm

www.salary.com

http://jobstar.org/tools/salary/sal-surv.htm

http://swz-hoovers.salary.com

Location

If you like the buzz of the dense impenetrable urban jungle, than you are unlikely to be happy working in a small village miles from the nearest multiplex. Equally, if you're lover of verdant rolling pastures the prospect of working in the middle of Manhattan may be abhorrent. Realistically, not everyone gets to choose where they live and work. Social and economic forces may dictate location. But for those people who are able and happy to relocate they could do worse than check out Employment Review's annual America's Best Places to Live and Work survey (www.bestjobsusa.com/sections/CAN-bestplaces2001 / index.asp). The survey looks at figures such as cost of living, unemployment rates and predicted job growth. It provides in-depth information on 20 cities that, according to the survey, provide the best employment opportunities.

If you are located in the US and interested in the costs of relocating a useful resource is the *Wall Street Journal's* real estate pages (http://homes.wsj.com/relocation). The section on relocation contains articles on aspects of relocating throughout the US. If you are considering relocation within the US you will also need to check on the relative costs of living. Once again the *Wall Street Journal* provide a good online aid with its salary calculator that calculates relative salaries at locations throughout the US (www.careerjournal.com/salaries/calculator/index.html).

If you are a globetrotter at heart and harbor a desire to travel the world while pursuing your career then one website worth looking at is that of the overseas jobs newspaper *Overseas Jobs Express* (www.overseasjobsexpress.co.uk). For information about all aspects of relocation there is the relocation journal website (www.relojournal.com).

Reputation

Another useful indicator is a company's reputation among its peers. The definitive survey of corporate reputation is America's Most Admired Companies published annually in *Fortune* magazine. Chosen from the one thousand largest US companies (ranked by revenue) and the 25 largest US subsidiaries of foreign-owned companies, companies are sorted into the top 10 for each industry category (www.fortune.com/fortune/mostadmired).

To create the industry lists, 61 in total, Clark Martire & Bartolomeo (CM&B) asked the thousand executives, directors and securities analysts to rank companies in their own industry on eight criteria from long-term investment value to social responsibility. Similarly, to create the top ten list CM&B asked the participants to name the five companies they admired most, regardless of industry. The result is a list of the most respected companies in the US currently headed by General Electric and Cisco Systems.

Some information is available remotely via the Internet. Among the many surveys published by *Fortune* is the annual Best Place to Work survey (go to www.fortune.com and click on the link on the left-hand side). From 234 candidates 100 'best' companies are selected. To make a selection, over 36,000 employees are surveyed by the Great Place to Work Institute of San Francisco, the consulting firm that created the survey. Companies also undergo a culture audit, in which they explain their philosophy and practices.

The Great Place to Work Institute conducts a similar exercise in the UK, which is published in the *Sunday Times* as the 50 Best Companies to Work For (www.greatplacetowork.co.uk). For this list almost 16,000 employees are surveyed representing a cross-section of businesses ranging in size from 500 to 100,000 employees with turnovers between £25 million and £20 billion.

The online version of the magazine *Fast Company* contains a useful A-Z directory of fast companies – those that the magazine considers to be the 'world's most interesting and innovative companies'. The listings include employee responses to a number of questions such as: "The decision-making processes at this office most resemble: A: The Indy 500 – fast and efficient. B: A monster-truck bash - fast, but dirty. C: A freeway at rush hour – slow and easily bottlenecked. D: A tractor pull – painfully slow and lumbering" (http://fcke.fastcompany.com).

For those thinking of joining the denizens of dot.com workers it is worth taking a look at the obscenely named fuckedcompany.com. The website is a memorial to dot.coms who have powered down their PC's for the last time. A section on rumors in the industry contains employee comment and can be useful to gauge morale, conditions and viability at dot.com companies mentioned. It is not foolproof but it proved a reasonable barometer during the dot.com meltdown of 2000/2001.

If you become a member at www.vault.com (free) you can peruse a databank of company guides. Although some only carry basic information, most of the major corporations are covered with corporate snapshots that reveal details about the company's background, getting hired and other aspects of company culture such as workload, dress code and attitudes towards minorities.

Questions of culture

Finding out if a company is financially viable, conveniently located and undertakes the kind of activities you wish to be involved in is one thing. Determining whether you and the company are potential soul mates, or at least a good fit, is quite another. The company that is the leader in the field that you wish to work in may be financially robust. It may even be growing and recruiting. It may seem the obvious place to apply for a job. But, and it is a big but, would you fit in?

The key to a good fit is corporate culture. Corporate culture is a term which Edgar Schein, an academic based at the Massachusetts Institute of Technology, is widely credited with inventing. Schein describes culture as "a pattern of basic assumptions – invented, discovered, or developed by a given group as it learns to cope with its problems of external adaptation and internal integration – that has worked well enough to be considered valid and, therefore, to be taught to new members as the correct way to perceive, think, and feel in relation to those problems". Culture, in other words, is the way things are done around here.

These basic assumptions, says Schein, can be categorized into five dimensions:

◆ **Humanity's relationship to nature** – while some companies regard themselves as masters of their own destiny, others are submissive, willing to accept the domination of their external environment.

- ◆ **The nature of reality and truth** – organizations and managers adopt a wide variety of methods to reach what becomes accepted as the organizational 'truth' – through debate, dictatorship, or through simple acceptance that if something achieves the objective it is right.

- ◆ **The nature of human nature** – organizations differ in their views of human nature. Some follow Douglas McGregor's Theory X and work on the principle that people will not do the job if they can avoid it. Others regard people in a more positive light and attempt to enable them to fulfill their potential for the benefit of both sides.

- ◆ **The nature of human activity** – the Western world has traditionally emphasized tasks and their completion rather than the more philosophical side of work. Achievement is all. Schein suggests an alternative approach – 'being-in-becoming' – emphasizing self-fulfillment and development.

- ◆ **The nature of human relationships** – organizations make a variety of assumptions about how people interact with each other. Some facilitate social interaction, while others regard it as an unnecessary distraction.

These five categories are not mutually exclusive, but are in a constant state of development and flux. Culture does not stand still.

Corporate culture is not just an abstract notion. It is a consistent thread woven through the fabric of everyday working life. Some companies will define their values and elucidate their corporate philosophy and culture in writing. Take Hewlett-Packard for example. The company's co-founders David Packard and Bill Hewlett took the trouble to enshrine the corporate culture of their high-tech company – including respect for others, community, and hard work - in The HP Way written in 1957. Pharmaceutical giant Johnson & Johnson has its Credo penned by founder General Robert Wood Johnson in 1943.

However, a company can have a strongly defined corporate culture without an accompanying document that encapsulates it. Take Southwest Airlines. Its corporate culture is summed up by its legendary founder and chairman Herb Kelleher: "Well, first of all, it starts with hiring. We are zealous about hiring. We are looking for a particular type of person, regardless of which job category it is. We are looking for attitudes that are positive and for people who can lend themselves to causes. We want folks who have a good sense of humor and people who are interested in performing as a team and take joy in team results instead of individual accomplishments."

For Kelleher, a match between employee and corporate culture is vital. So should it be for you. You will have to live and work with your company's culture day in, day out. The hours you work, your rewards, your interaction with your co-workers, work-life balance, how you manage and how others manage you, office environment, dress; corporate culture will pervade and affect all these. At home you can choose the lifestyle that suits you, at work, corporate culture determines your work style.

If you assessed your values and discovered the desire to earn large sums of money and be accorded status is extremely important to you then you may be able to survive in an organization where corporate culture is unsuitable but the pay and benefits are adequate compensation. For most people however working in an unsuitable corporate culture will be a huge drag on their career. It can make life a misery, and prevent them from advancing in their career and fulfilling their potential.

CAREER ADVENTURER

DONNA MARTIN *on researching corporate culture*

Title/Position: Senior Vice-President, Human Resources
Company: Faulding Pharmaceuticals
Industry: Pharmaceuticals

'I ask a lot of questions from a lot people, the same questions across the board to a variety of people regarding how they work, and how they communicate in the organization. I look for visible and invisible signs of that. Part of it involves sensing as you watch people interact in the organization. Is what they're telling you borne out by what you see and hear, as well as by what you don't see and don't hear, in the physical environment?

For me it's also about how I feel, there either is a chemistry or there is not. Chemistry is about my ability to communicate and be communicated with. Is the communication level such that we have an understanding that matches? Is there a sense of common direction? I also look for a certain energy level in an organization, and I think you feel that as you walk the halls. Walk around the halls and feel what it's like to be there. Ask employees what they like about being there, and what would make it even better for them?

Ask for the opportunity to do what you can inside the organization before you accept an offer. Ask. They may not offer it to you, but ask. It's in the organization's control, but I love it when a candidate asks if they can walk around and see more, and to talk to people in different positions. It tells me that they have a different level of interest.'

CAREER ADVENTURER

JOHN REESE *on culture and finding a job*

Title/Position: Business Services Visionary
Company: In transition

John started out as a computer programmer and systems analyst and later focused on delivering groundbreaking business services systems. He has worked for large corporations such as Citibank as well as founding his own company iSearch which had revenues of over $10m a year.

How has the Internet changed job seeking?

'The Internet has now made it incredibly convenient to apply for a job. The good news is that each job seeker can easily press a button and apply. The bad news is that companies are now inundated with electronic resumes, far more than they used to receive on paper. So they need a system to filter those resumes.

My advice to job seekers is to use the Internet. But the best way to find jobs has always been, and continues to be, networking with people, whether through employee referral programs or any other networking process. And do your homework. Research the companies that you want to work for. That's trivially easy now on the Internet.'

How can you find a culture that suits you?

'Fairly early on you need to decide what size organization, and what kind of organizational culture, you feel comfortable with. Those are critically important.

If what you really want is to have someone pay for your MBA program, go to a large corporation. You're less likely to get that kind of support in a small, feisty organization. If you're looking for more degrees of freedom and more potential rapid growth, that might best afforded to you in a smaller company.

Go where your passion is. If you can't get passionate about your current job or where you can take it, leave. I say that assuming that you are not just looking for a 9 to 5 paycheck, but that you want to get a meaningful component of who you are out of your work.'

Culture clues

So how do you find out what a company's culture is like? If it's a big public company then its corporate culture may be well known. If it's a small company the specialized trade press, specialized trade directories and the local press (local to the location of the business, that is) are likely to be the only media sources of information. They may not provide much information but don't knock them. Any relevant snippet may prove useful – awards for local businessmen, details of activities, etc. These are all points of reference, possible points of contact outside of the work environment and at least a potential conversational reference for when you attend an interview or a company tour.

Corporate websites may reveal clues through pages on corporate values. Giant pharmaceutical company Merck lists five values on its website (www.merck.com/overview/philosophy.html). Microsoft, the software behemoth, has a page on its corporate website titled "Living our values", (www.microsoft.com/mscorp/values.htm). It is the same with many other large companies. Even smaller companies may give some indication of their values on their website.

Other useful sources are business books and corporate biographies. Bestseller *Built to Last*, Collins & Porras (Harper Business, 1997) examines a selection of enduring well-known companies including a discussion of values. Many large organizations will have some form of corporate biography in print, authorized or unauthorized. Books such as *The HP Way, How Bill Hewlett and I Built Our Company*, Packard (Harper Business, 1995) or *The Nokia Revolution the Story of an Extraordinary Company that Transformed an Industry*, Steinbock (McGraw-Hill, 2001). Most will give a feel for the company culture as well as providing a useful background. Biographies and autobiographies of business executives will often serve the same purpose.

A great deal of this information should be taken with a sizeable pinch of salt. A huge boulder-like piece of salt is often appropriate. No company is Utopia.

Inside information

For many companies it is not possible to determine what the company culture is like without actually working there or speaking to someone who does or has. This is true even for internationally famous companies, Fortune 500 companies, FTSE 100 companies and other large public companies that receive acres of press coverage. They may give extensive details of their corporate culture on their website, but inside information from former or current employees is still the best way to get a real feel for what it is like to work for them.

Unfortunately, getting the dope from the inside is not always that easy. Most companies like to control their image. This means access to employees through a direct approach to the company is likely to be closely controlled. It is still worth approaching a company directly if you take the right approach. 'Strategic questioning of the corporate people can be helpful,' says Sylvia Milne, partner of Catalyst Career Strategies, "if you know how to read between the lines and ask very focused questions.'

'Find a role model in the particular position that interests you and spend time both during work and off the job with that person,' advises career adventurer Joyce Barrie of Joymarc. 'At work so that you can actually see what it takes, and off the job so that you can find out what the disadvantages are. When someone is doing the job, they can make it look easy and effortless. People see only the end result. It's only by talking to that person off the job (e.g. over lunch) that you can find out what it takes to be successful in that job, as well as what's not so great about it, things you might not be able to figure out for yourself while watching what's going on. You may discover that the nitty-gritty of what it takes to get there may outweigh the potential benefits for you. It's very personal, what works for you may not work for someone else."

Another good resource is the WetFeet site (www.wetfeet.com/research/companies.asp). While there are very basic company details on thousands of companies, a select few, mostly household names, have expanded details. For these companies there is an indication of the company's culture and values revealed by their answers to some set questions.

For example:

Q: Day-to-day, what makes working for your firm different from working for others?

Q: Most brochures speak only to the plusses of working for a firm. Are there any challenges or downsides you'd like to discuss?

Q: What percent of your professional staff is female?

Q: Does your firm sponsor community service activities?

While some company's answers read like a PR puff others are refreshingly frank. UBS Warburg, for example, doesn't mince its words when discussing workload. The prestigious investment bank "demands a high level of commitment from its employees, which is rewarded accordingly. From an early stage, recruits can expect major responsibility, a demanding workload and periods of working long hours."

Likewise the US National Security Agency, which while not flagging up the possibility of taking a bullet in the line of duty, highlights another slightly less painful downside to the job; 'there's a bureaucracy you have to work within, which some people feel stifles their creativity'.

Congratulations also to management consultants the Boston Consulting Group who correctly and honestly note: "Learning to handle the lifestyle takes time, and some people never become comfortable with the fast pace, occasionally long hours, travel, and continual change. Consulting and BCG are probably not for everyone."

It is this kind of honesty that is an invaluable guide to career adventurers. It doesn't take much intelligence to realize if you have strong family commitments and need to be at home evenings and weekends then working as a consultant for the Boston Consulting Group is not a good idea. Indeed, working as a management consultant for any of the big consulting firms is not a good idea. But it is better for both you and the Boston Consulting Group that you find this out now and not after the interview, as by then you will have wasted everyone's time.

CAREER ADVENTURER

FIONA BAILEY *on Corporate Culture*

Title/Position: Director of Culture
Company: Safeway plc
Industries: Retail

Fiona is director of culture at UK retail chain Safeway. Her role is in her own words 'to refine and develop a culture strategy vision, goals, measurable objectives for the business and act as a catalyst and champion (and critic) where needed.' In addition she controls internal communication developing action plans for cultural change within Safeway, benchmarking progress and measuring it.

"The match between corporate culture and potential employees is vital . . . recruitment criteria must align, and you should not compromise . . . a dress hanging on a hanger may look fantastic but it might look dreadful on YOU!!

Involve employees in the process and enable the interviewee to find out more about the working environment before she makes up her mind. Recruiting the wrong fit for culture leads to frustrations, higher labor turnover and extra work and frustration for those left . . .

If the values mean anything then they should be the key attributes to drive business success and therefore are important to embed in all recruitment and retention strategies.'

So what are the tell tale signs to look out for to determine a company's culture?

'Symbols (visual ones like the meeting room decor, posters, reception, dress code); rituals – meeting culture, communication up and down; the attitude of interviewer – hierarchical, interest in YOU. Open? Honest? Willing to admit the company's faults? What do the people look like in their demeanor? Do they look happy? Miserable? Are there pictures of staff or company achievements on the wall? What stories do people tell?'

What are the questions to ask to find out about an organization's culture?

◆ How is effort rewarded (non-financial too)?
◆ What opportunities are there for my ideas to be heard and for people to listen to my feelings?
◆ How will I be looked after as a new starter?
◆ What is the "hours" culture?
◆ What is the company's attitude to risk and failure?
◆ What is the culture of the company and its guiding values?
◆ And its core purpose?
◆ What behaviors and management styles are rewarded?
◆ How accessible is the senior management and the board?
◆ How does the company communicate with its people?
◆ How does it involve its people in the business? Teams? Cross-functional teams?

4. NETWORKING

Finding out more about prospective employers and the world of work is not just a matter of tapping a few questions into a search engine. If it was, everyone would do it. The fact is that some people have an innate, uncanny ability to tap into useful sources of information and inspiration. They are the networkers.

Networking is one of the core skills of career adventurers.

There are many different views on networking, many different approaches. (In the dictionary networking is defined as "to interact or engage in informal communication with others for mutual assistance or support" and a network as "a group, system etc. of interconnected or cooperating individuals".)

So what's the point of networking? To get a job, right? To start your career in the right direction and keep it on track? Yes, yes and again yes. The end goal is the job, but networking is about more than just getting a job. Creating and maintaining a network is arguably the most valuable career investment you will ever make. Jobs change. But a network, if properly cultivated and tended, will last a lifetime.

Think of it as a game where the idea is to meet as many interesting people as possible and be as useful to them as possible. The by-product of the game is this, when a hirer has a position they need to fill the first name that pops into their head is yours.

If you treat networking this way you will avoid coming across as desperate which is a bad thing and have fun which is a good thing.

Networking at its most basic involves contacting friends and family on a regular if infrequent basis. We don't call it networking, of course, we call it keeping in touch. But many of the same skills and disciplines are involved. Networking is essentially about keeping in touch with a lot of people. At its most complex it can involve plugging into professional networking organizations and maintaining tens or even hundreds of contacts, at frequent intervals. You can use the telephone, email, face-to-face contact, letters or the fax. Networking comes in many guises, so anyone can do it, even the painfully shy, given enough planning and practice.

Why is networking so important? Consider this statistic, some 60-90 percent of all job positions are identified through networking. Traditional methods, trawling the job ads, surfing the Internet jobsites etc., do work but only a very small proportion of jobs are ever advertised this way. Job ads can also be unreliable; too often they are already filled by the time you apply.

Hirers will inevitably pick someone with the requisite talents that they know over someone they don't. It's not difficult to work out why. The hirer is more inclined to trust a candidate referred from a trusted source. A candidate who has been referred by an existing employee is also likely to know more about the company, have made a decision about whether they are a good match for the company and the position, and are therefore more likely to be a good fit. The applicant can tailor their approach based on the inside information. Candidates who have gained inside information through informational interviews and networking have a clear advantage.

Networking comes more easily to some people than others. Not everyone has a personality suited to the gregarious pursuit and assimilation of personal contacts.

Shyness can inhibit your career prospects. Researchers have found that those who are shy tend to begin their careers later than non-shy people. They are also more apt to refuse promotions. They choose careers that are less interpersonal and are more undecided about which field to pursue.[1] Once in a career, 'shy people have a harder time developing a career identity – an image of themselves as competent or successful within a career track'. The good news is that shyness need not last a lifetime. It can be beaten. Many of the best networkers have had to overcome personal inhibitions.

Here a few tips for the naturally reclusive:

- As described below, start with your friends and family – people you feel comfortable talking to.
- Try to forget, initially at least, that you are building networks for the purpose of acquiring a job and furthering your career. Concentrate on building friendships and relationships that are mutually beneficial. You scratch their back, they scratch yours.
- Avoid small talk; only contact people when you have a reason to do so.
- Be a good listener.
- Be passionate – if you talk about things that you are passionate about you will forget your inhibitions.
- Identify worries/barriers and draft an action plan to deal with them.
- Pluck up the courage to arrange a meeting – often it's the hardest part of the process. It's usually the "before" that is more of a problem than the "during".

'Like many issues of confidence, social phobia is best overcome through the gradual and systematic exposure to situations that create anxiety, a technique called systematic desensitization," explains the psychologist Robert Sharrock of YSC. "A hierarchy of situations, starting with the most easily achieved to the most demanding, can be created in order to create a sense of accomplishment as goals are achieved. The risk of reclusivity is that the anxiety is never confronted, so remains unchecked over the years, and can even deteriorate as individuals form work routines to minimize their social exposure. The compulsive accountant or actuary could be (admittedly, somewhat stereotyped) examples.

'Having said this, it is important to understand precisely what lies behind apparent cases of social phobia. Some individuals simply do not need people. They like to work in a relatively detached and self-contained manner. They come across as 'cold fish', but can be highly rational, analytical and penetrating in their business thinking. They may be able to form networks of contacts when they can see a clear purpose for so doing, but they are unlikely to be rewarding people to be with. Such individuals work best in roles requiring analysis, logic and objectivity, finance and planning roles, for example.'

'On the other hand, there are those who underlying social needs are higher, but they find contact with others quite threatening. These are more emotional individuals who can form very close enduring relationships, but who find initiating contact difficult. Such individuals can be helped significantly using the above techniques of so-called systematic desensitization. They work best where these aspects of their emotions, possibly feeling threatened by others – work to their advantage rather than disadvantage. Examples may be quality or project implementation roles. Certainly not sales!'

CAREER ADVENTURER

HARVEY MACKAY

Title/Position: CEO, writer, business speaker
Company: Mackay Envelope Company
Web: www.mackay.com

Harvey Mackay knows how to network. It has helped him achieve his career goals. Chairman of a company with annual sales of some $85 million, he is also the author of a series of best-selling business books, his first book was in the *New York Times* best-seller lists for 54 weeks. He has been acclaimed as one of the United State's leading corporate speakers. Despite these accomplishments and an array of plaudits from the great and the good (including the bizarre juxtaposition of Robert Redford and Billy Graham), on his business card Harvey Mackay has a single unfashionable description of himself: salesman.

The very word takes you back to the days when salesmen (sales women were yet to be invented) arrived carrying a heavy bag of samples and an equally weighty arsenal of persuasive phrases. The truth is that no one wants to be called a salesman even if selling is what they do. "There are no jobs unless someone buys something yet, according to business cards, there are no more salesmen," laments Harvey Mackay. "There are a variety of different names which are used. Any word but selling."

This is strange. After all, selling is the very essence of business. Robert Louis Stevenson, author of *Kidnapped*, never clinched a corporate sale in his life but was shrewd enough to observe "Everyone lives by selling something".

And born salesmen are addicted. Now in his late sixties, Harvey Mackay is a rich man. Yet, he still gets a kick out of closing a deal for his company which sells envelopes. After a speech to a corporate audience he is more likely to be found pitching to sell them some envelopes than standing idly around taking the plaudits. "I don't have to do it," he admits. "A born salesmen who still enjoys it gets a thrill out of getting a new order." He goes on to recount a recent trek he made across America in the middle of the night so that he could give a speech to a potential envelope purchaser. Once a salesman always a salesman.

The essence of selling, according to Harvey Mackay, is networking. "Networks," he believes, "are as thick as blood." During the dot.com boom, networking was elevated to something approaching an art. At specially designated weekly meetings bright young things clutching business plans sought to network their way to venture capitalists.

Harvey Mackay does not network with a glass of wine in his hand on a prescribed night of the week. He networks with total dedication. If he is scheduled to go to Kansas City, he will extricate the names of all the people he knows who are based in the city and decide which he needs to meet. His database contains 9,500 names assembled over the last forty-odd years. "It is not a question of collecting business cards by just walking around a room," he says. "I have studied successful people and the common denominator is that over their lifetime they nourish a network of contacts. I see all the people I meet as potentially important to my happiness and my business life."

For all the technology now available, Mr. Mackay regards networking as a highly personal activity. Firing off a shoal of e-mails to people whose business cards you have collected is not what he has in mind. "Nothing could be done without a one-on-one relationship. It is still a one-on-one world," he says.

Harvey MacKay's networking vigor is applied to all his activities. Preparation is all. "Prepare to win. Then prepare to dazzle," he advises. "Due diligence is more than a legal concept. It is the means for making new friends, customers and members of your network." He prepares in detail before each and every of his seminars for around 10 hours per speech. An appearance in Taiwan saw Mackay espousing his selling message in Mandarin. He routinely checks into a language school to bolster his knowledge of the local language. In a business filled with Americans whose world-view regards Canada as international, Harvey Mackay is a surprising internationalist. "I do my homework. I don't leave it to chance. You can't rely on Yankee humor or colloquialisms to get by." His ambition is to visit every country in the world, he jokingly bemoans the break up of the Soviet Union for the obstacles that this presents him.

His books are thoroughly American in tone, if not outlook. Their titles are typical of a uniquely American brand of homespun, high achieving, self-improvement *Dig Your Well Before You're Thirsty, Swim With the Sharks* and the most recent addition to his aphoristic canon, *Pushing the Envelope.* "Getting through the fence to the top dog is easy, if you know the gatekeeper," is typical of his brand of advice.

In essence, his message is that business hasn't changed. Strip business down to its basics and it is still about people selling things to each other. The great proponent of the hard sell was Dale Carnegie and Harvey Mackay treads in his footsteps. He wears his salesmanship with pride. If he does his homework, he shows it off. His networking system may reveal someone has an enthusiasm for stamp collecting. When they meet, he uses this knowledge to re-establish a bond. He does his homework and will tell you so. Like all great salesmen, his enthusiasm is there for all to see. His company's dictum is "Thank God it's Monday". If you are tired of networking, you are tired of life.

You already have a network

Networking begins at home. For networking beginners the best place to start is with people they already know. This way the networker can ease into the process and expand their horizons as confidence increases. "But I don't know anybody worth contacting", is a common complaint. But for the majority of people a few moments of contemplation will reveal this as patently untrue.

You may be familiar with the six (or seven) degrees of the Kevin Bacon puzzle. For those who don't know, Kevin Bacon is successful Hollywood actor who has starred in, among others, that celluloid classic *Tremors*. The aim is to link Kevin Bacon with any other actor using only six (or seven) connecting steps. So, for example, how is Carrie Fisher connected to Kevin Bacon?

The answer:
Carrie Fisher was in *Star Wars* with **Harrison Ford** who was in *The Fugitive* with **Tommy Lee Jones** who was in *Batman Forever* with **Val Kilmer** who was in *Heat* with **Robert DeNiro** who was in *Sleepers* with **Kevin Bacon.**

An amusing if pointless pastime you say. Possibly. The point is that it illustrates the power of networks. It is said that if you pick any person on the planet you are only seven steps away from connecting with them. Ridiculous? Well consider it this way. Do you know the US President to talk to? Probably not. But try aiming a little lower and working your way up. Do you know a community leader or local politician, or if not, do you know someone that knows them. Because your local political representative will know the regional political representative, who will know someone in government, who will know someone who knows the US President. And in only six steps.

Your connection to the US President may not be of much practical use in career terms. But, apply this theory to useful contacts within companies you would consider working for, and you will see that networking is a very powerful career skill.

Your network might include the following for example:

◆ Family
◆ Friends
◆ People you know less well through clubs, societies etc.
◆ Old school friends – alumni organization
◆ Work colleagues and ex-colleagues
◆ Teachers, lecturers, personal tutors and other academics
◆ Members of your church
◆ Members of the local community – councilors etc.
◆ Politicians – local representative
◆ People you see on a regular basis – local shopkeepers, bartenders etc.
◆ Professionals – your lawyer, doctor, dentist (although it's not always easy to talk to the dentist)
◆ Other businesspeople – bank manager, hairdresser
◆ Local business organizations – chamber of commerce, Rotary Club

These are all potential contacts. Get chatting with the ones that you see on a fairly regular basis. Find out what makes them tick, what their interests are. Learn to listen, it's one of the most important skills for a networker.

Adventure 8

Write down a list of people you know well. Then split them into three groups:

1. People who have the ability to hire you or influence the hirer.

2. People who know about the kind of work/job you want to do – people who work/or have worked in that field, who know the skills, qualification type of personality required etc.

3. And finally people who aren't in (1) or (2) but might know someone who is.

You will probably end up with a lot of names in group (3), fewer in (2) and fewer still in (1). But with some successful networking under your belt the numbers will even out.

With the people you know best and trust, ask them for feedback, and advice on your technique. When you have more confidence from building and improving your close contacts try stretching your comfort zone a little. Strike up a conversation with fellow passengers when you are traveling. If you are stuck in a queue try light conversation with your neighbors. On holiday, watching a sports game,even out shopping, you may be surprised; a good contact can come from the most unexpected encounters.

Professional networking

Some networks, of course, open more doors than others. This explains the enduring appeal of exclusive clubs. Businesspeople have always been a clubbable lot, but the networking-obsessed new economy spawns new possibilities.

Clubs have a long history. The nineteenth century was the heyday of gentlemen's clubs in Britain. In places like the Athenaeum, the Carlton and the Reform Club, political debate gave way to more pragmatic concerns. The idea that the vulgar conduct of business should be left at the door was wasted on the new arrivals. Today, businesspeople have their own power networks. The business club has come of age. The old clubs are being elbowed aside by new, better organized, and more commercial models.

New technology opens new doors. A global economy demands global clubs. Reaching across national borders, they can provide access and instant introductions around the world.

Networks of influence

Belonging to an intellectual network has cachet. Consider the Strategos Institute, part of Strategos, the consulting operation founded by management guru and academic Gary Hamel. To the select few, Strategos offers membership of its Institute, "a consortium of successful companies who are addressing the most fundamental business challenge of our time". The Strategos Institute offers two levels of membership, general membership or full partner level. General members can participate in two of the four research streams the Institute is pursuing, while partners can participate in all four. Partnership has its privileges, a one-day workshop with Gary Hamel designed expressly for the company. Easy payment terms are available.

But for serious network effect, the Global Business Network (GBN) is hard to beat. Founded by scenario-planning guru and former Shell executive Peter Schwartz and four friends in 1987, the idea emerged around a pool table in a Berkeley, California basement. The five co-founders envisiged a worldwide learning community of organizations and individuals. GBN's Explorers Club is there to help companies make the "transition from the old to the new economy".

Today, GBN is based in Emeryville, California, in a former tractor factory, and has around 100 client members including the government of Singapore, as well as big corporations. Small fry need not apply. Corporate membership costs $40,000 annually and individual members are invited to join only if they can "contribute remarkable insights, provocative ideas and deep experience".

In return for their membership cards, thrusting executives get the chance to hob-nob with each other at seminars and conferences, picking up lots of fresh ideas and perspectives on the way. They belong to an exclusive club that includes business gurus, show-biz doyens and a former Apollo astronaut.

Leading GBN members and advisers include the management luminaries Michael Porter, Gary Hamel, Esther Dyson, Edgar Schein and Arie de Geus. Bill Joy, co-founder of Sun Microsystems is another GBN member, as is John Kao, author of Jamming and founder of The Idea factory. Kevin Kelly of Wired magazine, and artists including Brian Eno, Peter Gabriel and the novelist Douglas Coupland are also GBN members or advisory members.

Education, too, remains a primary route to networking. The traditional power networks such as Ivy League, Oxbridge and Grand Ecoles are being augmented by business schools. Business schools are taking the educational club to new heights. The b-schools alumni associations are among the most powerful executive clubs. They help graduates develop their careers, update skills, make new contacts and generally open doors in the world of business, politics and beyond. At the bigger and better known schools, the alumni networks are worldwide fellowships. From Boston to Beijing, and most cities in between, there will be a member of the alumni network who is only too pleased to make alumni feel at home.

With 22,500 members, the French business school INSEAD's Alumni Association has members in 120 countries throughout the world. But when it comes to clubbing, the American business schools make their European cousins look like amateurs. With more than 60,000 active alumni worldwide, in terms of pure networking muscle Harvard Business School is in a class of its own. At the last count, no fewer than a quarter of the directors of the Fortune 500 companies were Harvard alumni.

People don't go to business school just for the learning. Induction into the alumni club is part of the deal. In return, the business school expects regular donations. In a business world of ambiguity and alienation, clubs offer certainty and a sense of belonging. That isn't going to change. If you can't beat them, you might as well join them.

CAREER ADVENTURER

FRANCO SAMA *on networking*

Title/Position: Producer/Consultant
Company: Samaco Productions
Industry: Entertainment
Location: West Hollywood, CA

In addition to his work at his production company Franco provides career counseling to industry professionals.

'I call the networking process 'establishing, nurturing, and developing relationships'. It's critical. There are so many networking groups and organizations. Pretty much every major organization in the entertainment industry has some form of networking gathering. I'm a fan of 'Women in Film,' they have breakfasts and luncheons. I also go to the one at the Friar's Club, the Creative Alliance and others.

In general the whole purpose of these events is to network and meet people who can further the action of your project. They're built for that. So you don't walk in wondering whether you should give out your card – that's the purpose of the function.

Personally, I've never, ever walked away from an event without making a significant contact. There's an important factor here though, which is part of what I teach in my class. What most people do when they go to these things is they go and collect cards, which is lovely if what you are looking for is a nice big card collection. Then they put them in a file and don't do anything with them.

I teach people not to take the card if they're not going to use it. And if they do take the card to follow up within 24 hours and be on the phone with them or these days it's just as well to email. You need to do that and continue to do that every 60 to 90 days, you need to be in constant communication with your network. Otherwise when you need them six months from now they won't know who you are. Remember what I said before, it's about establishing, developing and nurturing relationships. Simply collecting a business card doesn't do any of those things.'

The next step: the infoview

You've contacted all the people you feel comfortable with. You have even made occasional contacts with strangers through chance meetings. Now it's time to home in on your target. By now you should have identified some people who work in the field that you hope to work in. Contact them and arrange an informal meeting, an informational interview.

The purpose of this meeting is NOT to ask for a job. Repeat: Do NOT ask them for a job! It's a surefire way of blowing a contact before you have even started. They feel used; you get nowhere. Instead, over coffee, or over a beer, avail yourself of their expertise. Explain to them that you want to find out more about the industry and you were hoping they could help. Then subtly pump them for information. What is it like working in the industry? What advice would they give for someone trying to break into the industry? What are different companies like to work for? Most importantly do they know anyone else you could talk to?

An informational interview is nothing more than you, talking to (interviewing), someone who knows what it is like to work in the industry you want to do the kind of work you want to do work for the company you are thinking of joining or any combination of these. Someone that knows more than you do. You get the chance to pick their brains. This is one of the preliminary objectives of networking.

Treat the informational interview as you would a job interview from the point of preparation. Research the industry your target works in and the company they work for. Dress appropriately i.e. whatever you expect them to wear and then a little bit smarter etc. (see the passage on interviews in Section Three for more information).

Note the use of the word "interview". This implies that someone is asking questions and someone is answering them. In this case you are the one doing the asking so it pays to be prepared. Here then is a random selection of questions to ask at informational interviews:

◆ What are your work responsibilities?
◆ What is the career path like? What are the opportunities for advancement?
◆ What do you dislike about your job?

◆ What is the atmosphere like where you work?

◆ What is the company's attitude towards flexible working?

◆ What kind of hours do you work?

◆ Does your company reward its employees well?

◆ What skills/qualifications/personality characteristics does someone need to do your job?

◆ How did you get started?

◆ What advice would you give to someone who wanted to work in the same field as you?

After the meeting, you should:

◆ Make notes to remind you of any personal interests or other details the contact mentioned. It may seem a little impersonal but in reality it's just common sense. Unless you are the kind of person who can memorize a pack of cards, knows the names of the characters and the actors who play them in every film you have ever seen and remembers the words to the Eagles classic Hotel California without having to hum after "On a dark desert highway", then you will inevitably forget most of what your contact tells you. Especially when the list of contacts grows into double figures.

◆ If you do take notes, however, the next time you make contact it will be easier to strike up a rapport, knowing as you do from your notes that Mr X is a Lakers fan and likes dangerous sports.

◆ Thank your contact for taking the trouble to meet you. First, because it is polite to do so. Second, because it will remind the contact that you exist in a good way. Email is a good means of doing this. "Always follow up" is one of the cardinal rules of career adventuring. Whether it is post-interview, after networking, during the mentoring process, following up with a polite thank you is essential.

◆ Follow up the contacts that you gain through these informal meetings, using a similar strategy. This time it is a referral. You can introduce yourself with "So-and-so suggested you might be able to spare me a few moments/give me some advice etc." If you handle it well, most people will be flattered. Remember, too, to thank them if their advice pays off.

Adventure 9

Like any relationship networking should not, and cannot if it is to be successful, be all take, take, take. Ideally networking is a win-win situation. All parties in a network should gain something. It's not always a straightforward reciprocal benefit. A might provide B with a lead who might in turn help C who refers A to a good contact.

An easy way to make sense of how networking is a two-way street is to make a list of people in your network and then list how they help you and you help them. If there are any gaps you need to fill them in quickly.

WHO YOU ARE NETWORKED WITH	HOW YOU HELP THEM	HOW THEY HELP YOU

Netting the big fish

When it comes to landing that prized job the people who really matter are the decision makers, the hirers and firers. Depending on the size of the company, hirers can be anyone from the founder or CEO in a small-to medium-sized company, to a departmental or business unit head in a large company. They can also be someone in the HR department, although the HR department will work in close liaison with line management.

Getting to these people is not easy. If your networking has been successful or plain lucky, you may have already cultivated some of these contacts. If not then it will be a case of cold-calling or, at best, lukewarm calling.

The difficulty in getting to hirers, is negotiating the screeners, the people whose job it is to make sure that the hirer is not unduly bothered throughout the day, leaving them to concentrate on more important and weightier matters than dealing with speculative telephone calls or emails from would-be networkers. Reaching the hirer, without annoying the screener or coming across as a stalker, requires careful strategy and planning.

There are a number of approaches:

1. **Try bypassing the screener.** This is not easy, but it is possible. Prepare to be astonished. Hirers do answer their own telephone sometimes. They may have their own private line. If you can get hold of the number then you have a head start. Alternatively try phoning when the screeners are likely to be absent, early in the morning, lunch times, late in the evening.

2. **Cultivate the screener** (or anyone else who could provide a route to the hirer). If the screener cannot put you through, don't just meekly hang up. Be straight, let the screener know who you are and why you wish to speak to the hirer. Tell them you are interested in finding out more about the company, industry etc. Ask if they could suggest anyone else who might be able to help you. Note and remember the screener's name. Try not to be too smooth or smarmy, but actively cultivate the gatekeeper and you may find that the gate opens.

3. **Subterfuge.** How important is this job to you? Most job applicants who apply through conventional means will experience rejection after rejection before they meet with success. Rejection is painful, even for the most thick-skinned person. If you can get an edge and cut down on the rejections, then why not? Find out what the hirer does in their leisure time. Do they play golf? Go riding? Regularly frequent a particular bar? Belong to a certain club? Go to the local church?

Can you do any of these things? If the answer is yes then join up. Go to the bar, play golf at the club, join the hang-gliding group. But be sensible. Take someone else along, that way you enjoy yourself and avoid sticking out like a sore thumb or coming across as Mr Nofriends. And don't sign up for the local soccer team if you're hopeless at football, and don't know your off-side from your elbow. You will only succeed in making a fool of yourself.

If you're lucky you may get to know the hirer in this way. They may get to know you. They may get to like you.

Presentation

It is a well-worn cliché that first-impressions count. Well-worn but true. Pay attention to it.

Gut feelings

In the early 1990s Nalini Ambady, a psychologist at Harvard University, conducted an experiment into the nonverbal aspects of teaching[2]. Ambady intended to use videotapes of teaching fellows from which observers would be asked to judge the effectiveness of the teachers by viewing the tapes with the sound off. However, before she could start the research she encountered a problem. Ideally at least a minute's worth of video footage was needed for the observers to view. When she viewed the clips there was only ten seconds worth of film with the teachers on their own in the frame i.e., without the students also being visible. It was important that the teachers be viewed alone because watching the students' reactions would bias the opinions of observers. Ambady went ahead anyway.

The results were startling. Despite the brief ten-second clip the observers had no problems rating the teaching fellows on a fifteen-item checklist. Nor did they have any problems with a five-second clip. Or a two-second clip. But this wasn't the most startling aspect of the research findings. Ambady also asked students to evaluate the same teachers after a semester of teaching. A semester spent in the same room observing the teaching fellows at close quarters. The results of the video observers and the students showed a high correlation. The verdicts on the teaching staff were virtually the same. Two seconds or several months it makes no difference. People make snap judgments about character and personality. Acting on unconscious cues, maybe a smile, a mannerism or a gesture, we instinctively classify, categorize and type strangers.

The problem is that we then tend to extrapolate that judgment about an individual to other situations. If we believe A behaves this way in one situation then we believe they will also behave this way in other situations. Not necessarily true. But more on this in Section Three.

Dress

For all networking meetings you have a choice of dress. You can dress in a way that reflects who you are. Or you can dress in a way similar to those in the kind of position that you want. If the two are the same then any decisions about dress are straightforward. If they are not you must decide which is the appropriate mode.

The general rule is dress for the occasion, and then dress in a similar manner to your contact. So if you are playing golf, golf gear is obviously appropriate. If you are meeting a contact from a new economy company at a bar, smart casual, if that is what they wear at work, is correct. If the person is a lawyer, it is probably worth putting on a suit. If they're a lumberjack, it's probably not. It sounds trite but polish your shoes. You probably wouldn't go on a date with scuffed, unpolished shoes, don't go networking in them either.

Telephone manner

'Hi, you have reached the voicemail of Jeffrey Jones senior vice-president marketing. Please leave a message after the tone and I will get back to you as soon as possible." Beep. "Um . . . ah . . . I'm calling about . . . umm . . . ah . . .' Beep. Sounds familiar? If not, you can skip this paragraph. If, however, you hate leaving messages on voicemail then there is nothing for it but practice and preparation. Practice by leaving a message on your own answering machine. Keep doing it until you are happy with the results. It should contain all the salient information; who you are, when and why you are calling, your contact details. It should be 'um' and 'ah' free. Plan what you will say in the event of hearing a voicemail message, this way when you hear the dreaded recorded message you will be ready. If for any reason you are not ready, hang up, don't try and fail. Don't rely on them ringing you back, better to tell them that you will try again.

The eradication of 'um's', 'ah's' and other interjections is as important in general telephone manner as it is in speech. If your speech is peppered with such asides don't worry. Practice will eradicate them. Learn to speak at a moderate pace, deliberately and assertively. Think before speaking. Don't speak for the sake of it. Practice by recording your speech and playing it back. Check the recording for distracting habits; gabbling, slurring your words, and altering your tone as if you are asking a question even if you're not. Keep practicing until you are happy with the results.

Remember that important contacts will be telephoning you. 'Hi, we're not here, we're out enjoying ourselves' or your three-year-old daughter practicing her expanding vocabulary may not be what you want your valuable contacts to hear when they get through to you. Record a professional sounding voicemail/answering message, and if you cannot be sure of who will pick up the phone, get another line, or a professional answering service.

CAREER ADVENTURER

JEAN-FRANCOIS LOUMEAU *on networking*

Interviewee:	Jean-Francois Loumeau
Title/Position:	Director Business Development
Company:	Faulding Pharmaceuticals Plc
Location:	United Kingdom

Networking in the industry is an important element of being able to reassess your market value on a regular basis. You have to organize yourself to get to know as many people as you can in this business. Keep your personal contact database as accurate as you can. Update it regularly by participating in international seminars, professional association meetings, professional licensing group meetings, and so on, to keep yourself abreast of what's going on in the business.

Large pharmaceutical companies rationalize their product portfolios, and products are offered for divestiture, which creates some interesting opportunities. You can get early warning signals on such opportunities through networking. Today there are a number of former pharmaceutical executives who are on the market as consultants as a result of all of the mergers and acquisitions. You can also get to know a lot of opportunities through those consultants who may be busy networking within their previous companies.

The way you conduct your business reflects on your level of professionalism. These people tend to remember how you've handled business with them, and that's the best way to "polish" your networking.

6. TRADITIONAL METHODS FOR JOB SEARCHING

The traditional methods of job search listed below still exist. You may find your perfect job this way. But we doubt it. Try to think of it like this. What if you wanted to buy a bunch of flowers as a gift? Which method do you think would bring the best results:

- ◆ Asking someone else to buy them for you.
- ◆ Responding to an advert purportedly selling flowers.
- ◆ Doing some light research on flowers, deciding which you like, asking around for recommendations on where to buy them, and going to a flower shop to buy them yourself.

Hopefully you chose the third option, if not, you either work for Phone-a-Flower or some similar company or need to re-read the section on networking.

Scanning the job ads

Learn to read between the lines. 'Salary up to £30,000' often means only a person with requisite skills and experience gets £30,000 and for some strange reason that never seems to be you (or anyone else). An alternative is OTE (On Target Earnings) £30,000, but just how tough are those targets?

Job ads often cram in every skill that could possibly be required. It's not uncommon to see computer positions, for example, asking for applicants with language skills that include C+, Perl, CGI, UNIX, HTML, Java, Visual Basic, php, and who knows what else. Sure, there may be some programmers who are fluent in all of these. Most programmers, however, specialize. And when you see a list of languages like this in a job ad for a webmaster then you know something strange is going on. If a long list of skills is demanded take it with a pinch of salt. Assuming you can do some of them well/brilliantly you could still be in with a shot.

Experience is slightly trickier. If they say they want a 'person with 10 years commercial property underwriting' for an insurance job it probably means that 5 to 7 years will do. Six months will not. Five years liability experience, as well as five years property and it might be worth applying.

A word of warning: be careful when applying to a blind classified ad, one that conceals the identity of the employer. It is not always easy to tell who is running the ad. You could end up applying to your existing company and being fired for your efforts.

Classified ads also have a nasty habit of being just filled. However, the agency who ran the ad will always be happy to find another position for you if they can just have your details, CV, etc. Which leads us on to the next possibility.

Living with the middlemen

Don't be surprised at how happy agencies are to help you; it is how they make their living. However, are they truly as concerned about finding the perfect career for you as you are? You are the one who will be stuck in the job. Don't let them railroad you into a bad career decision. Treat them like a travel agent. If your heart is set on the Valley of the Kings and the majestic beauty of Egypt's archeological heritage, don't be tempted by an all-night disco cruise from the UK to Scandinavia with as much alcohol as you can drink thrown in. Even if it is available right now. You will only be disappointed.

Which isn't to say that placement or personnel agencies are a complete waste of time. On the contrary, specialist agencies can be very useful. They will deal with all the major corporations in their field and will have seen countless candidates in the course of their business. They can be a good gauge of your chances of getting the job you want. The keener they are, the better your chances. And if you are unrealistic in your aims they can provide a much-needed dose of realism before you lay siege to your target company directly.

So, by all means use personnel agencies to sound out the market. They may even get you the job you want. But try not to be too disappointed if they don't and don't be seduced into straying from your chosen career path by the honey-tongued agency staff. A word of warning here, too. Agencies have been known to mistakenly distribute resumes to an individual's existing employer. We know of instances where an employee's details have landed on their boss's desk. If the boss has no inkling that you are thinking about leaving, this can cause problems.

Also in the middlemen category are headhunters. Headhunters contact you. Probably by telephone. Usually uttering the telltale 'Is it a good time to talk' line. Your boss may be seated next to you when this happens.

As a general rule you do not contact headhunters. This is because headhunters are the crème-de-la-crème of the professional job-search fraternity. They deal in individuals with reputations for high profile jobs. Word of mouth, gossip, rumor, innuendo, the media, these are what bring high-flyers to the attention of headhunters.

Fay reprise

So what of our career adventurer Fay? Fay enthusiastically flung herself into her research. She visited the websites of all the major US airlines. She contacted a friend of a friend who was flying for American Airlines. The pilot put her in touch with several people who worked for different airlines. The pilot also convinced Fay to broaden her career horizon. She explained that although women had been accepted as pilots for commercial airlines only relatively recently, Bonnie Tiburzi was the first woman pilot employed by a major carrier when she became a flight engineer on a Boeing 727 with American Airlines in 1973, it was much more commonplace today. In fact in 2001, as American Airlines was celebrating its 75th anniversary, the company numbered over 400 female pilots among its employees.

The pilot also suggested reading a few books on airlines including *Nuts: Southwest Airlines' Crazy Recipe for Business and Personal Success* by Kevin Freiberg and Jackie Freiberg (Bard Press, 1996). By the time Fay had got halfway through the book she knew that Southwest Airlines was the company for her. Through the pilot she arranged to meet someone from Southwest who in turn arranged for her to be shown around the Southwest HQ in Dallas, Texas. Fay applied to be a flight attendant and was accepted. She's also taking flying lessons.

RESOURCES

Navigating the Job Application Process

@Brint.com BizTech Network – Lauded by *Business Week, Computerworld, CIO, Fast Company, Fortune,* Harvard Business Publishing, *Information Week,* and the *Wall Street Journal* among many others, Brint is the premier knowledge portal and global community network for e-business, information, technology, and knowledge management, which pretty much applies to all businesses today in one way or another. A quick click on 'careers' takes you to 'The Information Professional's Career Page™', but the page is chock full of helpful links for all job-seekers on career, resume and interview skills and resources (scroll to the bottom half of the page; beware however, many of these links are no longer valid). For IT professionals there are also extensive links on the changing role of the CIO, professional development, associations and societies, and job and salary surveys. There are also voluminous links to business directories arranged by category to industries in a variety of languages, and much, much more of vital interest to career adventurers. **www.brint.com**

Careerbuilder – This great site offers practical guidance on job hunting, writing and formatting cover letters and resumes, job interviews and negotiating offers. It also addresses work-life issues, including balancing work and family, getting ahead, and dealing with workplace issues and transitions. You can search for a US-based job here as well via a well-designed search utility.
www.careerbuilders.com

Career Journal Europe – The European edition of the Wall Street Journal is a terrific resource for jobs in the UK and in Europe. The site enables jobseekers to customize their homepage with *Career Journal* information, enter their resumes into a confidential database (partnered with Futurestep.com), and receive new job listings by email that match criteria that they enter. Hundreds of resource articles are helpfully arranged into several categories: job-hunting advice, manage your career and salary and hiring information, among others.
www.careerjournal.com/default.asp?strGlobalizationRegion=EUROPE
(the *Journal's* mirror site for Asia is
www.careerjournal.com/default.asp?strGlobalizationRegion=ASIA, and
for the US it's simply **www.careerjournal.com**.)

Job Asia – This is a great site, primarily in English, for searching for jobs in Asia, including Australia, as well as the UK and US. There are resources available for recruiters (e.g, Asia b-school rankings) as well as jobseekers.

Choose from three resume templates to easily enter your personal information and submit your resume online. Six different search tools are available, including one for researching companies and another targeted for the financial services industry, but you have to register (free) to use the most advanced search tools. **www.jobasia.com**

Monster – The granddaddy of job-hunting websites, this US-based monster devours the competition when it comes to comprehensive job-search resources on the web. The novel 'JobZilla' feature helps you find jobs that fit your passions – from beer and club hopping to socializing and watching sports. Simply enter your passion and hey presto! Out pops a handful of relevant jobs and professions, along with a recommendation for a book related to that topic. The career center gives customized information arranged by industry or profession, articles and resources on cover letters, resumes, interviews, salaries, seasonal jobs, and more. You can also obtain overview information on hundreds of companies, and of course build and post your resume and search for jobs in monster's massive database (over 1,000,000 listings). **www.monster.com**

WetFeet – Lookout Monster, you're about to get your feet wet! WetFeet actually provides a powerful complement to Monster for job applicants. Unlike Monster, it is not a resume-posting site. WebFeet's consumer portal gives detailed information on companies, careers, industries, and salary benchmarks that career adventurers can use throughout their career expeditions. Free expert advice, newsletters, and discussion boards cover everything from negotiating a pay rise to writing better cover letters. In addition to the extensive free information provided, WebFeet publish in-depth insider guides to dozens of companies and industries ($24.95 each for the print version, 20 percent discount to members, $16.95 to download). For companies, WetFeet features its award-winning web-based recruitment technology and recruitment marketing, research, and consulting services to optimize web-based recruiting efforts and reduce overall time-to-hire. Corporate clients include Merrill Lynch, KPMG Consulting, PricewaterhouseCoopers, J. Walter Thompson, Xerox and Procter & Gamble, among many others. **www.wetfeet.com**

Notes
1. Azar, Beth, When Self Awareness Works Overtime (APA Monitor. November 1995).
2. Ambady, N & Rosenthal, R 'Half a Minute: Predicting Teacher Evaluations from Thin Slices of Nonverbal Behavior and Physical Attractiveness' (*Journal of Personality and Social Psychology* 64: 431 41, 1993).

"Our worst fear is not that we are inadequate, our deepest fear is that we are powerful beyond measure. It is our light, not our darkness that most frightens us. We ask ourselves, "Who am I to be brilliant, gorgeous, talented and fabulous?" Actually, who are you not to be?"

Marianne Williamson, *Return to Love*

(Quoted by Nelson Mandela in his 1994 inaugural speech)

THREE
OPENING DOORS
MAKING YOUR FIRST MOVE

In this chapter you will learn how to:

■

Write a resume

■

Construct covering letters

■

Impress at interview

Negotiate the best salary and perks.

1. RESUME WRITING

Networking will find you an opening, but only very rarely will it secure you a job.

The odds of a successful application may shift in your favor, but who knows how many other arch-networkers will be competing for the same position. Your career in the sun awaits. The sandy shores of the tropical island on the horizon, the beach barbecue, the glistening tanned bodies, the evening cocktails, may all be nearer, but they are still tantalizingly out of reach.

To secure your sun lounger, your penthouse office suite, your cubicle on the cube farm – whatever personal workspace awaits you – there are several more hurdles to overcome. The essential elements of the process are: the resume, the covering letter, the interview, the offer and acceptance, and pay negotiations.

Your networking skills should have allowed you to get a foot in the door. Each step on the way offers you a chance to force the door a little wider open, or for the recruiter to slam it shut again.

You know you deserve a chance, that your talents deserve a stage. Now is your chance to shine. The first step is to produce some marketing materials. Like any product or service you need to let the recruiter know that first you are available and second what you can do. Some promotional literature is called for. There are two main elements: the resume or curriculum vitae as it is also known; and the covering letter.

The door-opening resume

Your resume is a brief account of your professional or work experience and qualifications. The purpose of the resume is to get you an interview. No more and no less. No one is hired on the strength of their resume alone. A good resume gets you through the door, then it's up to you. The purpose of the covering letter is to get the recruiter to read your resume.

Resume writing is a science (or art depending on your perspective) all of its own. Advice on how to write the perfect resume abounds. There are articles in print, websites focusing on the subject and even whole books running to more than one hundred pages devoted to how to draft a resume covering just one or two sides of paper.

Advice is conflicting. Should you, for example, include a so-called career objectives statement? 'No' say some, such a statement written too broadly is a waste of space, too focused and it may unnecessarily rule you out of the running for a job. Of course you should, say others, it demonstrates to the employer what you want to do. The one thing that you will learn for certain from a study of resume writing resources is that there is no one right way to write a resume. There is, however, a wrong way, or at least a list of don'ts.

DON'T

◆ Waffle or use – over descriptive or flowery language.

◆ Write the resume on the back of a camel delivered to the offices of the employer, have an airplane trail it in the sky, use rainbow – colored paper or any other wacky idea you may have to make it stand out. Generally speaking wacky is out – there are a few exceptions noted further on.

◆ Spatter your resume with action verbs, having taken them from a list such as the one detailed later in this section without giving any thought as to whether they actually apply. It just looks like you've taken them from a list – which you have.

◆ Write a novel, a novelette, or even a short story. Instead write a one or two-page selective autobiography. Write a resume.

◆ Include personal details such as age, marital status, race, sex, religion or political affiliations, unless the details are especially relevant to the job.

◆ Include your existing, previous or target salary.

AND NEVER, EVER

◆ Lie. (Careful wording to accentuate the positive is another matter.)

The career adventurer's resume

As noted earlier, there are different approaches to resume writing. The chronological type is the most popular. It focuses principally on education and work experience presenting, both in reverse chronological order. Skills and achievements are brought out in the work experience section.

The main alternative is the functional resume. This approach focuses on skills and achievements rather than work experience. Instead of listing jobs in chronological order accompanied by details of achievements, tasks etc., the resume headings are functional, such as 'communication skills' or 'business management'. Work experience is then incorporated within each functional heading.

The functional approach is more difficult to complete effectively. As such it is best avoided. However, where an employment history is haphazard and/or peppered with gaps then the functional method enables candidates to present themselves in a better light.

Finally, there is a third approach favored by the career adventurer. This approach to resume writing combines the best facets of the chronological and functional types of resume to enable the candidate to get the essential information in front of the hirer in the best possible format.

Start by considering the person who will be viewing your resume: the recruiter. What does a recruiter want?

A recruiter wants to recruit the best possible applicant to fill a vacancy. This does not necessarily mean the person with the best formal qualifications. Neither does it mean the person with the most experience. More likely it means the person who has the best combination of qualifications, skills and experience and is the best fit with the organization and co-workers.

A recruiter is usually a very, very busy person. If he or she works in a large organization they may see thousands upon thousands of resumes in the course of a year.

A recruiter has read every possible pitch you can imagine and then some. They can spot a terrible resume at a hundred paces. They have a very large waste bin within easy reach. Picture recruiters opening your letter and reading your resume. What are they going to do with it?

What does the recruiter want?

First, the recruiter wants their life to be made as easy as possible. This means an easy-to-read, clearly presented resume, in a convenient format and in language that doesn't make them cringe. Next, they want a resume that contains the details of an outstanding candidate; a candidate with the appropriate skills for the particular job, the appropriate experience, any necessary qualifications and that little bit extra that sets them apart from the crowd. Finally, they want an absence of negative points that might weigh against the positives.

Given the above, the recruiter, providing they are not having an off day, will invite the applicant for interview. It's as simple as that.

A recruiter is usually a very,very busy person. If he or she works in a large organization they may see thousands upon thousands of resumes in the course of a year.

Content

A resume should contain: educational and professional qualifications; career history; relevant personal information; a summary.

Summary

The summary is your elevator pitch – a term derived from Silicon Valley to describe how you would impress someone if you only had their attention for a few seconds during an elevator ride. It goes at the top, after your name and contact details (telephone/email), and is the first thing the recruiter will read. The summary is make or break. It is your big opportunity to arouse the interest of the recruiter. It should scream out to them that here is someone they will want to interview. By focusing on the skills and experience that are relevant to the position for which you are applying, it allows you to both declare your suitability and set the agenda for your interview. The summary should bring together skills, experience, qualifications and personal characteristics in a single short and persuasive passage that makes it obvious that you are the best person for the position.

Qualifications/skills

What can you do? This is the section where you tell the recruiter the wonderful skills you possess. All skills listed should be relevant to the job. They should include job-specific skills e.g. 'Computer programming: programming several languages including php, perl, java and unix' for a computer programmer or 'Languages: can speak fluent Mandarin, Japanese and Korean' for a translator. As well as personal traits/characteristics, 'resilient and cope well with pressure', and transferable skills that carry from one job to the next, 'Communication: strong-communicator who enjoys and excels at delivering presentations and other public speaking'. Don't list too many or too few. The ideal number is between three and six core skills/traits that tie in with the skills/traits required by the employer.

Professional qualifications that add substance, prestige or directly relate to the vacancy should be listed. Thus, while qualifying as a lawyer might not obviously relate to a senior management position in retail it demonstrates a strong academic background as well as an ability to think quickly and laterally, and make a good case for just about anything. It is also seen as a prestigious qualification. A swimming proficiency certificate however, is unlikely impress, unless you are applying to be a lifeguard, swimming instructor or similar.

Education

The more senior the position you are applying for, the less important your education, particularly your early education, is to the recruiter. This is because other factors such as skills and experience are more relevant to suitability than what school the applicant attended or what class of degree they received. In this case, only college/university, and post-graduate education need be listed (in reverse order). An exception might be if you attended a particularly prestigious school.

If you are just starting out on a career and have little work experience, or seeking to change to a career for which you have little or no work experience, then education at a high school/secondary level may be useful in demonstrating an aptitude or interest in your chosen field. Similarly, you may need to make more of university and post-graduate education, by detailing a minor subject or outlining specialisms or research interests that relate to the work you want to do.

Career history

A procession of jobs trotted out in reverse chronological order so the recruiter knows what work you have done, right? Wrong. The clue is in the word. The all-important career history should be a *story* that relates a logical progression in the world of work from one position to the next. Taken as a whole, your career experience should be told in such a way that it supports your application. At each stage you should be able to demonstrate new and/or increased responsibilities and skills levels so that they lead naturally into the position you are applying for.

Format: Dates, full-time/part time, position, company, segment summarizing key role, bullet points relating accomplishments, tasks, skills and responsibilities. This is where you get to use action verbs. Begin sentences with an action verb, 'Managed marketing department', use numbers, 'of 150 people', 'Instigated new guerrilla marketing campaign that resulted in 50 percent year on year sales increase'. Even these statements are superficial. Go deeper. How did you manage the marketing department? What specific tasks did you perform? What kind of guerilla marketing tactics did you employ?

Always be as specific as possible. Generalized statements such as "worked for" and "responsible for" are a waste of precious space. Recruiters don't want to know what you were responsible for, they want to know what you did, in what ways the responsibility manifested itself. They want to know about the nitty gritty. The devil really is in the detail. When it comes right down to it, "wrote copy for web-based promotional material, visualized and executed design of flyers, booked projectionist and conceptualized advert projected onto Houses of Parliament" is a lot more informative than "organized guerilla marketing campaign."

Note that the normal rules of grammar are suspended for the duration of the resume. Personal pronouns my, their, etc. are unnecessary as are definite and indefinite articles, a, an, the. This does not mean, however, that you have free license. Write your resume in a tight, punchy style. Avoid any urges to be humorous, sarcastic or ironic. Similarly, avoid slang and abbreviation.

Don't undersell yourself, if you built a new IT system for the company then say so. Don't oversell yourself though. If you, and a team of nine other people built, an IT system for the company, don't claim all the credit.

Work experience that is less important or irrelevant can be listed in a catch-all brief section headed 'Other work experience' with the most basic of details. Elaborate only if relevant to the work you are applying for.

Presentation

Presentation is critical. In the book Brilliant CV (London: Prentice Hall, 2001) Jim Bright and Joanne Earl asked a selection of professional recruiters what they looked at in resumes. The three common factors were:

◆ Layout
◆ Relevant experience
◆ Qualifications

Remember recruiters see thousands of resumes. They are looking for an excuse to whittle down the pile. They actively seek to eliminate candidates. Don't make it easier for them.

Key presentation points include:

Paper – Good quality paper but not too good. The computer scanning of resumes is becoming common practice. A heavy weight paper will make this more difficult. Don't use flimsy paper such as common copier paper either. The color should be a crisp white, no fancy colors.

Type – Use an easily read common typeface such as Arial, or Times New Roman. Or try something slightly different such as Tahoma or Verdana. Choose a point size that is legible, but still allows you to keep to two sheets of paper 10, 12, 14. Make sure headings and body text are consistent point sizes. The color should be black.

Layout – There are several layouts that work. These all strike a balance between white space and blocks of text. The standard practice is to set headings and text hard to the left with a small margin. Bullet points can and should be used to break up the look of the page. Sensible spacing between sections avoids the resume looking like an instruction manual. Don't use lines or underlining. The practice of scanning resumes does impose some restrictions on layout. Lines of above 75 to 80 characters can be wrapped, pushed onto the next line, by scanning programs thus destroying carefully a planned layout. Bear this in mind.

Other points – No graphics, yes that does mean no photographs of yourself, no matter how stunningly attractive you are and how many articles you have read asserting attractive people do better in business. Remember the cliché 'that beauty is in the eye of the beholder'. The recruiter may not share your self-confidence. Photographs introduce the possibility of bias and discrimination; don't send them.

Don't fold the resume – If you mail it, do so in a cardboard backed envelope. This imbues it with value. Subconsciously, the recruiter will regard it as a valuable document because the way it is presented encourages him to do so. Print the resume on a good quality laser printer. It may cost a little more than an inkjet. But think of it as not wasting your money, rather than spending extra.

ACTION VERBS

Accelerated	Boosted	Conserved	Devised	Expedited
Accomplished	Briefed	Considered	Diagnosed	Explained
Achieved	Broadened	Consolidated	Differentiated	Explored
Acted	Budgeted	Constructed	Directed	Expressed
Activated	Built	Consulted	Discovered	Extended
Adapted	Calculated	Contacted	Dispensed	Extracted
Addressed	Calibrated	Continued	Displayed	Fabricated
Adjusted	Captured	Contracted	Dissected	Facilitated
Administered	Catalogued	Contrasted	Distributed	Fashioned
Advanced	Categorized	Contributed	Diverted	Filed
Advertised	Centralized	Controlled	Documented	Finalized
Advised	Chaired	Converted	Doubled	Financed
Advocated	Changed	Conveyed	Drafted	Fixed
Agreed	Charted	Convinced	Drew	Focused
Aided	Checked	Coordinated	Earned	Followed
Allocated	Clarified	Corrected	Edited	Forecasted
Altered	Classified	Corresponded	Educated	Formed
Answered	Coached	Counseled	Effected	Formulated
Analyzed	Collaborated	Created	Eliminated	Fostered
Applied	Collated	Critiqued	Empathized	Found
Appraised	Collected	Cultivated	Employed	Founded
Approved	Combined	Customized	Encouraged	Fulfilled
Arbitrated	Communicated	Cut	Enforced	Furnished
Arranged	Compared	Decided	Engineered	Gained
Assembled	Compiled	Decreased	Enhanced	Gathered
Assessed	Completed	Defined	Enlarged	Gave
Assigned	Composed	Delegated	Enlisted	Generated
Assisted	Computed	Delivered	Ensured	Governed
Attained	Conceived	Demonstrated	Entertained	Grossed
Audited	Conceptualized	Described	Established	Guided
Augmented	Concluded	Designated	Estimated	Handled
Authorized	Condensed	Designed	Evaluated	Headed
Awarded	Conducted	Detected	Examined	Heightened
Balanced	Conferred	Determined	Executed	Helped
Began	Configured	Developed	Expanded	Hired

Honed	Maximized	Pioneered	Reduced	Showed
Hosted	Measured	Placed	Referred	Simplified
Identified	Mediated	Planned	Refined	Simulated
Illustrated	Merged	Played	Regulated	Sized
Implemented	Met	Predicted	Rehabilitated	Sketched
Improved	Minimized	Prepared	Related	Sold
Improvised	Mobilized	Prescribed	Remodeled	Solved
Incorporated	Modeled	Presented	Rendered	Sorted
Increased	Moderated	Presided	Reorganized	Spearheaded
Indexed	Modernized	Prevented	Repaired	Specialized
Influenced	Modified	Printed	Reported	Specified
Informed	Monitored	Prioritized	Represented	Spoke
Initiated	Motivated	Processed	Researched	Sponsored
Innovated	Narrated	Produced	Reshaped	Staffed
Inspected	Navigated	Programmed	Resolved	Standardized
Inspired	Negotiated	Projected	Responded	Started
Installed	Netted	Promoted	Restored	Streamlined
Instigated	Observed	Proofread	Restructured	Strengthened
Involved	Obtained	Proposed	Retrieved	Structured
Issued	Opened	Protected	Reviewed	Studied
Itemized	Operated	Proved	Revised	Suggested
Joined	Orchestrated	Provided	Revitalized	Summarized
Judged	Ordered	Publicized	Routed	Supervised
Kept	Organized	Published	Sang	Supplied
Launched	Oriented	Purchased	Saved	Supported
Learned	Originated	Qualified	Scheduled	Surpassed
Lectured	Outlined	Raised	Screened	Surveyed
Led	Overcame	Ran	Searched	Sustained
Liaised	Overhauled	Rated	Secured	Synthesized
Listed	Oversaw	Reached	Selected	Systematized
Listened	Painted	Realized	Separated	Talked
Located	Participated	Received	Served	Targeted
Logged	Performed	Recommended	Serviced	Taught
Maintained	Persuaded	Reconciled	Set	Tended
Managed	Photographed	Recorded	Sewed	Terminated
Marked	Piloted	Recruited	Shaped	Tested
Marketed	Pinpointed	Redesigned	Shared	Tightened

Totaled	Transformed	Troubleshot	Upgraded	Volunteered
Traced	Translated	Tutored	Used	Weighed
Tracked	Transmitted	Uncovered	Utilized	Welded
Traded	Traveled	Undertook	Validated	Widened
Trained	Treated	Unified	Verified	Won
Transcribed	Trimmed	Updated	Vitalized	Wrote

Preparing to write

Writing a good resume requires careful preparation. You need to dredge your memory and any other sources, old resumes, job adverts and job descriptions, for all pertinent information and then collate the information on several pieces of paper.

On one sheet of paper write everything you think the employer is looking for in a potential applicant. Hopefully there will be plenty of clues. The job advert, if there is one, will reveal information in its careful use of language. 'We are looking to recruit an *experienced* and *focused* individual', 'you will undertake *business analysis* for new systems and *manage* new and ongoing *projects in conjunction* with the relevant managers', 'you will also need experience of HTML, JavaScript, VBScript, Visual Basics and Visual Studio/Interdev'.

If there is a job advert it is important to understand all the terms contained in it. Don't just think that you understand, check that you do. The advert should reveal what kind of personal characteristics or traits the employer is looking for. Also what kind of knowledge, training, skills and experience is required? Underline key words and familiarize yourself with the language. Think about what it actually means.

When you have finished you should have a pretty good idea of exactly what the recruiter is looking for. Then, on a separate sheet of paper, write down in chronological order your work experience and your accomplishments, as well as the skills and knowledge you used to achieve them. After completing a chronological list of your work experience, start a list of skills and technical qualifications. Make sure you cover areas such as communication skills, organizational skills, creativity, teamwork and leadership, initiative, problem solving, management skills, social and interpersonal skills, positive personality traits, attitude towards change and IT skills. Write down examples of each. Sort your skills out into three groups: job-specific technical skills; transferable skills; and personality traits.

Ask yourself questions such as: Why should an employer hire me? What are my strengths and weaknesses? What makes me particularly suited to this job/industry/company? How did I learn from mistakes/experience in the past? Then, write down the answers to these questions.

Once you have done this you will have a clear idea of your skills, achievements, qualifications, work experience and personality traits. You need to know these inside out, not just for the purposes of writing your resume, but also for the interview process. Now, armed with the knowledge of what the recruiter is looking for and what you can offer you can proceed to write your resume matching one with the other. Don't leave too long between your preparation and writing a first draft as it is important to have the material fresh in your mind.

And remember a resume is a living, evolving document, a document that you should continually return to and update. If you have followed the advice in this book so far you will have narrowed down the number of possible employers and thus the number of resumes required. Nevertheless, you will inevitably need to produce more than one. While the one-size-fits-all approach is not to be used for resume writing some elements, experience and skills, may remain largely the same from resume to resume. The Career Adventurer must, however, we repeat *must*, tweak each resume to reflect the needs of the prospective employer.

Last-minute check

After your final draft but before final printing make a last check:

- ◆ **Look** – It should be easy to read, correct color and weight of paper, readable font size, no creases or tears.

- ◆ **Content** – Does your resume address the requirements of the job you are applying for? Does it do you justice? Have you brought out your key attributes in the first couple of paragraphs? Have you used concise language throughout, check to see that you can't replace phrases or groups of words with a single word, or substitute a more appropriate word. Have you put your personal contact details down?

And finally there should be absolutely *no*, that's *no* spelling mistakes or typos. It is, after all, a short document, and as most word-processing software packages come complete with a spell checker there are few excuses for misspelled words.

RESUME WRITING RESOURCES

Reading
Jackson, T., *The Perfect Resume,* (Doubleday, 1990).
Good, E & Fitzpatrick, W., *Does Your Resume Wear Blue Jeans?* (Prima Publishing, 1993).
Lewis, A & Moore, D., *Best Resumes for Scientists and Engineers* (John Wiley & Sons, 1993).
Bright, J & Earl, J., *Brilliant CV* (Prentice Hall, 2001).

CAREER ADVENTURER

KENNY ENDO
Title/Position: Taiko Artist
Company: Kendo Music
Industry: Music

'"Taiko" is the word for drum in Japanese. It is also the description of an art based around performance of that instrument. Each taiko is carved from a single piece of keaki (zelkova) tree trunk. The skin is made from cowhide. In one type of drum, the skin is mounted by pulling the skin tight and pounding tacks into the wooden body. In the other type, the skin is lashed on with rope.

Taiko drums come in various sizes, but the big ones have a huge sound. When you have a group of ten or more people playing these drums, combined with movement and voice patterns of encouragement to each other, it is dynamic and exciting.

Kenny, what led you to become a professional taiko artist?

I had a background and career in Western percussion before I got started in taiko in 1975 with the Los Angeles-based Kinnara Taiko group, while I was a student at UCLA. I graduated from UCLA in 1976 and moved to San Francisco where I studied and worked with the San Francisco Taiko Dojo until 1980. They performed all year round and had a teacher from Japan named Seiichi Tanaka. In 1980 I moved to Japan to further my Taiko studies. I lived and worked there until 1990.

In 1987 I received a Natori (a license and stage name in the classical drumming field, the type of drumming used in the Kabuki theater). Around the mid-1980s I began to compose music for taiko and melodic instruments. My compositions have influences from Western drumming and world music, in addition to Japanese music.

Since 1990 I have lived in Hawaii and received my MA in music (ethnomusicology). I established a school for taiko, the Taiko Center of the Pacific, and released three CDs featuring my original compositions (Eternal Energy, 1994, Hibiki, 1998, Jugoya, 2000). I keep a schedule concentrating on performances, composing and collaborations.

What first ignited your interest?

In the fourth grade I started playing drums and percussion in school bands. I started playing drum set in pop bands when I was thirteen years old. When I heard kumi taiko for the first time in 1973, I was very impressed. The sound was so powerful that not only could you hear it with your ears, but you could also feel it with your whole body. It was also something that was part of my cultural heritage, and I wanted to learn more about that.

How do people react when you tell them what you do professionally?

Even in Japan people think of this as something people would do at the festivals. So they are quite surprised that someone can actually make a living doing this. In the US it is even more on the fringe of being an accepted career because there is less of a cultural context for the art. But the best way for people to judge the art is to have an opportunity to see and hear a performance.

If anyone were to choose this as a career I would encourage them, it's not easy, but something that can definitely be quite satisfying. Hang in there, be patient, persevere and have passion.'

2. THE COVERING LETTER

With the invention of e-mail, the art of letter writing has begun to fall into abeyance.

Supplanting the preferred form of written communication for lovers and businessman alike, e-mail has both vandalized the English language, or at least rendered grammatical form redundant, and threatened to make the practice of letter writing a quaint historical irrelevance.

But the extinction of letter writing is still a little way off. Which is good news for people who are used to organizing ideas into paragraphs. Bt bd nws fr txt mssgrs.

During the course of your job searching you can expect to write several types of letter:

◆ Letters replying to job adverts
◆ Letters soliciting work
◆ Thank you letters
◆ Follow-up letters
◆ Acceptance or rejection letters

Of these, the first two merit consideration here, although it is important to emphasize that you should never forget to write follow-up letters (after applying for jobs, interviews, attending job agencies etc.), or thank you letters (to everyone who has helped you in your quest for work).

The covering letter should accompany your resume when you apply for a job that you know is available either by word of mouth or through adverts. The speculative letter should be sent to prospective employers regardless of whether not there is a position available. The job of both letters is to sell you to the employer as a kind of person that they would want working for them.

Covering letters and speculative letters are the same in that they:

◆ Sell you by focusing on your benefits, skills, experience, and personal qualities that make you the right person for the position.

◆ Articulate your qualities succinctly but creatively, striking a balance between brevity and detail.

◆ Accentuate the positive, omit the negative.

◆ Accompany your resume.

Covering letters and speculative letters are different in that they:

◆ Are addressed to different people: the covering letter to the person specified in the job ad; the speculative letter to the person that you have identified as the appropriate recipient within the organization.

◆ Open in a different manner, the covering letter with a restatement of the job as defined in the advertisement (its title if stated), the speculative letter, with a statement of what kind of position you're interested in, or area you wish to work in, what you are able to offer the employer and why you want to work for that particular company.

Writing the letter

The letter you write has only a few brief moments, less than a minute, to make the right impression. From the hundreds of letters read by the recipient yours must stand out and be memorable for the right reasons.

To avoid a reply of the standard "thank you for your interest, we have no suitable position available moment but we have placed your letter on file" type, avoid the following common mistakes:

◆ A stiff formally worded letter, letters should be conversational in tone. The days of "referring to yours of the fifth inst.", are gone. Formal letters are only appropriate if demanded by professional circumstance as may be the case with professions such as the law and medicine.

◆ Over familiar and jokey letters, the idea is to write free-flowing text but not to be too chummy. Avoid using slang and colloquialisms.

◆ Obvious grammatical errors, if you are worried about grammar buy one of the many dictionaries of grammar available. If your blunders are slight, it is unlikely that they will count against you, or even that they will be noticed, unless you are applying for Professor of English or similar, that is.

◆ Spelling mistakes and typos, dyslexia apart, there are few, if any, excuses for spelling mistakes in such a brief document. Don't rely on your computer's spellchecker, try typing in "fro" instead of "for", for example, and see if the computer notices. Get someone to proof/read the letters. Spelling mistakes and typos can be a "straight to the wastepaper bin" offence.

◆ Over use of the first person pronoun, the use of I, creates a friendly tone. But use 'I this' and 'I that' and friendly becomes repetitive, egotistical and unimaginative.

◆ Stating irrelevant skills/characteristics/qualifications , space is at a premium in your letter. Do not waste it on irrelevant information.

◆ Addressing the letter to the wrong person, misspelling their name, or using "to whom it may concern" (lazy), show some initiative by finding out the right person to send letter to and how to spell their name properly.

◆ Writing an overly long letter, just four or five paragraphs will do, enough to cover one side of A4. Four or five flowing and informative paragraphs. Each one expressing a main idea and then embellishing upon it.

Your letter should include the following elements: a paragraph relating your skills/characteristics/qualifications to the position available, or a paragraph outlining what kind of work you wish to do and how it relates to your skills/characteristics/ qualifications. Two or three paragraphs outlining the highlight of your career achievements and your particular strengths. An indication of why you are looking to change your existing job. A paragraph explaining what you hope to achieve with your letter, i.e.,selection for interview or obtain a meeting to discuss possible opportunities within the organization. And your personal contact details.

Some recruiting professionals suggest a more succinct approach when applying for an advertised position via the Internet.

Ms XX

My name is Bill XXXX and I'm responding to your job advertisement for Lead Website Designer. Briefly my career has covered:

◆ Computer Graphics Degree at Nerdington University (obtained a first).
◆ Five years as web developer in small web design agency.
◆ Good working knowledge of industry software including Photoshop, Flash, Illustrator, Dreamweaver and Coldfusion.
◆ Led multi-million pound project to design and build interactive website for Fortune 500 company.
◆ Developed and implemented computer design training program for new employees.
◆ Member of Design Council and government consultative committee on new media design.

I am currently working for XXXX so please call me at home on XXXX after 6.30 PM GMT or e-mail me at x@y.com.

Yours,
Bill XXXX.

The writing process

Some people find it difficult to put pen to paper, or struggle when faced with a blank computer screen and word processor. The secret is to get the words down, any words. Just spill out your thoughts and ideas for the letter's content. Then loosely arrange them in paragraphs, without worrying too much about length. Now organize them so that they have an internal logic. Condense the contents of each paragraph into bullet point and arrange them in a way that has a logical order. Each paragraph should serve a purpose. Discard anything that is superfluous. Next rewrite and rewrite – and rewrite. Finally when you're satisfied show several other people whose opinion you respect.

LETTER WRITING RESOURCES

Reading

Beatty, R. *The Perfect Cover Letter,* (John Wiley & Sons, 1989).
Frank, W. *200 Letters for Job Hunters,* (Ten Speed Press, 1990).
Hansen, K & Hansen, R. *Dynamic Cover Letters,* (Ten Speed Press, 1990).
Krannich, C & Krannich, R. *Dynamite Cover Letters, and Other Great Job Search Letters,* (Impact Publications, 1992).

CAREER ADVENTURER

FRANZ LANDSBERGER *on hiring*

Title/Position: VP Human Resources, Bioscience Division
Company: Baxter, Europe
Industry: Pharmaceuticals

Franz Landsberger started at Baxter, the healthcare company, in April 1990 as the Compensation and Benefits Manager for Baxter Germany. After a year and a half he became the overall HR Director for Baxter Germany, and then HR Director for the Bioscience division. Before Baxter Franz worked in EDP, electronic data processing, which has since become IT. He started as a programmer working in a couple of small companies in Germany that had international parents. Working in a small company gave Franz the opportunity to do everything from bookkeeping to office/finance and HR management to serving as a commercial director. Here is what Franz has to say from the hirers' perspective:

'While working as a commercial director, we increased in size from 50 employees to 180 in just two years. That experience made me realize that hiring is the key job in an organization. Hiring the right people is what makes your organization successful. If you make the wrong choices, you can become bogged down with lots of HR issues.

From that point forward I focused my career more exclusively on HR. My background in various business areas (e.g., budgeting, strategic planning, commercial director) strongly supports my HR work. I am much better able to assess job candidates, and to know what to look for in terms not only of skill sets, but also in terms of "fit", which is much more important. Skill and "will" both have to work. The candidate has to fit with the team and company cultures that are in place, to find this out is an art rather than a science. It is both very challenging and rewarding, especially when we can successfully do it across country and cultural borders; that's great!

You have to understand what kind of applicant is sitting in front of you. I'm not a big fan of written tests, because I think the key thing is that the company and applicant take time to sit down and get to know each other. I use a lot of probing questions to try to find out how an applicant is wired. For example, how do they like to operate; do they prefer to work in a more or less structured environment? Are they creative? Risk-taking? Do they prefer to follow strict operational procedures? Do they like to be accountable? What has made them successful? How have they been dealing with their employees? And so on. I also point out how we work in terms of management process and culture, which underlies the management process.

Be very open with each job candidate. Clearly state the job requirements and your expectations. Remember, this person is not an employee yet. Depending on your first rough judgment, either bring the interview to a quick end or turn it into a real "selling the job" exercise. Be up front with them from the beginning. I've been hiring people since about 1982, and with a few exceptions over these many years, I have gotten the team and everyone I have wanted on board.'

CAREER ADVENTURER

DONNA MARTIN *on recruiting*

Title/Position: Senior Vice President, Human Resources
Company: Faulding Pharmaceuticals
Industry: Pharmaceuticals

How do you approach recruiting?

'It depends a whole lot on what the position is and its level in the organization. In looking at more senior level positions, I first validate background and skill sets, and set that aside. Then the first factor is does the person know what has made them successful? If they don't know, they can't repeat it.

The candidate must also have an ability to fit into the particular culture. Does what they express give you a sense that they will be able work within the culture that either you have or are attempting to create?

Then there's a third piece that goes along with the other two. Does their competency level and behavioral self complement the existing organization? They don't have to match it exactly, but do they mesh well with it and will they help you get to where you want to go?'

3. THE INTERVIEW

'Two of my interviews stay with me to this day, in fact I wake up at night in a cold sweat thinking about them', says one career adventurer who is now a successful writer and researcher.

'In the first I was being interviewed for a job as a commodity broker. Everything was going well; I had struck up a rapport with the interviewer, and as far as I was concerned the job was as good as mine. Then I was asked whether I had a good grasp of economics. I foolishly replied that I had an excellent understanding. Out of the blue the interviewer asked me to explain a technical aspect of inflation, which to my embarrassment I couldn't.'

'In the second interview, as I sat in a queue outside the interview room I inwardly scoffed at the candidates surrounding me who were wading through what looked like a large technical manuscript. When I was called for interview my first surprise was to be greeted by a panel interview; my second was to be thoroughly grilled on relevant legislation and regulations, the large thick manuscript everyone else was reading. More embarrassment. Needless to say I didn't get either job.'

Most career adventurers have an interview horror story to tell. Yet in many cases what turned out as a nightmarish, embarrassing experience need not have been that way at all. An interview requires the interviewee to take certain basic steps, say and do certain things, and avoid saying and doing certain other things. In a way an interview is a game with its own rules. Play by the rules and you stand a chance of being recruited. Flagrantly break the rules, and you can forget about the job. Twist and bend the rules and you can dramatically shift the odds in your favor.

There are a number of types of interview:

- **One-to-one** – just you and the interviewer, the most common format.

- **Panel/team interview** – the interviewers gang up on you. Intimidating if you are not used to it.

- **Structured interview** – all interviewees are asked the same questions. Questions are not always obvious in their intent. Can be daunting.

- **Unstructured interview** – a general chit-chat. Well not quite, but without a set agenda there is more scope to steer the interview in the direction the interviewee wishes.

- **Telephone interview** – usually conducted when geography rules out a face-to-face meeting. Ask the interviewer if they can ring back if you're not ready.

- **Video conference interview** – face-to-face with help of modern technology. Treat it as a live face-to-face interview rather than a virtual one.

◆ **Second, third, interview** – often, but not necessarily, more relaxed than the first. At least you know you're in the frame.

CAREER ADVENTURER

JONATHAN HILL *on interviewing*

Dr Jonathan Hill works both in his own psychology business, and at the Center for Applied Psychology, at Leicester University in the UK, where he investigates employment interviewing policy and practice. Before that he was Research Director in the London office of the Gallup Organization.

In preparing for interview you can either be true to yourself, or you can put on an act. These hints are mainly for someone who wants to be true to themselves. But if you do decide to construct a fresh identity make sure it has some personal relevance to the direction you really want to move towards. Otherwise you may end up getting a job which is simply not you.

A month before
Conduct a review of your previous work experience and personal qualities with a primary focus on your strengths. Increasingly, progressive employers are more interested in strengths rather than weaknesses. They want to heighten your peaks rather than fill in your troughs because that way lies the route to competitive advantage. Be ready to support your strengths in a way which answers the kind of question that you have been asked at the interview. For example:

1. Factual Issues – *Be ready to answer factual questions accurately. This means accuracy about dates, salaries, job titles and company names as they were at the time of your employment, and as they are now. Do not approximate your responses to factual questions. Integrity is increasingly valued in business life, not least because of regulatory pressures. So be ethical.*

2. Values – *Be clear about the two or three key values that mean the most to you in your life and career. These values are at the core of your being. They might include a deep commitment to customer service, an authentic desire to help others learn and grow, strong family values, honesty and/or professional standards. Whilst flexibility in team working, skills acquisition and hours of work, are appreciated by many employers, 'flexible values' are not really held in such high regard. Let your values shine through the interview.*

SAMPLE QUESTIONS: *What do you most strongly believe in? Which values are most important to you?*

3. Motives – *Understand clearly your own needs and desires – those that are enduring and have lasted many years. What really drives you? Do you need power or achievement or popularity? In other words are you a leader, a beaver or a socializer?*

SAMPLE QUESTIONS: *In your previous work, what gave you the biggest sense of satisfaction? What kind of work do you most enjoy? Leading others, helping others or just getting on and doing the work yourself?*

4. Relationships – *Which of these questions applies to you?*

Are you a relationships quick starter? Or a long-term investor? A net-worker? A team-player? Or a one-to-one advisor or coach?

◆ *Quick starters make friends swiftly and often. They may also lose them just as easily.*

◆ *Long-term investors may keep friends for many years, deepening the relationship as time goes by. Both can be good, depending on the job.*

◆ *Networkers like to expand their circle of contacts, so that each year their Christmas card list gets longer, as they seek to sustain the social architecture of their constituency or power base.*

◆ *Team players love to be part of a small group.*

Depending on the requirements of the work or career, employers may look for evidence in your interview responses that you are more than just a 'good realtor'. These days it is the quality and duration of customer relationships which are most important in building a business. So be ready to talk about your experience of dealing with different types of customer, as well as different kinds of colleagues.

A SAMPLE QUESTION MIGHT BE: *How would you describe your best customer? Or, how did you deal with your worst customer?*

5 . Expertise – *Technical questions are the ones we all dread. But will you be expected to know all about a particular software package or procedure, or technique? While you can mug up your technical knowledge a month before, remember that these days, owing to the pace of change, willingness to learn is just as important as current knowledge. Be ready to talk about how you have* *acquired your knowledge and skills, and what you are studying right now in order to stay abreast of your profession or career.*

SAMPLE QUESTIONS MAY INCLUDE: *Could you talk me through the process that you used for X situation? How did you acquire your skills and knowledge? Where did you learn your knowledge of X? From whom did you gain your knowledge of X? What are you studying now to build your skill base?"*

Interviewing styles

Today, most organizations employ two principal styles of interviewing: the traditional interview and behavioral interview.

The traditional interview – This uses conventional questioning to discover whether the interviewee has the appropriate skills and experience, the requisite personal characteristics and traits, and is a good fit with the organization. Questions are likely to include the ubiquitous "Tell me why I should hire you", "What are your strengths and weaknesses" and "where do you see yourself five years from now". Books abound on questions typically asked at job interviews.

The behavioral interview – These attempt to probe a little more deeply into the background of the interviewee. The interviewer uses questions to assess the interviewee's behavior in different work situations. Questioning usually proceeds along lines such as "Tell me about a time when you needed to use your initiative to achieve a certain goal", what follows is an examination of how you reacted in a given situation. The theory is that past performance and experience in dealing with certain situations are the best guide to an individual's future performance. In a traditional interview you might be able to bluff your way through, as most traditional interviews require no hard and fast factual information about your skills and experience. In a behavioral interview where the interviewer can probe into real situations in your past, bluffing is not an option. Some organizations such as the management consulting firm Accenture have been using this method for sometime, and it is becoming more common. You can expect to be interviewed in this way at some point in your career.

Interview formats

The structure of the interview itself will vary. But many run along the following lines:

◆ Introductions and preamble (puts you at your ease)
◆ General questions put to all candidates
◆ Specific questions arising from your resume
◆ Clarification about the position
◆ Answering your questions
◆ Close

In an ***unstructured interview*** a canny interviewee can determine the required response from the question and deliver it. If the interviewer is inexperienced or untutored in the art of interviewing the interviewee may even take control of the interview steering the direction of the conversation into areas with which they feel comfortable.

A ***structured interview*** is a whole different ball game. Take a look at these two questions.

A: 'Describe a few situations in which you had several tasks to perform at the same time? How did you cope?'

B: 'Your boss gives you two tasks to perform. You realize it is possible to complete one, but not both tasks within the deadline. What do you do?'

Question A, a common type of question asked during unstructured interviews, is easy to answer. The clue to the answer is in the question. The question is about coping, dealing with pressure and stress. The interviewee can relate the answer to previous experiences. It is possible to steer the answer into a pre-planned answer.

Question B, is more difficult, it is neutral in tone, it poses a hypothetical problem, but does not allow you the room to maneuver the answer into territory you feel comfortable with. It is not entirely clear what information the question is designed to elicit. Worse, however you answer the question it reveals something about your personality. Throw in a trained impassionate interviewer furiously taking notes and it is easy to see why structured interviewees are the bane of interviewees and the friend of the recruiter.

CAREER ADVENTURER

JONATHAN HILL *on interviewing*

Interview preparation: a month before

Whilst the preparation undertaken a month before addresses what Douglas Bray has called 'Life Themes' – recurring and predictable patterns in your life and career to date, during the week before you may wish to focus on the categories of question that a modern, forward-looking employer may plan to ask you.

There are at least four kinds of question: situational, behavioral, conceptual, and personal.

Situational questions *deal with hypothetical situations, though they may model incidents that may actually occur in the job on offer.*

Typically situational questions start with the phrase: 'What would you do if…?'

Situations present opportunities for you to use your imagination, demonstrate your experience, parade your values, portray your relationships style or prove your expertise. If you rely solely on your previous experience you might narrow the scope of your answer. If the situation is an emergency, you will have to think on your feet, drawing on your strengths and values as well as your expertise. If the situation is not an emergency, however, you could choose to respond at first by asking for more information, or saying that you would first seek more information (though you might not get it), to show that you have some capacity for investigative or diagnostic thinking, and that you do not rush in where angels fear to tread.

Illustrative situations *used might include:*

◆ *Dealing with a customer complaint (listen, calm, soothe, resolve).*

◆ *Dealing with a colleague with troubles, or with performance problems (diagnose, agree course of action, continue to monitor and support).*

◆ *Handling a loan enquiry (show interest in the upside, then practice due diligence).*

◆ *An extension of the situational question is the case interview, favored by some management consultancies, in which particular business scenarios are described and you have to say what you would do in that situation.*

Behavioral Questions – *Here the interviewer is seeking evidence from your past behavior that you have the competences for a job or career. Typically the line of questioning starts with the phrase 'Have you ever?' or 'When did you last…?' The best responses are specific and tied to a place, a time, a person or an event. You are the main character whose initiative directs the drama to a tangible outcome or conclusion. The interviewer may probe with further questions such as 'What happened next?', or 'How did you follow up?'*

The critical aspect in answering behavioral questions is to do a rapid memory search and choose judiciously the appropriate event or incident from your own repertoire. A moment's thought to select the best example will make the rest of your response and follow-up responses a little easier to support with factual details that are relevant to the interviewer's quest for evidence. Add some energy, enthusiasm and interest to your response so that it carries conviction.

Conceptual Questions – *Perhaps the most famous of these is "What are your strengths and weaknesses?" Do not be tempted to trivialize your answer. While it may seem a simplistic line of enquiry, the undertones may be very serious. What's more, many people really do not have a clear idea about their own talents, limitations and potential. Do some research concerning yourself, be crystal clear about your best contributions, and ask your friends and family for their opinions. Summarize three strengths and one limitation. Be prepared to illustrate these by reference to specific behaviors or challenges which you have addressed. If asked, be ready to say how you cope with your limitation, either by partnering or delegating, or using a system, or by learning at least some of the basic skills involved. Explain how you intend to cultivate your strengths so that you may move from good to excellent.*

Another conceptual question is 'How would you define the ideal workplace?'

Your challenge is to 'create a brand'. Few people can do this instantaneously, so prepare a list of concepts which will help you to define the brand. Think also about your ideal colleague, your ideal boss, your ideal client and your ideal job. Draw upon your values and motives so that your identity has some coherence with your aims and ambitions, and these color your interview responses.

Personal Questions – *Examples of personal questions include those that deal with your current payment package, your references, your willingness to travel or change locations, your likes and dislikes and your plans for the future. Such questions should not be intrusive, and if you feel they are, you may decide to*

> decline to provide full details *(**see box on illegal questions**)* or to buy time to
> check back with your partner or mentor before answering.
>
> However, questions about your future career plans are legitimate and you should
> have well rehearsed answers. Timescales add weight to your answers, as do
> plans for further learning, and financial goals in relation to, for example mortgage
> repayments. People who have clearly defined plans for their future may be seen
> as more thoughtful, conscientious and discerning than those who simply claim to
> go with the flow.

THE RULES OF ENGAGEMENT

Prepare

When you wrote your resume, you conducted research into the company/industry you intend to work for/in. You wrote the resume to meet the requirements of the prospective employer, as well as extol your virtues. The resume was good enough to get you the interview. Now the interviewer will check that the person in front of them corresponds to the person in the resume. They want to reassure themselves that the person in front of them will be able to do the job they are recruiting for. And, that the person in front of them will fit into the organization.

Before the interview, review your resume. Your interviewer will do the same. They will look for career gaps, faltering career progression, missing skills, weak personal characteristics or traits, and they will ask you questions about them. In turn you will need to counter with answers that allay any misgivings the interviewer may have.

Present the right image

Be confident. But don't be arrogant. Remember you have been called for interview because the recruiter likes your resume. That's probably a third of the battle won. Impress the recruiter at the interview, and the job could be yours.

Presentation is important. First impressions are critical. You are unlikely to spend long with your interviewer. They must make a decision based on what they see. The onus is on you to make the best impression you can in the short amount of time available. Right or wrong, they will make a judgment about you based on your appearance. The way you dress should fit in with the culture of the organization you're planning to join. If the employees wear smart casual then so should you, if they wear suits then you should wear a suit. If you are unsure how people dress in the organization, you could do some discrete reconnaissance. Observe the people entering and leaving the building for a while. Once you have established what type of dress code, err on the side of smartness. So if you wear smart casual, make sure you live up to the "smart" part. Avoid "loud" clothes, fashion statements or extremes i.e., tuxedos or combat fatigues. Above all make sure you feel comfortable in your clothes, it will improve your performance. Other aspects of personal appearance are also important. Neat hair, clean teeth, fresh breath, clean shoes, tidy nails, zippers (done up); well-groomed is the way to think of it. Before you go into the interview check your appearance in a mirror.

Let your body do the talking

Studies have repeatedly shown that between 80 and 96 percent of human communication is non-verbal. In other words, the actual content of what we say carries less weight than the way we say it. Body language, in particular, speaks volumes. Send the right body language signals. When you greet the interviewer/s make sure that you shake their hands with a firm grip, smile and look them in the eyes. It may sound corny but it works. Don't reserve your good manners for the interviewer. Be polite and friendly to anyone else you meet within the organization, they may have an input into the hiring process. The person who hands out refreshments in the lobby may be your interviewer.

During the interview avoid the following:

◆ Picking or scratching your nose (it happens)
◆ Swearing
◆ Using slang, over-using technical jargon
◆ Yawning
◆ Fidgeting, tapping (pen, pencil or fingers)

- Over-familiarity
- Rocking or swinging from side to side in your chair
- Umming, aahing, 'you know', humming
- Not finishing your sentences
- Gesticulating wildly
- Falling off your chair

When you sit down, sit up straight, try to relax, avoid slouching, don't cross your legs or fold your arms (defensive). During the interview be positive, coherent, and enthusiastic. Would you hire someone who was sullen, unresponsive, and negative?

Answer questions correctly

Once you have created a good impression by portraying the right image the next obstacle to overcome is the questioning. Whatever questions your interviewer asks, there is a right way, and a wrong way to answer them. Or more correctly, an answer your interviewer wants to hear and an answer that they do not.

There are books that deal solely with the subject of interview questions. You may buy these books, you may even memorize the questions and answers. The best preparation however, is to understand why the recruiter is asking a particular question. If you understand the underlying sub-context then you can supply the correct answer.

The point here is that each question you are asked is asked for a reason. The interviewer is digging for information and it is not always obvious from the question what that information is. Your job is to read between the lines, to avoid the pitfalls and traps, and provide the information that the interviewer wants to hear. Negotiating a way through the interview questions minefield is difficult, but by no means impossible. And remember to think to before you speak.

For a behavioral interview it is possible to prepare beforehand. As you know that the interviewer will be asking about real-life experiences select illustrative examples from your past to use in the interview. Each experience should illustrate as many desirable skills or traits as possible. The situations should also include an incident where you coped with adversity and preferably turned it into a positive outcome. Armed with these mini-case studies you will be able to cope with most behavioral interviewing.

Adventure 10

Here are a few likely questions. How would you answer?

- ◆ How do you handle criticism?
- ◆ What salary are you on?
- ◆ What are your main weaknesses?
- ◆ How do you handle criticism?
- ◆ Why do you want to work here?
- ◆ What was your last boss like?
- ◆ Where do you see yourself five years from now?
- ◆ You don't appear to have spent very long with your previous employers. Why is that?

Now think again and consider the sub-text:

◆ **How do you handle criticism?**

Wrong answer: "I hate being criticized."

Because the question means: How hard a time are you going to give your boss when they criticize you especially if it's me.

Right answer: "I always welcome constructive criticism."

◆ **What salary are you on?**

Wrong answer: "I'm on $20,000."

Because the question means: How little can I get away with paying you.

Right answer: "What kind of salary are you expecting to pay?"

◆ **What are your main weaknesses?**

Wrong answer: A long list of weaknesses.

Because the question means: Let's watch you dig a big hole for yourself.

Right answer: A weakness that is not relevant to the job, a weakness that is not really a weakness, "I'm not very good with practical things like fixing cars, etc." is good if you are going for a job as an accountant. Or "I can be a bit of a perfectionist sometimes".

◆ **Why do you want to work here?**

Wrong answer: "Because the pay is excellent."

Because the question means: Here is your chance to impress me with your knowledge of the company, the job and the skills required.

Right answer: Impress them with your knowledge of the company, the job and the skills required.

◆ **What was your last boss like?**

Wrong answer: "They were a complete b**@!!*".

Because the question means: Are you loyal to your boss or do you badmouth them when they are not around?

Right answer: If you hated working with them. "I enjoyed working with them" (an exception to the 'never lie in interviews rule'). If you enjoyed working with them extol their virtues a little.

◆ **Where do you see yourself five years from now?**

Wrong answer: "At your principal rival on a bigger salary after you've spent lots of money training me".

Because the question means: How ambitious are you, and do you have unrealistic expectations that can't be fulfilled.

Right answer: Along the lines of "It's difficult to say, here certainly, doing a job I enjoy and having advanced in my career".

◆ **You don't appear to have spent very long with your previous employers. Why is that?**

Wrong answer: "Because I get bored easily."

Because the question means: If your track record shows you only stick around for a year or so, why will be any different here?

Right answer: "I'm looking for a long-term position but I need to be challenged by my work. The companies I've worked for so far didn't continue to challenge me."

ILLEGAL QUESTIONS

In many countries certain questions are prohibited by law (usually discrimination legislation). Whether a particular question is illegal depends on the exact phrasing of the question and the legislation in force in that state or country. The type of subject matter that is usually out of bounds includes:

◆ age
◆ ancestry, birthplace, ethnic origin, place of origin
◆ family status, marital status, sex, sexual orientation
◆ color, race
◆ creed, religion
◆ citizenship
◆ criminal record
◆ disabilities
◆ membership of organizations
◆ personal circumstances
◆ personal appearance, size, weight, height

The problem with illegal questions usually arises when they are asked not because the interviewer is malicious, but because the interviewer is ignorant of the law. If you are asked an illegal question you have several choices.

You can refuse to answer the question outright, pointing out that it is an illegal question if necessary. The problem with this course of action is that you risk offending the interviewer, especially if they are ignorant of the law.

Alternatively you can answer the question. However, if you do this you run the risk of providing information which counts against you in the mind of the interviewer.

Possibly the best strategy is to gauge why you are being asked the particular question and then try to provide enough information to satisfy the interviewer without prejudicing yourself.

Take whichever course of action you feel most comfortable with. If the question is an illegal one don't be pressured into revealing information you wish to keep private.

Ask the right questions

After receiving a grilling at the hands of the interviewer they will invariably ask you if you have any questions. Regardless of how grueling the interview was and how much you want to escape from the room/rest on your laurels/relax/dash to the rest room, the correct answer to this question is 'yes'. Why? Because it shows you are genuinely interested in the company and the job. It shows you have an inquiring mind. It smacks of enthusiasm and initiative.

To avoid the situation where your mind goes blank and you can't think of anything to ask it is best to prepare a few questions beforehand. You need to ask questions, because not asking them shows you in a bad light. Asking the wrong questions, however, will do you no favors either. Questions such as 'What time can we leave the office?', 'Will we have to work weekends?', 'Will there be a lot of extra work?', 'What is the company's disciplinary policy?' merely flag you up as a potential shirker and troublemaker. It's easy to undo all the good work done in the interview by asking a poor question.

Instead, your questions should elicit useful information. Keep the questioning passive and not aggressive, you do not want the interviewer to feel that he has lost control of the interview. Suitable questions include 'What kind of opportunities are there for vocational learning and obtaining extra qualifications?', 'What kind of career advancement can be expected assuming you are a suitable candidate for promotion?' or 'When can you expect an answer? Best to leave this one until last.

Give the interviewer what they want

To give an idea of what recruiters look for during an interview here, according to respected headhunting firm Boyden International, are five traits essential for most managerial positions:

- ◆ **Motivation** – to establish whether a candidate is sufficiently motivated recruiters will ask questions such as: How do they handle stress? Are they independent self-starters? How persistent are they in achieving objectives? You need to demonstrate commitment and motivation in past situations.
- ◆ **Problem-solving** – rehearse a situation where you used problem-solving skills successfully before you go for the interview. Then when you are asked to recall a situation you will be ready with your answer.
- ◆ **Communication** – communication skills are vital to most managerial jobs. Public speaking, presentations, lectures, if you have experience of this kind make it clear at some point. And remember good communication is as much about listening as it is about talking.
- ◆ **Social and interpersonal skills** – recruiters look for qualities such as empathy (see the section on Emotional Intelligence in Part Four), insight, consideration for others. These days, qualities such as assertion, charisma and a commanding presence are supposedly less desirable (although the recruiters of Fortune 500 CEOs seem to have ignored this).
- ◆ **Organizational skills** – one of the hardest to master and most important skills a good manager can possess. More specifically, if you can demonstrate delegation and time-management skills you will impress the recruiter. An inability to delegate has sunk many a manager. At the very least, you should arrive at the interview on time and well-prepared.

A NOD AND A WINK

FRANK BERNIERI, Professor of Psychology at the University of Toledo conducted some revealing research into the effects of non-verbal communication during job interviews. Over a period of six weeks he trained two people to conduct job interviews. The interviewers then conducted interviews with ninety-eight volunteers. After each interview lasting between 15 and 20 minutes the interviewer completed a six-page evaluation of the interviewee.

Bernieri hoped that the research would give an insight into whether interviewees trained to apply certain-non verbal techniques, mimicking posture for example, during the interview could obtain a better report than their untrained counterparts. It turned out that they couldn't.

The really interesting findings however, came when Bernieri's student Tricia Prickett used the video and reports to test the popularly held notion that 'the handshake is everything'.

She asked volunteers to write a report on the applicants based only on viewing a video clip showing the candidate entering the room, shaking the hand of the interviewer, sitting down and being welcomed. Just fifteen seconds of video. The resulting reports showed a remarkable correlation with the reports of the interviewers, even though the interviewers had been trained for six weeks.

What message should the career adventurer take from this research? Not that it's a waste of time preparing for interviews. Even if you make a star entrance, if you blow the rest of the interview it will still count against you. Instead think of it this way. In the first 30 seconds you have a chance to make a lasting impression. Take that chance. Then reinforce that positive impression with a great interview performance.

IT'S ALL ABOUT FIT

JACQUELINE DE BAER is founder of de Baer Limited, a sort of designer label for companies. The company designs and manufactures staff uniforms for the likes of Marriott Hotels, Boots Opticians and the Odeon Cinema in London's Leicester Square. It has helped introduce innovations such as fleece jackets and even jeans to help employees feel more comfortable sporting their company colors.

Headquartered in London, de Baer has manufacturing bases in a number of other countries. It employs some 70 people, and has a turnover of around $13.5 million. As the company grew, however, de Baer was concerned that the original culture was becoming diluted. Determined to maintain the excitement and informal approach to business that had inspired her original designs, yet still managed to expand the business de Baer turned to corporate values.

After some soul-searching, she distilled the company's values down to four: fun, integrity, openness and learning. She then set about inculcating them into the company's DNA. 'Defining and communicating the company's values is very powerful. The values can guide you in all sorts of ways, especially in speeding up decision making. We are very clear on what we are all about.'

How does this affect new recruits? De Baer explains: 'I recruit against the values. Every new person to join at management level has a benchmarking telephone interview to identify their values before being asked to the first formal interview.'

The aim is to weed out applicants who don't share the values before they reach interview stage. At other levels within the organization, questions aimed at identifying values are incorporated into the first interview.

'Basically, we have a set of criteria based on our brand values. Before a candidate is called to interview, we check against these. Then, I personally interview every candidate. I don't look at their skills at that stage, I look at them as people against our brand values.'

So much for theory, but how does it work in practice? 'We've developed some questions which give us an idea of how people fit against the culture', she says. 'One of our key values for example, is learning. So I might ask about how training was managed at an applicant's previous company. If they say it was handled by the HR department then that tells me one thing. If they say they liked to be actively involved in training their staff and making sure they had as much information as possible, then that tells me they are likely to fit our culture.'

Bronwe Lawson joined de Baer in August 1999 as an account manager. Prior to joining the company the 29-year-old worked as a project manager for a fashion garment company involved with import and export, but didn't enjoy her job. She recalls the interview process at de Baer.

'I was invited to a first interview with the personnel manager and my line manager. At that interview they asked a lot of questions about my personal values as well as my skills and work experience. For example, they asked where I would like to go on holiday and the books that I was reading. The questions were over and above assessing whether I could do the job', she says.

'Then, at the second interview, I had to give a presentation based on information I'd been given about the company and my own research. They're interested in your personality and style as well as the content. If you can do the job but don't fit in, then you won't get the job. After that the interviewing team told Jacqueline that they'd found a good candidate and she interviewed me. She asked some tough questions that I had to think hard about. I remember she asked me to talk about a current affairs story I'd read that I thought would affect me. She also asked about work situations and how I had dealt with them in the past.'

The end result, in Lawson's case, is a happy de Baer employee. It may sound time and effort intensive, but Jacqueline de Baer insists it isn't more expensive than traditional recruiting. 'If anything it saves us time and money. Because our HR dept and any recruitment agencies we use have such a clear idea of what character traits are important to us, we don't waste time – and therefore money – by doing lots of interviews with unsuitable candidates. I have no idea how long it takes our competitors to find staff – but it takes us less time than it would if we did not have these criteria in place.'

Quantifying the benefits is difficult as Jacqueline de Baer frankly admits. But she believes they are tangible: 'I don't have figures for how long our staff stay compared to the rest of our industry. But we have a large number of long-standing employees who have been with the company for over five years. I think that speaks for itself.'

Adds Bronwe Lawson: 'It's tough to get in here, but I can see why it's so important to recruit against the values. Every one has a different personality, but the company is always looking for the same values. I think it's quite an informal culture; very motivating and exceptionally team-oriented. I've never seen another company where people pull together to solve problems the way they do here. People always go the extra mile. I don't think that would happen if they weren't really motivated about the job.'

Techniques to succeed

There are always new suggestions on how to succeed at interviews. None are foolproof, but they might enable you to view interviews in a new light.

The 'Zelig' technique

In the classic Woody Allen film *Zelig*, the hero turns into the characters he finds himself with. Standing beside Adolf Hitler, Allen metamorphoses into an unlikely Nazi. In an interview it can be helpful to mirror the body posture of the person interviewing you. The theory is that this puts you more "in tune" with them and a rapport can be established more easily.

Beyond mirroring body language, there is personality matching, which includes mirroring voice timbre and speed, and other attributes of personality. So if the interviewer talks at a slow tempo in a lowish voice, the clued-up interviewee in personality-matching mode will match the pace and tone of the interviewer's speech. A note of caution. Only pursue this strategy if you feel comfortable with it. If the interviewer is female with a high-pitched voice and rapid delivery and the interviewee is male with a naturally gruff, bass voice then it is unlikely that the interviewee would feel comfortable with mirroring the voice of their interrogator. Even if they felt brave enough to try it, it may well come across as both absurd and "put on". "Put on" is the equivalent of fake, a quality the interviewee does not want to be associated with.

Assuming you are comfortable matching the voice of the interview, next, you can mirror the posture, lean forward if they do, or cross legs if they have, for example. The desired effect is a subtle echoing of the interviewer. Exaggerated gesture and obvious mimicking must be avoided at all costs. If, however, you strike the right balance (and pose) achieving that all important rapport will become a lot easier.

The fiction-into-fact technique

This is based on the theory that if you say or do something for long enough you and in a knock-on effect, others will eventually come to believe it. In

Greek mythology Pygmalion believed so strongly that his ivory statue of a woman was real that the goddess Venus gave it life. Thus, if you practice smiling over an extended period then eventually you will smile without realizing it and hopefully feel happy into the bargain. Interestingly smiling seems to be infectious. If you smile, other people smile, although if you are going to try this be careful where you do it.

How is all of this of any use to an interviewee? The trick is to tell yourself, and get others to tell you, how good you are at certain activities, how talented you are, how confident you are, etc. Then, at your interview you will exude confidence and star quality.

The seeing is believing technique

A technique commonly employed by sportsmen and women, visualization involves the mental enactment of the task about to be undertaken with a successful outcome attached. Gary Lineker, a famous English soccer team player, used to visualize scoring goals before a game of soccer. It appeared to work as he was one of his country's top goal scorers. Similarly Edmund Hilary climbed Mount Everest many times in his head before he scaled the peak for real.

Use this technique to walk through the interview in your mind. Imagine the questions you might be asked and your responses. Imagine asking questions. Imagine getting the job. How will it feel?

CAREER ADVENTURER

FRANZ LANDSBERGER *on hiring*

Title/Position: VP Human Resources, Bioscience Division
Company: Baxter, Europe
Industry: Pharmaceuticals

What are the factors that help you know when you've found the right person for a position?

'I guess it's a mixture, a little basket of things. There is always an intuitive element that is hard to quantify. Another very important factor is to have the applicant meet with his or her new boss and two or three future peers, so that we have at least three to five people interviewing at management level. I make it very clear that if one of those interviewers has a question mark or a 'no', we start an internal probe to find out why. If we don't come back with a resounding 'yes' from everyone, I don't hire.

We should only hire if everyone involved says yes, and it's easy to see why. If a new hire comes in and does not meet expectations, the interviewer with reservations about that person will come back and say 'See, I knew we should not have hired that person'. They will be looking for evidence to support their opinion.

Don't decide by yourself; take the help from a couple of others. Ask them to go into the chemistry and cultural aspects. Sit down and talk about it together: what did you see here? What questions did you ask?

I take a lot of time with the hiring process. Ninety-five percent of the people I've hired are still working in the company. Strategically speaking, take enough time to hire. Don't wait too long, but align your management on the vital importance of the interview process. If they can't make time for appointments for interviews, you should challenge them if they really need to fill the job and if they are committed in building the best team. It has to be an important event for your managers. The job candidate takes time off from her/his job to be interviewed, travel to you, etc.

The hiring process does not finish by signing an employment contract, it continues once the person joins. You have to have your landing and integration plan for them; it must be clear that they are welcome. You can't forget to order the phones for them. You have to be ready for their arrival. Have flowers on the table for them. Very simple, it's not expensive, but do it. Let them know that you value them. You didn't hire them just because there's a free seat available in your firm.'

4. COPING WITH PSYCHOMETRIC TESTS & ASSESSMENT CENTERS

They liked the resume. They loved your interview. Then, just as you were counting your chickens, along comes the psychometric test.

Psychometric tests are yet another part of the interviewer's arsenal. They are reasonably common in the selection process and you are likely to come across them at some point during your career. The idea is that the tests further help the recruiter to match the individual's characteristics with those required by the position available.

The tests are not always encountered at the end of the selection process. Essentially, it depends on the type of test used as to when you will encounter it. Long in-depth psychological tests are time-consuming and costly to administer, making them more suitable for screening a small group of candidates towards the end of the selection process. Short-term, less in-depth tests can be used for screening a large number of candidates to whittle them down prior to the interview stage.

Whenever you encounter the psychometric testing you should be told in advance that you are to take one, leaving you time to prepare. And there is no harm in asking the organization you're applying to whether they use psychometric testing. Forewarned is forearmed.

Types of tests

Although there are many different types of psychometric testing they can be loosely divided into two categories, ability (or aptitude) and personality.

Ability tests
Often referred to as tests of maximum performance, ability tests assess what you can do. They give an indication of your reasoning, decision-making, problem solving and other skills or aptitudes you may have. Ability tests, such as standard IQ tests, are often encountered early on in the selection process and used as a screening tool.

Personality tests

Often referred to as tests of typical performance, personality tests show what an individual is likely to do. They are not tests in the strict sense; rather they are indicators of type. There are no incorrect answers as such. However, by demonstrating certain preferences, you can manifest a personality that is not suitable, in the recruiter's opinion, for the job. This type of test is often used later on in the selection process to shape and structure second interviews.

Taking the tests

Taking psychometric tests, particularly the ability tests, is just like taking any other test. It is a case of back to school. All the tips your teachers gave you about taking school tests hold true for taking a psychometric test.

Ability tests will often be conducted under examination conditions and there will invariably be a time limit imposed. The trick here, just as it was at school or college, is to divide the time available by the number of questions, and then try to stick to the average time allotted for each question.

You may have experienced that 'running out of time' panic. It's not conducive to high-quality test answers, so try to avoid it.

You may have the sudden plunging stomach experience when you turn over the question paper and discover that you have trouble understanding the questions, let alone answering them. The way to avoid this is, of course, revision. Find out from the recruiter what type of test you will be taking and, if possible, who the test provider is. The majority of test providers have websites illustrating the type of test they offer. Some even have practice tests and sample questions that you can take online. There are also many books that offer the opportunity to take practice tests.

As well as preparing by practicing tests, try sharpening up your mental skills generally. Do crossword puzzles and mental arithmetic puzzles. Most daily newspapers will carry a puzzle section of some sort, do them. If you are a chess player, chess problems are an excellent way of honing your mental acuity.

As with all tests you should read the questions properly. It is unlikely that there will be trick questions but not impossible. Many questions in ability tests are deliberately framed in an ambiguous manner.

Team assessment

Another type of test you may encounter is the team assessment test. This is where a group of candidates are gathered together and given tasks to perform. It may be indoors or outdoors and the tasks can vary from getting from one line to another using only milk crates and wooden planks to completing a wooden block puzzle.

The point of group testing is to see how you function within a team, how you interact with your colleagues. Are you a leader or follower? Are you passive or active? Are you a good listener? Do you take direction well? Are you open to the ideas of others?

Team assessment can be very revealing of a person's character. Once the individuals are absorbed in the task they can easily forget that they are being scrutinized. It is difficult to maintain a façade during a team assessment. People's guards come down and they revert to type.

Remember, this will happen to you. If you wish to contribute and perform well during the task, as well as presenting yourself in a good light, you must try to remain a little self-conscious and aware that you are being observed.

If you've done your preparation properly you'll already know what type of person, what skills and characteristics, the recruiters are seeking. During a team assessment try, if you can, to demonstrate some of these traits.

Positive roles that you can play during a team assessment include:

- ◆ **Facilitator** – helping to get things done
- ◆ **Diplomat** – keeping the group together by resolving conflicting opinions
- ◆ **Creator** – generating ideas
- ◆ **Implementer** – taking ideas and putting them into action
- ◆ **Leader/coordinator** – taking a leading role, directing and coordinating the actions of others

Negative traits that should be avoided during an assessment include:

- ◆ **Being overbearing** – assuming a leadership role is alright as long as (a) it doesn't come across as a struggle for supremacy; (b) you are naturally a leader and comfortable with being leader; (c) you do not lead in a dictatorial and autocratic manner smothering the life out of the rest of the group.

◆ **Negativity** – employers want can-do people. Comments that include words such as 'can't', 'shouldn't', 'mustn't', 'don't', 'never' etc. should be avoided. If you wish to criticize suggest alternative courses of action, could it be done in a positive way. Try 'Why don't we do it in this way' or 'How about this' rather than 'That's wrong' or 'Don't do that'.

◆ **Passivity** – while you want to avoid coming across as overbearing, you must also avoid seeming meek, timid or passive. Employers like people who are motivated, who have energy, who are self-starters. If there are lots of other people trying to make a contribution you may be inclined to sit back and let them get on with it. You cannot afford to do this. Even if you know how to complete the task or have great ideas, the recruiter will never find out unless you show them. Being active doesn't necessarily mean taking charge, or doing something in a practical sense. It might mean coming up with and explaining ideas or solutions. Problem solving is, after all, a highly valued skill within organizations.

◆ **Marking and selection** – Recruiters make selections from test results in different ways. One approach is the top-down method. The recruiter decides how many candidates they wish to select and then counts down from the highest score until the required number is achieved. Alternatively a recruiter may set a cut-off score selecting anybody who achieves a higher mark. Cut-off scores are set objectively and represent the minimum level at which an individual can be expected to perform the job well.

CAREER ADVENTURER

JONATHAN HILL *on psychometrics*

'*If you are to be tested on either verbal or numerical critical reasoning, obtain some practice questions and rehearse your ability to deal with the problems they pose.*

You may also wish to study your own personality, perhaps using one of the web-based questionnaires. Treat such an exercise as a piece of personal research, and whilst looking for consistencies in the results, do not give too much weight to any one profile. Much may depend on the kind of boss you have, since some can help you polish your personality and encourage you to celebrate your best features, whilst others simply wear you down and undermine your self-confidence.'

INTERVIEW RESOURCES

Reading

Effective Answers to Interview Questions, (Jist Works Inc., 1989).

Yate, M *Knock 'Em Dead With Great Answers to Tough Interview Questions,* (Bob Adams Inc., 1992.

Krannich, R & Krannich, C *Dynamite Answers to Interview Questions,* (Impact Publications, 1992).

Leeds, D *Smart Questions: Interview Your Way to Job Success,* (Harper Collins, 1993).

Fry, R 101 *Great Answers to the Toughest Interview Questions,* (Careers Press, 1994).

You may wish to further research your strengths by purchasing a copy of *Now, Discover your Strengths* by Marcus Buckingham and Don Clifton, and completing the web-based questionnaire using the unique pin-number provided with each copy. The book was published by the Free Press in 2001.

5. SHOW ME THE MONEY

Pay negotiation. It's tricky but it has to be done. And if you don't want to feel undervalued it has to be done well.

You may think that your employer ideally wants to pay you as little as they can get away with. This may be true. It is just as probable, however, that your employer will be happy to pay what's fair and reasonable.

If you have followed the advice in this book until now then you have avoided all questions regarding salary. Only when you receive a firm job offer is it time to talk money. The following pointers will help you achieve the desired outcome – a reasonable pay package.

◆ **Prepare** – if you don't know your own market worth then you're not in a good position to negotiate a fair salary. Previous pay packages may provide a guide, but only a guide. Use the Internet to find out industry and job-specific pay levels. The

Internet has created a level playing field and evened up the balance of power between employer and employee when negotiating pay.

One web site, JobSmart, contains a wealth of salary related information with links to salary surveys for a host of different professions. Or if you are in the +$100 k bracket try Execunet.com for an idea of what top execs are being paid.
(See SECTION TWO for more salary links.)

Remember to take the cost of living into account. It varies from country to country, and within countries from region to region. It can even vary within different parts of a large city.

◆ **Be fair** – If you have done the research you will have an idea of the salary range you can command. This is a fair salary. If an employer wants the best person for the job they should be willing to pay at least within the salary range and hopefully towards the upper end. This is where you should pitch your demands.

◆ **Persist** – Recruiters are experienced negotiators. They negotiate pay hundreds of times. There may be moments when you are tempted to accept less than you want. This may be because you feel you are likely to lose the job. Resist the temptation. If what you are asking is fair and the organization wants you to work for them it should be prepared to pay a reasonable and fair salary. So as long as your requests are reasonable, stick to your guns.

◆ **Be flexible** – if your employer is unwilling to meet your straight salary demand be creative. Think of other ways that you can achieve an overall package with which you're satisfied. Benefits such as bonus payments, stock options, pension payments, company car allowance and mortgage subsidies, can all be used to shuffle the pay and benefits pack until the deck is stacked to your satisfaction.

Remember that failing to negotiate the best salary possible can be much more costly than you might think. Larry Nadler, Professor of Communication at Miami University of Ohio, has studied pay negotiating habits and concluded that because of the compounding effect of subsequent pay rises a $2000 increase secured at the age of 22 translates into roughly $150,000 extra income over a 40 year career.

Stephen Pollan, co-author of *Live Rich,* a book on negotiating, emphasizes the importance of securing the best salary and benefits package between receiving the

job offer and accepting it. If you don't use that opportunity for negotiating well you may never get another like it: "You are never more powerful than when you are responding to their offer", Pollan says, "because it is the one time that the employer may want you more than you want him."

◆ **Don't push your luck** – there's fair and there is greedy. If you keep upping your demands you risk alienating your prospective employer. At worst you may do yourself out of a job. They may meet your demands but resent you for being greedy. Your strategy could poison the atmosphere and your working relationships when you start your new job. If you compromise, your employer may be more favorably disposed to you in the long term.

◆ **Remember your goal** – don't lose sight of the objective. The point of the exercise is for you to obtain a salary that you are happy with. It is not a competition where you have to get one up on your employer. Sensible stock traders set themselves price limits. If a stock rises to a certain price they sell and take a known profit. If a stock price falls to a certain limit they sell and take a known loss. Sensible stock traders learn not to see trading as a personal battle between them and market. Be professional; set to yourself a salary target. If you reach the target accept the salary. Remember, too, that this job is just a way station on your career adventure, not the final destination. Whether it is taking you in the right direction may be more important than the immediate financial return. The money may come later.

PAY & BENEFITS: THE ALTERNATIVES

MONEY

Bonuses: Signing-on bonus, signing-off bonus, performance-related bonus, on-target bonus. There lots of different bonuses you can ask for.

Mortgage Subsidy: Subsidized mortgages can be worth a lot of money. On the negative side they can also have quite a tie-in effect.

Profit sharing: But remember you can only share profits if there are profits.

Salary: Whatever the recruiter offers they will expect you to counter.

Severance pay: Golden parachutes are highly desirable. Who wouldn't want to receive a large lump sum when leaving a company? If you can negotiate a golden goodbye, congratulations. They are usually the province of senior executives and highly talented staff.

Stock options: During the dot.com boom these were the must-have accoutrement for any self-respecting job seeker. However, the dot.com bust showed stock options in their true light and left many a poor employee crying into their stock portfolio. Remember, stock options are sensitive to the vagaries of the stock market.

PERKS

Tech gear: Laptops, PDAs, mobile phone and other essential tech accessories for the road warrior.

Flexible hours: Employers can be surprisingly accommodating over flexible hours but often only after you have been with the company for a specified period. Similarly, if you want to work from home, get clarification on the position now.

Health insurance: Can improve an invaluable perk.

Holidays: Extra days, days in lieu, carrying over untaken holiday, flexible arrangements.

Relocation: You may be able to squeeze more relocation expenses out of the employer if your needs are unusual or greater than the average.

Tuition fees: Large companies usually pay for course fees where qualifications are taken at the behest of the company. If you are lucky you may be able to get other extras, such as books and other course materials paid for.

The art of negotiation

Founder of a web-based email company, Sabeer Bhatia, knows how to negotiate. He could have sold Hotmail to Microsoft for tens of millions. Microsoft came to the table with a team of six. Bhatia elected to negotiate alone, this way he could avoid divide and rule tactics. The Microsoft team returned every fortnight for two months. Then Bill Gates invited Bhatia to Redmond for a chat.

Bhatia asked for $700 million. Microsoft offered tens of millions. Bhatia said no. Microsoft offered $200 million. Bhatia said no. Microsoft offered $300 million. Bhatia said no. Microsoft offered $350 million. Bhatia's staff at Hotmail quietly suggested he should secure their future by accepting. Bhatia's management team said he should accept. Bhatia said no.

When the deal was done at an undisclosed price, 2,769,148 of Microsoft shares were exchanged for ownership , a value of $400 million at the time of the deal. Some might question whether it was great negotiating, stubbornness or plain foolhardiness. In the end the outcome justifies the means. One of the golden rules of deal-making is: don't underestimate the value of what you are offering.

Not everyone possesses Bhatia's innate gift for negotiation. But even the most inept negotiators, the kind who come away from the used-car lot having paid full price for a motor car, but still feeling pleased about the deal they made, can learn to avoid common negotiating pitfalls. In a 2001 Harvard Business Review article Professor James K. Sebenius, *Harvard Business School* professor and founder of its negotiation unit, outlines six errors[1].

Mistake 1
Neglecting the other side's problems. You can't negotiate effectively unless you understand your own interests and your own no-deal options. But since the other side will say yes for its reasons, not yours, agreement requires understanding and addressing your counterpart's problems as a means to solving your own.

As an eighteenth-century pope once noted about Cardinal de Polignac's remarkable diplomatic skills: 'This young man always seems to be of my opinion [at the start of a negotiation] and at the end of the conversation I find that I am of his'. In short, the first mistake is to focus on your own problem exclusively. Solve the other side's as the means to solving your own.

Mistake 2

Letting price bulldoze other interests. Negotiators who pay attention exclusively to price turn potentially cooperative deals into adversarial ones. These 'reverse Midas' negotiators use hard-bargaining techniques that often leave potential joint gains unrealized. That's because, while price is an important factor in most deals, it's rarely the only one. Wise negotiators put the vital issue of price in perspective and don't straightjacket their view of the richer interests at stake.

Mistake 3

Letting positions drive out interests. Three elements are at play in a negotiation. Issues are on the table for explicit agreement. Positions are one party's stand on the issues. Interests are underlying concerns that would be affected by the resolution.

Great negotiators understand that the dance of bargaining positions is only the surface game; the real action rakes place when they've probed behind positions for the full set of interests at stake. Reconciling interests to create value requires patience and a willingness to research the other side, ask many questions, and listen.

Mistake 4

Searching too hard for common ground. Conventional wisdom says we negotiate to overcome the differences that divide us. So we are advised to find win-win agreements by searching for common ground. Common ground is generally a good thing. Yet many of the most frequently overlooked sources of value in negotiation arise from differences among the parties.

Conducting a disciplined 'differences inventory' is at least as important a task as is identifying areas of common ground. While common ground helps, differences drive deals. But negotiators who don't actively search for differences rarely find them.

Mistake 5

Neglecting BATNAs. BATNAs are best alternative to a negotiated agreement they reflect the course of action a party would take if the proposed deal were not possible. Negotiators often become preoccupied with tactics, trying to improve the potential deal while neglecting their own BATNA and that of the other side. Yet the real negotiation problem is "deal versus BATNA", not one or the other in isolation. Your potential deal and your BATNA should work together as do the two blades of scissors to cut a piece of paper.

Mistake 6

Failing to correct for skewed vision. You may be crystal clear on the right negotiation problem but you can't solve it correctly without a firm understanding of both sides' interests, BATNAs, valuations, likely actions, and so on. Yet the psychology of perception systematically leads negotiators to major errors.

Getting too committed your point of view 'believing your own line', is an extremely common mistake. And partisan perceptions can easily become self-fulfilling prophecies. Clinging firmly to the idea that one's counterpart is stubborn or extreme, for example, is likely to trigger just that behavior, sharply reducing the possibility of reaching a constructive agreement.

RESOURCES

Cohen, H *You Can Negotiate Anything*, (Carol Publishing Group, 1980).
Trump, D & Schwartz, T *Trump! The Art of the Deal*, (Random House, 1987).
Fisher, Ury & Patton *Getting to Yes: Negotiating Agreement Without Giving In*, (Penguin, 1991).
McCormack, M *On Negotiating,* (Arrow Books, 1996).
Miller, L *Get More Money On Your Next Job: 25 Proven Strategies For Getting More Money, Better Benefits and Greater Job Security,* (McGraw-Hill, 1998).

For a slightly different take on negotiation try Scene 15 Harry the Haggler from the film *Monty Python's Life of Brian:* 'Four? For this gourd? Four?! Look at it. It's worth ten if it's worth a shekel.' Etc. http://www.stone-dead.asn.au/movies/life-of-brian/scene-15.html

The counter-offer

When you are offered a job and negotiate a decent salary package don't think the application ordeal is over. There is still the counter-offer.

You tell your existing employer that you are leaving; that you have been offered another job and more money. Your employer naturally asks you why you're leaving. Unless they are pleased to see the back of you, they will want you to stay. The departure of an employee causes ripples in the social structure of the workplace. Other employees have to bear additional workload until the position is filled. Dissatisfied co-workers may be prompted to leave. Filling the vacated position cost the company money. Whichever way you look at it, it is inconvenient for the employer.

At this point your employer will do one of two things. Either they will wish you well on your new adventure, or they will do everything within their power to keep you at the company. If the company adopts the second course of action always remember that it did nothing to keep you until it was forced to do so when you chose to leave. Employers can be unscrupulous in the methods they adopt to retain would-be leavers. They may badmouth your future employer, tell you how the new employer is in trouble, rumors they have heard, anything to sow the seeds of doubt in your mind. Alternatively, they may tell you that the company is going through a difficult period, how your co-workers will suffer in your absence. It is the whole guilt-trip thing.

Then on top of this there is the counter offer. Your existing employer may offer:

◆ More money
◆ More perks
◆ Promotion
◆ Anything you want
◆ Any combination of the above

Or, as is often the case, your employer *promises* you any combination of the above.

And if you get a hard and fast offer which is an improvement on your existing pay package, and an improvement on the pay package you have negotiated at your prospective employer, then what do you do? The obvious answer is to stay where you are. This way you negotiate better terms for yourself without all the hassle of moving. Closer inspection however, reveals that the decision is not so straightforward.

First, consider your prospective employer. They'll have to start the job search process over. Any headhunters involved will also be out of pocket, and be made to look unprofessional. So what, you say. Why should the impact on your prospective employer/headhunters/recruitment agency bother you if you're not moving. The reason is reputation. Reputation makes careers. Blow your reputation by letting people down and it will affect your value in the market. You can guarantee that it will color any future interaction between you and the prospective employer/headhunters/recruitment agency.

Next, take your current employer. Yes, they came up with a better package, but don't think that they enjoyed doing it. No one likes having a gun held against their head, your employer will make a mental note that you wanted to leave and plan accordingly, they will resent your course of action, and even if you remain future progress may well be difficult. They may question your loyalty.

Finally, what about your own position? While you may have negotiated a better benefits package for yourself you have both damaged your reputation and destabilized your position with your existing employer. The financial gains may only be short term.

So what decision should you make if your current employer makes a counter-offer? The answer is think about why you wanted to move in the first place. If your current employer was rewarding you sufficiently, if you're being challenged by your work, if your job satisfaction was high, would you have wanted to move? Nothing has changed. All that has happened is that your employer has been forced into temporary counter measures. The underlying reality, your employer's ethos, its attitude towards you, is unchanged. Remember the reasons that caused you to move. Be brave, take the new job.

The job offer

'We are pleased to offer…' Eventually this will be the letter that lands in your mailbox. Congratulations, you managed not only to get a foot in the door, but to barge your way through it; you have been offered the job. The application ordeal is not quite over yet though. You still have to accept.

The acceptance letter should include the obvious statement of acceptance, as well as an expression of enthusiasm and gratitude. Equally important is an outline of the principal points of the employment, as you understand it. This means reiterating the position and job description and any explicit duties you have agreed that you will be undertaking, as well as the pay and benefits.

You do this to avoid any misunderstanding. In the 1880s, Ralph Waldo Emerson became America's first lecturer known to have received a fee. He received $5 for himself plus a bag of oats for his horse. After completing the lecture he had to argue whether the oats were included in the agreed payment or not.

Career adventurers are unlikely to find themselves arguing over a bag of oats but something far more important (unless you're a horse) such as salary or stock options. If you turn up to work only to find that the Lear jet you were promised has mysteriously transformed into a railway season ticket, or the salary in the region of $60,000 turns into $30,000 plus on target bonuses, or the 35th floor penthouse office suite is in fact just another cubicle, then your employer will not be able to accuse you of misunderstanding if you have clearly outlined your expectations in the acceptance letter.

If you are fortunate enough to receive more than one job offer then you will have to write a letter declining one, or several, of the jobs you are offered. In this case do not be brutal. While you may wish to indicate on what grounds you made your decision to decline, offering an opportunity for the company to counter-offer, it pays to remain on good terms with prospective employers. You never know when you might be reapplying.

If it is clear after, or even during, an interview that you are no longer interested in working for a company, let them know as soon as possible. It's professional, and it saves everyone concerned time, money and stress.
Finally, when you receive a letter of rejection and most of you will at some point, don't just bin it. Write back, say you are disappointed, ask for feedback, and say that you would be willing to be considered for another position if one

became available. This can't do any harm because if you were a complete no-hoper as far as the vacancy went then you're still a complete no-hoper; but if you were a borderline candidate, your response might just tip the scales in your favor in the event of another position becoming vacant.

Notes

James K. Sebenius, *Six habits of merely effective negotiators*, (Harvard Business Review, April 2001).

"The ultimate measure of a person is not where he or she stands in moments of comfort and convenience, but where he or she stands at times of challenge and controversy."

Martin Luther King, Jr

"I know quite certainly that I myself have no special talent; curiosity, obsession and dogged endurance, combined with self-criticism have brought me to my ideas."

Albert Einstein

"That which does not kill me makes me stronger."

Nietzsche

FOUR
THRIVING IN THE JOB JUNGLE
HOW THE WORLD OF WORK CAN WORK FOR YOU

In this chapter you will learn how to:

■

Cope with your new role

■

Identify and acquire a mentor

■

Use internal networking to consolidate your position

■

Learn how organizational politics affect you and your next move.

1. SETTLING INTO WORK

Today's the day you start your new job.

Not just any job; the first job in your career adventure. You have been thinking about this moment for weeks, maybe months, even years. Yesterday you were on the outside, with your nose pressed up against the glass, gazing in at all those people who were doing what you wanted to do. Today you become an insider. You've taken time to find out what makes you tick and what you really want out of life. You have plotted and planned and worked to get the best job you can, the best for you. You have made it. Congratulations. Give yourself a pat on the back. Take a minute to bask in your success. Now you can sit back and enjoy yourself, right? Wrong.

Your 60 seconds of self-congratulation are over. It's time to get down to work. In the last chapter, you learned how to beat off your rivals to secure your new job. Now you have to prove yourself.

First, remember how lucky you are that you have got this far at all. Despite what you may think, receiving a firm job offer is no guarantee that you will ever start the job. Take the graduates recruited by some of the world's leading management consultancies in 2001. High-flying graduates taken on by management consultants Accenture were asked to take an extended summer holiday before starting with the firm. Difficult economic conditions meant that of 570 graduates starting jobs, 400 were asked to delay their start. To soften the blow they were given their signing on fee of $9,000 as well as being paid half their monthly salaries. It may seem like a dream arrangement, being paid to go on holiday, but the downside is the element of uncertainty introduced at such an early stage in the individual's career. At least the graduates joining Accenture were better off than some of their counterparts at PriceWaterhouseCoopers. In the UK, the firm was forced to lay off nearly 100 graduate trainees before they started work.

Hand-holding

If you're middle or senior management you might be lucky enough to be given a coach to help you ease in to your new job.

Cranfield School of Management's Professor Andrew Kakabadse, an authority on management and leadership, believes it takes a year for an executive to settle into a senior post and three years to make an impact. If only executives had that kind of time. Today they are likely to be assessed after only a few months.

To make the transition into a new company culture a little easier, some recruitment consultants offer coaching services. The coach acts as a sounding board and hand-holder. They should have in-depth knowledge of the culture and working practices of the executive's new firm. This means that they can help steer the new executive around the inevitable pitfalls that beset someone new to an organization. In less enlightened times being assigned a coach might have been seen as a sign of weakness and had a stigma attached to it. Instead, today, coaching is seen by some as denoting status, a mark that an executive has been earmarked for better things.

The majority of people starting a new job, however, will not have the benefit of a guardian angel. For them, the first day at work is a time of high stress. They're in an unfamiliar environment, with strange rules and new people. You may be one of those people who strides into a new environment and is immediately at ease. If so, you are in the minority; your challenge is to avoid seeming too brash. Most people feel some trepidation when starting a new job. Most of us have been through a similar experience, even if it was not in the workplace. Remember your first day at school? You survived that experience, you will survive this one.

True, there are additional complications. If you didn't fit in at school for the first 90 days, if your schoolwork wasn't up to scratch, if you broke the rules occasionally, you were unlikely to be thrown out onto the sidewalk clutching your satchel. Work is different. New jobs usually come with probation periods. Conduct yourself poorly during the probation period and you could find yourself out on your ear, with all your hard work and effort to get in wasted. But this is how it should be. No company wants an incompetent employee. If you and the organization you work for don't fit together, it's best to find out quickly. Otherwise you will both be unhappy in the long run.

The first 100 days

Few are exempted from this process of judgment. The performance of a US President during the first hundred days in office is subjected to intense scrutiny. Incidentally, your company may have a financial incentive to make a thorough assessment of your performance after 90 days. If you were discovered through a recruitment agency then your employer will have to pay between 15 and 30 percent of your first year's salary in fees. These fees often fall due at the 90-day mark.

You should get used to assessment. It didn't use to be this way. Your grandfather didn't have to prove himself so frequently. Once he was in, as long as he toed the company line, he could probably expect to remain with his employer for life. Those days are gone. You will be judged continually throughout your working life. Develop the right working habits from the beginning and not only will they enable you to survive your own personal hundred days, they will serve you well throughout your entire career.

So, what do you need to do?

Make an impression

As with networking and interviews, first impressions count. Treat your first day at work as you did your interview. Dress appropriately but conservatively. Set out early to avoid arriving late. Be friendly with everyone from the receptionist to the boss, it's not always clear who is who.

The youthful CEO at one technology company recounts how a new recruit, seeing him dressed in jeans and a sweatshirt, failed to recognize her new boss. It was only after he'd been quizzed about himself that he pointed out the misunderstanding. Even then she didn't believe him, assuming it was a prank. Her expression changed when he produced a copy of the company's annual report containing his photograph. Needless to say, it wasn't the first impression that she had hoped to make.

Be organized. If you're not naturally organized make a conscious effort to change the habits of a lifetime. Plan your day in advance (obviously this may not be possible for the first few days). Use a notepad or personal organizer, write down your thoughts as they occur, names, telephone numbers, e-mail addresses and other important information you need to remember. In fact, scribble yourself a note about anything you might forget. If you are not familiar with the computer/telephone system and need to use it to do your job, write down the basic operating instructions. It will save you embarrassment and time later on.

Get connected

In 2001, a television show called *Shipwrecked* aired in the UK. The premise: a group of young people, deposited on a tropical island in the South Pacific had to survive together for several weeks. After only a few episodes, however, one of the group was voted off the island by fellow castaways. Why? The reason given at the time was that the individual was stealing provisions. But when the experience was over, several other castaways admitted to taking items. Even at the time that the unfortunate person was voted off, a few of her co-conspirators claimed joint responsibility.

So why was this individual ejected and not her accomplices? Because she failed to bond sufficiently with her fellow castaways. Without allies she was isolated, and easily singled out as the fall girl. Tellingly, one of the co-conspirators admitted that after this incident, in fear of meeting the same fate, she made distinct efforts to form attachments with other members of the group.

Why is this story relevant to new employees? Because failure to fit in is one of the main reasons that employees don't make it through the probation period. To avoid an early exit you must take steps to bond with your co-workers. This doesn't mean being overbearingly friendly. You just have to be interested in them as people. In the first few days a good opening gambit is to ask for help. There is nothing wrong with this. It is not a sign of weakness, as long as you are not asking for help with core skills that were instrumental in landing you the job in the first place. (The new head of IT enquiring how to switch on his computer will not inspire confidence.) But asking for guidance on how to navigate in a strange environment with unfamiliar rules is perfectly natural and can help you make friends.

Another important part of getting connected is remembering people's names. There's always one person at a party who remembers your name even though you have only met them briefly once before. How do you feel about that person? Favorably. You are more likely to like them because they like you, or at least you are inclined to think that they like you because they remember your name. Of course, they may not care for you at all. They hardly know you, after all, but they do know the importance of remembering names. If you aren't good with names, it's worth writing them down.

Try this: when you are introduced to people repeat their name out loud. At the same time try to remember something about their appearance, the color of their tie for example, or the kind of glasses they are wearing. Then in future when you think about that first meeting you should be able to recollect saying their name.

Appear to know what you are doing

Inevitably it will take you time to learn the ropes at your new job. But if you appear all at sea you will only increase the chance of being forced to walk the plank when it comes to the end of your assessment period. You may not feel it, but try to appear confident.

If your job was an idea for a film could you pitch it to a film studio executive in under a minute? This exercise helps you to crystallize the essential elements of the job in your mind. As well as understanding your own role it is important to see where you fit into the bigger picture. How does your contribution affect the bottom line?

Another way of familiarizing yourself with your company is to read the annual report if there is one. This will include an account of the previous year's trading, where the business did well and where not so well, the chairman or CEO's predictions for the future and a detailed account of the organization's financial position.

To appear less of a fish out of water, 'own' your workspace. It may be the tiniest of corporate cubicles, but it is yours. Annex it. Introduce some personal touches, a few pictures, a nameplate, and your coffee mug, enough to make your workspace belong to you. It will help you appear a more integral part of the working landscape in your company. Don't overdo it though. Avoid clutter and crass keepsakes.

Start building your reputation

"The purest treasure mortal times afford/ Is spotless reputation." So said Mowbray in William Shakespeare's *Richard II*. England's greatest dramatist understood the importance of reputation. It was a theme that ran through many of his best plays, *Othello*, for example. Shakespeare reportedly observed of himself: "I am my reputation". You are, too. Within hours, if not minutes, of your arrival at your new job, word will have spread about what sort of person you are. It will be based initially on your manner and appearance. But in the coming days, weeks and months, it will encompass your work style, job performance and much more.

The word reputation, that which is generally believed about your character, is derived from the Latin, *reputatio* or reckoning, and is as important in the twenty-first century as it was in the sixteenth. In a world where individuals market themselves to employers like companies market brands to consumers, reputations don't simply speak volumes – they positively bellow. For free agents hoping to build their own client base, building a reputation is crucial. It's important, too, for employees who can expect to work for several companies during their working life carrying their skills, experience and reputation with them.

A strong reputation will help you stand out from the crowd. Reputation is built upon values as well as abilities. Society attributes certain values to a good reputation, values such as reliability, honesty and integrity. In addition, specific values that determine reputation may vary from industry to industry, from job to job. Cautiousness may serve a stunt man well but a sales executive less so. If you are not aware of your personal values system already, try articulating it with the help of one of the values inventories in Section One.

Once elaborated you must make a determined effort to live up to your values. This means consistency. If you build your reputation on honesty and reliability then take great care not to deviate from these values. Tell one lie, let one person down, miss one important deadline and it can undo months of good work.

Behavior consistent with your values over time, coupled with a continually high standard of work will build you a formidable reputation in your chosen career. Then, as the saying goes, your reputation will precede you. You will need to market yourself less as word-of-mouth does the marketing for you and the world beats a path to your door rather than vice versa.

For a cursory evaluation of your reputation try the online quiz at http://content.monsterindia.com/tools/quizzes/reputation.

Being outstanding and standing out

At some point in your first 100 days you will have to show up on the radar of the people who matter. These are the people who make hiring and firing decisions, bestow promotions, conduct reviews and determine salary. It may be your boss, your boss's boss, or someone else in the organization. But, if you are to make progress, it helps to get an early score on the board.

The best way to do this is to do something that gets you noticed. Something good that gets you noticed, rather than something bad. Good is usually synonymous with improving the bottom line. Any idea that saves on expenditure or brings in more revenue is likely to be well received, improving efficiency for example. The trick here is not to appear a know-it-all or smart-arse but an employee who has the company's best interests at heart (rather than your own).

A caveat here is that you don't want to be a creep, or land one of your new colleagues in trouble. A degree of enthusiasm is good. Obsessive behavior is not. Dropping an idea into conversation with your boss is likely to be seen as being helpful. Buttonholing the chairman in the elevator and berating him with a list of long overdue improvements will do little to advance your career. Nor will going over the head of your immediate boss. Bide your time. Learn the culture. Then make your move. Chances are if no one has come up with your brilliant cost-cutting idea so far and it's worth checking to find out if they have then they won't suddenly think of it tomorrow.

Other things to do and not to do:
- ◆ Don't shirk your work responsibilities. Keep personal telephone calls and emails to a minimum. At least until you are established. If you run out of work to do, ask for more, however much it pains you to do so.
- ◆ Under-promise, over-deliver is a cardinal rule in life and work. Start as you mean to go on. If you under-promise people will be pleasantly surprised when you turn in a better than predicted performance. If you promise the world and only deliver two continents they will be disappointed.
- ◆ Pin down your job description. Make sure you know what is expected of you.
- ◆ Keep a critical assessment of your own performance. Check with colleagues that your work is up to scratch.
- ◆ Go beyond the call of duty. Employees who go the extra mile stand out. Be enthusiastic. Volunteer for extra duties. (But remember the creep caveat.) Take on additional projects. Not only is it all invaluable experience, it is good for improving a career adventurer's prospects of advancement.
- ◆ Join in. It is sometimes tempting to opt out of work lunches, office parties and other bonding sessions. Make sure you attend, lest you offend. Otherwise you run the risk of appearing an outsider and missing out on all the useful gossip.

SURVIVAL: A BRAND NEW U

Branding is not just for corporations. In the late 1990s, the management guru Tom Peters wrote an article in *Fast Company* exhorting individuals to adopt the branding strategy of corporations. Like most brilliant ideas it seemed obvious the way Peters explained it.

Companies spend huge sums of money developing brand strategies. They collect the advice of academics, researchers, practitioners and commentators and distil it into a workable and effective brand strategy. How do we know it's effective? Because there are few people who do not have some sort of relationship with a brand. Whether it's a logo on a pair of running shoes a badge on car bonnet or a label on a shirt pocket nearly everyone is branded.

In the modern world of work, argues Peters, we are each CEOs of our own company, ourselves, our 'unit of one'. Therefore there is no reason why individuals cannot create a buzz about themselves just as Sony does about its Playstation, Walkman or other electronic goods, albeit with a smaller budget.

The starting point in defining your own brand is to look for the qualities that differentiate you. Ask yourself: How am I different from the next person? What are my key personality traits, characteristics, qualities, call them what you will, that define me as a person?

Companies frequently use a feature-benefit model when they create brands. For each feature offered by a product or service, a corresponding benefit to the consumer should be identifiable. Ask yourself: What do I do that adds measurable specialized added value? What have I done in the past that I can use to enhance my brand equity? This will give you an understanding of your personal brand values.

The next step is to market the brand. In today's society there are no prizes for shyness or modesty. Peters characteristically recommends that individuals 'market the bejesus' out of their brand.

As with corporate brands maintaining a high level of visibility is crucial for marketing your brand. Networking, presenteeism, attending and conducting meetings at work all enhance visibility. It is important to remember however, that with visibility comes potential pitfalls. Some companies have found out to their cost how easy it is to damage the brand. Individuals seeking to create their own personal brand have to be constantly vigilant. Behavior must be consistent with brand identity at all times.

As with most marketing there is a place for style in the process of creating your personal brand. Appearance matters when a brand is being judged. After all, branding is all about claiming a place in the mind of the consumer. In personal branding credibility and power are must-have qualities. Some of the most powerful brands are those that confer status by association. Similarly, the strongest personal brands will be those that others wish to be associated with. What this means in practice is that the individual must have something others want. Skills, contacts, good company, they all count. Ask 'Why would others want to associate with me?' Hopefully coming up with an answer won't be too much of a struggle. Whatever your answer is, a good sense of humor, wisdom, charm, cultivate it. If you succeed in effectively marketing yourself you will enhance your reputation.

Peters' take on branding the individual might seem light hearted and frivolous. It is anything but. Peters is spot-on in his observations. In the new world of work successful individuals will be those who have created their own brand. It's already the case. How many times do we hear that a successful person has charisma, personal magnetism and expertise in a particular field, an easygoing charm? Whether by design or not these people have created their own brand. They have established a reputation. And there is no reason why others who would wish to emulate their success should not consciously create their own brands. The power of brands is not limited to soft drinks and motorcars, breakfast cereals and candy bars.

As Peters says: 'It's this simple: You are a brand. You are in charge of your brand.'

Source: Peters, Tom *The Brand Called You Fast Company*, Issue 10, August 1997.

2. MENTORING

When Odysseus, King of Ithaca, left for the Trojan Wars (circa 800 BC), he was faced with a problem; who would look after the royal household and groom his son, Telemachus, for the throne in his absence?

Odysseus' turned to Mentor, his trusted companion, and instructed him to assume the role of father figure, advisor, counselor, tutor and role model to Telemachus while he was away. Greek mythology also tells us that the goddess Athena would speak to Telemachus in the guise of Mentor. Jump from the writings of Homer to the present day and the word 'mentor' has become part of our language, signifying a wise and trusted counselor, a sagacious adviser, a tutor.

Modern definitions of the term include that of Linda Phillips-Jones, one of the leading experts on mentoring, who describes mentors as 'skilled people who go out of their way to help you clarify your personal goals and take steps toward reaching them'. In her book *Mentors and Protégés* she describes some characteristics of mentors and the mentoring relationship[1]:

- ◆ Mentors are usually older than their protégés.
- ◆ Mentors frequently but not always initiate the relationship.
- ◆ Mentor-protégé relationships do not need to be particularly close.
- ◆ It is possible to have more than one mentor at a time.
- ◆ There are patterns and cycles in mentor-protégé relationships.
- ◆ Mentoring should benefit both partners equally.

In an organizational setting mentoring may cover the following areas:

Appropriate dress, conflict resolution, communication, company protocol and culture, ethical practice, leadership, networking, office politics, presentation, project management, time management, work-life balance.

Why have a mentor?

Mentoring has long been recognized as a beneficial practice in the private sector. In a survey of 1,200 top managers of the largest US corporations in the 1980s, for example, over two-thirds had been mentored[2]. In a later study of Fortune 500 CEOs, when asked what factors had contributed to their success, many CEOs referred to effective mentoring as a key factor[3]. Women have found mentoring particularly effective as a means of smashing the glass ceiling. In a survey conducted in 1996, of female executives interviewed 99 per cent had been mentored[4].

Although you are unlikely to enlist the help of a Greek god or goddess to advise you, a mentor can be just as useful to you during your career as it was to Telemachus. Indeed, mentoring is recognized as a very important adjunct to career development and many companies offer mentoring relationships. So how can a mentoring relationship help you?

A good mentor can:
◆ Expand your horizons and perspectives
◆ Help build your confidence and give you moral support
◆ Provide you with a professional role model
◆ Improve your skills level, and emotional and intellectual development
◆ Provide you with professional connections, and acquaint you with industry specific values and customs
◆ Provide objective feedback on a performance
◆ Help you enter and advance within your chosen career

Mentors can also be very useful in relieving one of the most significant factors in determining job satisfaction, stress. According to Linda Hill, consultant and Harvard Business School academic, even the most experienced managers often report feelings of conflict, ambiguity and isolation. 'The myriad of challenges encountered when one becomes a manager are difficult to shoulder alone,' she notes. 'Unfortunately, new managers can be reluctant to ask for help; it doesn't fit their conception of the boss as expert.[5]'

A good mentoring relationship is a win-win situation. Possible benefits to the mentee include:

◆ An increase in self-confidence and self-worth

◆ Better pay and benefits

◆ Better prospects for promotion

◆ Improved productivity and performance

◆ More rapid career advancement

Benefits to the mentor may include:

◆ An increase in prestige and status within the organization

◆ Enhanced communication and other interpersonal skills

◆ Greater self-worth

◆ More power

◆ Revitalized career

◆ Satisfaction from passing on knowledge

What does a mentor do?

The mentor's role varies according a variety of factors, including the quality of the relationship between mentor and mentee, the level of skills and knowledge of both parties, time available and organizational culture.

With an experienced mentor and relatively inexperienced mentee the mentor may take on the role of tutor, counselor, encourager, life-coach. If both parties are located close to one another they may, over time, develop a strong friendship.

For a more experienced mentee, the mentor's role may be closer to sponsor and facilitator. They may provide a sounding board; someone to discuss and explore ideas and experiences.

Roles of the Mentor

In the various literature on mentoring a number of specific roles associated with mentors have been identified.

Acceptor: as an acceptor the mentor provides unconditional support and encouragement for the mentee. With unreserved support the mentee will not be afraid to fail and will be encouraged to take risks and push themselves beyond their normal boundaries. Good mentors are fans of their mentees. They visualize how through their efforts the mentee will be improved to fulfill their full potential. In return, the mentor receives affirmation of their own qualities through the respect and trust and admiration of the mentee.

Counselor: the mentor can help the mentee with their personal problems. Ethical issues, such as the balance between maintaining personal integrity and values and career advancement or the struggle to maintain a work-life balance, can be discussed. If the mentor can empathize with the mentee, personal internal conflict can be worked through and resolved. If left undealt with, this internal conflict can cause withdrawal, interfere with career satisfaction and adversely affect the quality of work and quality of life.

Coach: the role of coach is one of the most important that a mentor can play. As a coach the mentor may provide crucial information about an organization's mission, vision and goals. They can suggest appropriate strategies for completing tasks as well as providing critical feedback. Linda Hill acknowledges the role of mentor as coach saying 'Given the complexities of their new responsibilities and all that they have to learn, new managers, no matter how gifted, still need coaching.' Without a mentor to coach them a new recruit will be at a distinct disadvantage, lacking critical information and insight about the organization.

Challenger: by pushing the mentee through the assignment of difficult and challenging tasks the mentor prepares the mentee for promotion and greater responsibility. Mentees must be prepared to work outside their comfort zone; the mentor can help break the barrier. Hill says, "Career theorist, David Thomas has shown that people who do not have access to stretch (challenging) assignments, or do not establish developmental relationships will actually lose skills over time."

Friend: the mentor as a friend may provide a different generational perspective to that that the mentee usually enjoys. They will also teach the mentee to be more comfortable when in the company of senior figures. The mentor may be re-energized by the friendship of someone younger than themselves and gain a renewed sense of vitality that enhances their life.

Listener: another essential and important role of the mentor is that of listener. Non-judgmental listening is a rare skill. Listening may sound easy but try out some of your friends and acquaintances and see how well they listen, and whether they judge or are critical. 'Dramatic listening is not just a rendezvous of brains; it is a uniting, a linkage, a partnership. Like all human connections, it requires constant effort and commitment,' says Bell.

Promoter: as a promoter the mentor exposes the mentee to influential people and situations that may benefit the mentee.

Inquisitor: the mentor as inquisitor adopts the methods of some of the great mentors of all time such as Buddha, Confucius and Moses. Like the great philosopher Socrates they teach by asking questions. The Greek philosophers called it Socratic dialogue. It involves the mentor leading the mentee on a path to wisdom, through effective and provocative questioning. When Fortune 500 CEOs were asked what made their mentors so effective, the most common answer was "They asked great questions".

Protector: as a protector the mentor prevents the mentee from taking unnecessary risks. In certain circumstances the mentor may shield the mentee from blame, or from taking credit. The mentor must be careful not to overprotect their charge and thereby inhibit their professional and personal growth.

Role model: the mentor as a role model influences the mentee through their values, behavior, and attitudes. These traits are adopted by the mentee as they mould their identity.

Sponsor: the mentor as sponsor acts as an advocate for their mentee both within and outside the organization. With only a single mentor acting as sponsor the fortunes of the mentee are very closely linked to those of the mentor. If the mentor leaves the organization, or falls from grace, then the career of the mentee is likely to suffer. It is better, and safer, for the mentee to obtain more than one sponsor if possible.

The perfect mentor, someone who can assume all of the roles above, probably does not exist. Rather than pursuing a fruitless quest to find the perfect mentor you would be better advised to assess which type will be most valuable to you, and then look for a mentor who embodies those qualities. It also pays to learn how to become a perfect mentee, so that mentors will want to take you on. Realistically assess whether you are an attractive proposition to a mentor. Are you ambitious, willing to confide in others, willing to learn? If you're not then why should a mentor give up their valuable time to help you?

What type of mentoring program?

Some organizations, including large organizations such as Federal Express, Johnson & Johnson, the IRS and the US Army, have constructed formal mentoring programs. One reason for this was that informal mentoring was taking place in insufficient numbers. These organizations found that a more productive mentoring experience can be obtained for a greater number of people through a structured program. This allows for the formal training of mentors to prepare them for the task. It also ensures that employees who were less likely to attract a mentor, if left to their own devices, could obtain one.

Yet informal mentoring has its own group of supporters. They maintain that the "chemistry" in an informal mentoring relationship is a vital ingredient for its success, and one often lacking in formal mentoring. The reason for this is that in informal mentoring relationships, there is no obligation on either party to undertake the relationship in the initial stages. Instead there is normally attraction/admiration/respect underpinning the initial contact. A stronger bond is likely to be formed in an informal mentoring situation. Fans of formal mentoring programs counter that the chemistry is unnecessary and the point is developing a professional relationship rather than one of 'best buddies'.

Ultimately, you will have to decide which style of program best suits you. This will depend on your own objectives as well as those of your company. If you already have a mentor and the company wishes to enroll you on it's formal mentoring program you will have to make some difficult decisions. It may not be easy to have two mentors, and devote sufficient time to making both relationships work. If, however, you're able to strike the right balance this arrangement can be very rewarding, particularly if you have a mentor within the workplace and one outside.

Finding a mentor

If you want a mentor, but your company doesn't have a formal mentoring program, and no one has seen fit to adopt you as their mentee, then the onus is on you to find your own mentor, in or outside the workplace.

Leading mentoring consultant, practitioner and author Dr Shirley Peddy suggests four keys to a perfect mentor match[6]:

◆ The ability to communicate. Both mentor and mentee need to be able to communicate. Otherwise mentor sessions become difficult, and a daunting and unwelcome prospect for both parties.

◆ Commitment to a two-way process. 'A relationship that is not mutually rewarding won't last,' says Peddy.

◆ Honesty. Both parties need to be honest and true to each other, and unafraid to share their successes and failures.

◆ A willingness to participate. If either party is forced into the mentoring relationship then it is unlikely to be a success. 'Nobody should be dragged kicking and screaming into the relationship, and neither should be asked to give beyond what they desire,' Peddy explains.

Drawbacks

Things don't, and won't, always go smoothly in a mentoring relationship. We are talking about two human beings after all, it is hard enough to form and maintain relationships in life generally, let alone within a formal work-oriented framework. Take all your personal foibles and quirks, combine them with all those of the other party in your mentoring relationship, and it is clear that there is potential for the relationship to breakdown.

You can help to avoid this by spotting danger signs early. Warning signals include:

◆ Poor training and poor follow-up

◆ Reluctance of mentor to take on difficult issues

◆ Passive behavior and an unwillingness to participate

◆ Poor communication

◆ Inappropriate behavior. The mentor is too autocratic/judgmental

◆ Forced participation. Fruitful mentoring is unlikely to rise from forced participation

◆ Unwillingness to commit time.

Formal mentoring programs should always be voluntary. Just because an individual has the requisite experience or seniority doesn't mean that they will want to be a mentor. Voluntary programs avoid resentment about being forced into mentoring relationship.

Finally, beware of the green-eyed monster. The reason you are entering a mentoring relationship is to advance your career and improve yourself personally. As a result, you may be promoted, and you will hopefully achieve great things in your career. When you tell your mentor of your achievements they will be both proud and pleased for you. Sadly, envy and jealousy are all too common human traits. It is best to remember this, whether you are mentor or mentee. If you gleefully brag to your mentor about the Oscar you have just won, and your mentor spent their life as a competent but not brilliant actor, you may stir up feelings of regret and jealousy. Be tactful. If you are a mentor, try to restrain any pangs of envy. Share the joy of your protégé. Be generous in your praise and proud of your accomplishment in helping them reach their full potential. Take pride in what you achieve together.

Equally be aware of the feelings of peers, co-workers and family. They may also be jealous of the close mentoring relationship you have formed. Be sensitive to the needs of your co-workers and family and discuss your mentoring honestly and openly so you can avoid any negative sentiment from these directions.

Occasionally, the mentoring relationship will fail. To cover this situation, it is wise to include a no-fault escape clause, so that either party can unilaterally walk away from the relationship if it is clear that is not working; part without blame and recrimination. If it is a formal mentoring relationship it may be possible for the organization to interview both parties to see if the relationship is salvageable. In the case of informal mentoring be clear from the outset on how both parties should approach breaking the relationship off if they wish to. This prevents embarrassment and bad feeling later.

Equally be aware of the feelings of peers, co-workers, and family. They may also be jealous of the close mentoring relationship you have formed. Be sensitive to the needs of your co-workers and family and discuss your mentoring honestly and openly so you can avoid any negative sentiment from these directions.

CAREER ADVENTURER

FRANCO SAMA on mentoring

Title/Position: Producer/Consultant
Company: Samaco Productions
Industry: Entertainment
Location: West Hollywood, CA

Franco was working as a consultant to car dealerships when he met a man who changed his career and his life:

'Around late 1995 I ended up in Albany, New York in the middle of winter. The man who owned the dealership where I was working posed a question to me that no one had ever asked. He said, "What do you really want to be doing in your life?"

My unhappiness must have been fairly transparent. I told him that my dream was to be in the entertainment industry and to be a producer of television and film. I knew when I was 12 years old that that was my dream. But even when I was twelve it wasn't a dream or a fantasy; it was a reality, a knowing. I always knew that I was going to be in the entertainment industry and surrounded by celebrities. It was like a self-fulfilling prophecy, part of the plan ever since I was a child.

So this gentleman Joe Gerrity literally changed my life. It turned out that he had just bought the car dealership, but he was a screenwriter with Steven Spielberg on ET. He went from Hollywood to Albany, and I was trying to do the opposite. He said that if I ever decided to pursue this, that he would help me. He taught me that it was all about who you know and networking. He planted the seed.'

Franco moved to Hollywood and worked first as publicist and then set up his own production company Samaco Productions:

'Joe Gerrity was my mentor the whole time. There were times when I was afraid, unsure or insecure. And he was the one person who believed in me, even when I didn't. He once sent me a random check for $5,000 when he heard I was about to produce my first short film. There's one thing I'm absolutely positive: as positive and aggressive a person as I can be, if I hadn't met Joe, I wouldn't be here.

Mentoring is a huge part of who I am and what I teach. I have created an entire structure around how to choose the right mentor, how to get one, and the appropriate protocol around having one.

It was with Joe Gerrity that I started to understand the importance and value of a mentor. At the time I didn't even realize that was what he was. Now I have mentors all over the place, in different aspects of the entertainment industry. I recognized early on that one person can't know everything. So if you're going to invite someone to be your mentor, choose someone in an area of expertise that you need, whose work you admire and respect, and who can help you further your career.

You can receive the benefits of mentoring every day if you set it up properly. For example, I have a lot of contractual situations in my business, but I don't understand anything about contracts, not the way a contract lawyer would. So I developed a friendship with a man who is the director of business and contractual affairs at a major television network. At first I took all of the steps that I now teach other people to take in getting someone to become their mentor. And now that I'm in this mentoring relationship with him, when these contractual situations, problems and questions arise, I have the ability to email a contract to him for his review and opinion, and he guides me. Normally you'd pay a lawyer $275 per hour to do some of the things that he does for me.

It's important that you recognize what the function and the purpose of this relationship is, and don't take advantage of it. The purpose is for you to learn from your mentor's experience and expertise. That's key.

Be clear on what your intentions are in the relationship. For example, if you're an actor and Brad Pitt is your ideal mentor, you're not looking for Brad to put you in his next movie, because that's not what this relationship is for. It's to learn from someone whose work you admire. He may turn around and offer you a role, but don't go into the relationship with any expectation of that, and don't ask him for it.

Most people are stopped by worrying that they don't have a shot at getting Brad Pitt on the phone to even talk about this. When I'm working with clients I ask them to make a list of ten people whose work they admire and respect. Then I give them a series of steps on how to reach the people on their list, and we've had success with that. For example, I have a 22-year-old kid right now who's only been here for two years. He followed the steps I gave him, and now he and Nicholas Cage correspond on a regular basis through email. That wouldn't have happened if he had limited himself as to who to include on his list. He took the appropriate steps and ended up with this mentoring relationship.

Make sure they understand what you are and are not asking for. The reality is that most people that you will want to mentor you don't have the time. Each person has their own idea of what it means to mentor someone. So you have to specifically define what it is that you are asking for. Set it up so that the minimum requirement is a 5 to 10 minute phone call with that person once a month. No one doesn't have 5 to 10 minutes a month, no matter how busy they may be. Also, ask for the ability to communicate with them via email to ask an urgent question in the event that something major should arise in between your conversations.

Begin by getting a commitment to that basic arrangement. Once you do that, you are in the relationship, and through that relationship you can build a bigger one. So start out with three or four months of 5 to 10 minute conversations each month, and you get your new mentor to warm to you. I've seen it evolve into full-fledged friendships eventually. For example, three years ago I was in a conversation with the managing editor of Entertainment Tonight *at Paramount. I gradually started placing a series of phone calls to him. It took a year and a half to get him to agree to go to lunch with me. It started out as a mentor relationship, then became more of a friendship. Now it has evolved to the point where I can go to him for just about anything.*

That's how it works, but you have to understand how to nurture that. Potential mentees naturally want to seize an opportunity. But they ask too much too quickly, which is a turn-off for people in positions of power. However, if you really understand the process, plant seeds early on in the relationship, and just get yourself in, you can work on developing something bigger over time.'

MENTORING RESOURCES

Reading

Phillips-Jones, L., *Mentors and protégés* (Arbor House, 1982).
Kram, K., *Mentoring at work: Developmental relationships in organizational life* (Lanham University Press, 1988).
Caldwell, B. and E. Carter (Eds.), *The principles and practice of mentoring. The return of the mentor: Strategies for workplace learning* (Falmer Press, 1993).
Clutterbuck, D & D. Megginson, *Mentoring Executives and Directors* (Butterworth-Heinemann, 1999).
Zachary, L., *The Mentor's Guide: Facilitating Effective Learning Relationships* (Jossey-Bass, 2000).

3. OFFICE POLITICS

"Of mankind we may say in general they are fickle, hypocritical, and greedy of gain."
Machiavelli

Machiavelli may have taken a cynical view, but he certainly knew about people. Organizations are hotbeds of political intrigue. All organizations. Why? Because they are populated by people. In small companies the politics may be confined to gossiping by the water cooler or coffee machine. In large organizations however office politics are the stuff that careers are made of. The higher up the pecking order you go, the more politics looms.

'Senior managers have competing agendas', says Dr David Butcher, senior lecturer at Cranfield School of Management and expert on the subject of organizational politics. 'It was ever thus. Management works that way. If you ask managers about what they do, they say that politics is part of their job. It is a purely notional view that says otherwise. It's high time we recognized that fact. But the theory is only now starting to catch up with the reality.'

Once you accept that a company, even a small one, is a political system, David Butcher argues, you can begin to make things happen. The political dimension brings new insights. 'As organizational structures become more loose, the power of individuals increases', Dr Butcher says. 'The question then becomes how to ensure that what is exercised is principled power. This refers specifically to differentiating between good and bad politics.'

'Politics is all about competing interests and competing value systems. We don't like politicians when they seem to be it for themselves. The same applies in business. When people think of politics in their company, they usually mean bad politics'

Principled politics, or good politics, is constructive rather than destructive. It is about balancing personal motives with organizational motives. Yet, according to David Butcher, it may involve many of the same processes and skills that we associate with the worst sort of political maneuvering. These include activities such as lobbying decision-makers behind closed doors; the use of stealth and influence; and being parsimonious with the truth. 'I know people who will deliberately travel on a long haul flight simply to sit next to someone they want to influence', he says. 'They know that six hours of drinking wine with someone can be a very effective way of lobbying. You can say it's Machiavellian, but it really depends on the outcome. What is certain is that you won't find it in the job description.'

According to David Butcher the worse scenario is when a manager goes to a meeting only to discover that the decisions have already been made in private discussions. In effect, the lobbyists have already won the day, and all that remains is to rubber stamp the decision. Be aware of the politics around you. You may not want to get too involved yet but you need to develop your political antennae.

For many people however, office politics is more prosaic. For a large percentage of workers, office politics is about scrabbling for promotion, preventing co-workers from getting one over on you, fighting to be heard – staying sane even. Yes, playing office politics can be wearing, stressful and downright damaging to your health. But then refusing to play the game can be equally detrimental to your career prospects. If you are the kind of person who would never think of jumping a queue, who believes that right will always overcome might, and who advocates turning the other cheek rather than taking an eye for an eye, then good for you. But if you want to get on it's time to get real.

To participate in the cut and thrust of office politicking, treat it as you would haggling in a market. Haggling for goods in a shop, even if it is only for a ten per cent discount, is something most have us have done at one time or another; even if it felt a little strange at first. In some cultures it is expected. In pay negotiations it is often assumed. If you can manage to haggle for goods you can cope with office politics. If you are forced to participate, think of it as the customary and common practice. It would be rude to refuse.

The reality is that a rudimentary understanding of office politics is essential for career adventurers. Organizations might well be better places and more productive if they eradicated office politics, but career adventurers are pragmatic people. They believe in realpolitik. Office politics exists, learn to deal with it.

Strategies for dealing with office politics

In William Golding's prize-winning novel *Lord of the Flies*, a group of schoolboys are marooned on an island after a plane crash. At first the boys construct an orderly society, based on the social morés, convention, manners and rules that have been ingrained in their psyches during their upbringing. They work effectively together as a team to build shelters, make collective decisions, hunt for food and manage to survive in some style. But slowly their ordered world descends into chaos and destruction. Power struggles transform the island paradise into a Hobbesian nightmare where life, for the weak at least, is 'nasty brutish and short'. Luckily for the boys, salvation comes in the form of a rescue party. Organizations, however, do not have William Golding to write a happy ending for them.

Whilst office politics may be reality, reducing the prevalence of political decision-making and the gossip, secrecy, rumor-mongering, power-broking, bullying, double standards, backbiting, badmouthing, lying, cheating, brown-nosing, self-serving, mistrust and other destructive activities that inevitably accompany it, could well prevent an organization, or its components from descending into a *Lord of the Flies*-like chaos.

If you have any influence over others, manage people, lead a team, run a division, you can play a part in reducing destructive politics:

◆ **Communication** – secrecy, rumor, gossip, innuendo, these are the friends of the office politician. Create an atmosphere of openness, communicate decisions and the reasons for decisions, communicate news as soon as possible, this way you dampen speculation and remove one of the principal weapons of the office politician.

◆ **Fairness** – judge people in an objective manner. Always base rewards on performance. It is never easy to remove personal feelings from the decision-making process. If you like someone it is easy to reward them. If you dislike someone it is easy to overlook them. Try to remove this subjectivity from your judgment. Look at the achievements, look at the results, and assuming they are real and gained in a fair manner, base promotions, pay increases and other rewards on these. In order to do this you will need excellent performance measuring systems. The same principle of objectivity and fairness applies to other decision-making processes, judging suggestions and work proposals for example.

◆ **Behavior** – try to avoid political behavior. It may be tempting to advance or favor someone because you can rely on them supporting you. The easy route, however, is not always the best route. Remember the effect on other possibly more talented workers when you advance a yes-man (or woman). You are sending out the message that brown-nosing pays.

Playing politics doesn't always mean compromising your personal ethics, knifing co-workers in the back and sucking up to the boss. There are other ways of playing and winning.

◆ **Hiding** – politicos crave attention. They like wheeling and dealing. Take any choice project within an organization, and it will be packed with politicians. Why? Because the important projects are where the power is. So if you wish to avoid politics, you could avoid glamorous projects.

This doesn't mean that you won't advance. On the contrary, within a less popular project away from the scheming and battling you may have the chance to shine. You should find it easier to implement your strategies and ideas. Ultimately, you may accomplish as much within the organization by seeking out the backwaters. That's where most of the real breakthroughs happen anyway.

◆ **Watching** – not everyone makes it to the top of the pile by trampling over others. Some people have a knack of saying and doing the right things at the right time. They rise through the ranks to positions of power and responsibility. Yet they seem to have no, or few, enemies and are almost universally liked. How do they manage it? Watch, learn and assimilate. Better still, sign up someone like this as your mentor. Patronage from a smart operator can be an invaluable aid to career success.

◆ **Do as you would be done by** – an aphorism applicable not just to work but life in general. If you treat others as you would wish to be treated, then you may get the best out of people rather than the worst.

◆ **Don't hoard** – it is tempting to hoard knowledge. If you know something useful it gives you an edge over your colleagues. So you hang on to that little piece of knowledge until you can use it to your advantage. It may well be to the benefit of the organization to divulge it straight away, but you still hang on to it. It's called intellectual meanness

Remember the popular kids at school. Were they the mean kids or the generous ones? How about the people you admire open, warm, friendly generous? Or cold, hostile and stingy? Don't be an intellectual Scrooge, if you know something and it is not confidential, offer it up.

CAREER ADVENTURER'S READING GUIDE FOR OFFICE POLITICIANS

Von Clausewitz, K & A. Rapoport, (Editor) *On War* (Viking Press, 1983).
Machiavelli, N., *The Prince* (Bantam Classics, 1984).
Sun Tzu, *The Art of War* (Oxford University Press, 1984)
Machiavelli, N., *The Art of War: A Revised Edition of the Ellis Farneworth Translation* (Da Capo Press, 1990)
Liddell Hart, B., *Strategy* (Meridian Books, 1991).
Schwarzkopf, General Norman, *It Doesn't Take a Hero : The Autobiography of General H. Norman Schwarzkopf* (Bantam Books, 1993).

CAREER ADVENTURER

MARK FASICK on office politics

Title/Position: Captain
Company: Pasadena City Fire Department, Pasadena, CA
Industry: City Services

'Don't fight the people above you. You might win the battle, but you won't win the war, especially if they have authority over your position. I've also learned not to make people look bad to make you look good. That doesn't work, and it only tears people apart. It creates distrust among your fellow employees. A good supervisor will see that happening and maybe take a closer look at the person that is trying to make his or herself look good at others' expense. That person may be trying to divert attention away from his or herself. Also, a good supervisor gives credit where it's due and does not take credit for someone else's work.'

CAREER ADVENTURER

JEAN-FRANCOIS LOUMEAU on office politics.

Interviewee: Jean-Francois Loumeau
Title/Position: Director Business Development
Company: Faulding Pharmaceuticals Plc
Location: United Kingdom

'I think that as soon as any human organization reaches a certain size, it has to face a certain level of corporate politics. I've worked in companies of varying sizes. Even in small-sized start-up companies a fair bit of corporate politics results from the way the CEO does or does not communicate his vision to his fellow employees and colleagues.

Politics are generated by organizational structures. As an organization grows bigger, people tend to defend their turf and make sure that their share of the pie gets bigger, or that their colleague next door doesn't step on their toes.

Politics are also encouraged by the attitudes of senior management. The degree of politics tends to diminish as the transparency of the CEO's communication mode increases. If, on the other hand, there is a lot of back office discussion behind closed doors, then corporate politics tend to resurface.

We've been through two attempted takeover attempts in a year. There's a lot of uncertainty and politicking in these sorts of situations. If that uncertainty is extended beyond a couple of quarters then the business starts hurting.'

4. GETTING ALONG

If there is one set of skills you can learn to help you cope with office politics it is interpersonal skills.

You may not like politicians, you may think them false, but if you have ever been in presence of a great politician it is almost impossible to resist their charm and charisma. Politicians are, are on the whole, people people, they may be schmoozers but they are accomplished schmoozers. If you make only one concession to office politics learn how to get on with the people in your organization.

Getting along with the boss

It's good to get on with the boss. It's not always easy but it is desirable. Bosses come in three main categories: good, mediocre and bad. Note, these are not synonymous with successful, moderately successful and unsuccessful. A bad boss can be hugely successful within an organization. This may say more about the organization than it does about the qualities needed to advance a career. Or it may mean that despite the boss's undoubted qualities, managing people, or even working with people, isn't one of them.

If you have a good boss, you are fortunate. They will see through the politicians among your colleagues, see beyond the fakers and reward your honest toil and sterling efforts with praise, additional responsibility, extra pay benefits and ultimately promotion.

If you have a bad boss, then commiserations are in order. All is not lost, however. The important point to remember here is that any boss has their own agenda. The key is to try to understand what that agenda is. If your boss is ambitious, consider how you can help him further that ambition. Some ambitious bosses (as well as some incompetent bosses) have an unfortunate habit of misappropriating credit for work done by others. If this sounds like your boss, do the work, but keep a separate record of what you have done.

At some point you will have a difficult decision to make. Either your boss will be promoted, if you have made yourself indispensable enough, you may well be towed along in the current. Even if you are not, you will have a patron higher up in the organization. Alternatively, your boss may be overlooked for promotion, in which case they are clearly an obstacle to your advancement. To bypass them you will either have to go over their head or move elsewhere in the organization (or leave). You will also have to start claiming the credit for your work which may further strain your relationship with your boss.

If your boss is particularly difficult and making life extremely unpleasant, it is worth having a one-to-one frank conversation. Be prepared to take the next step. If you burn your bridges at this point, your next step is either over your boss's head or elsewhere. Don't expect to go over your boss's head without irretrievably damaging the relationship. The damage done may be concealed but most bad bosses are like elephants, they never forget.

If you have an average boss you may be able to get by with just a little gentle and occasional nudging. An average boss is often amenable to suggestion. The key is to make them look good. This doesn't mean unwarranted flattery. As with a bad boss, it means gauging their needs and helping fulfill them.

MANAGERIAL GRID

The Managerial Grid was invented by Dr Robert R. Blake and the late Dr Jane Mouton. It seeks to identify an individual's management style. In it, Blake and Mouton set out to capture human interactions and management orientation in numbers and graphs.

The Managerial Grid was a way of characterizing managers in terms of their orientation towards employees (people skills) and towards production (task skills). This became a three-dimensional model with the addition of motivation as a third axis. What Blake and Mouton did, essentially, was to build on the two dimensional models developed by earlier theorists such as Douglas McGregor. McGregor had a bipolar design that ran between x and y. This, Blake and Mouton felt, was an inadequate formulation of all of the variations. It didn't satisfy their concept of what they were seeing every day at Exxon.

With the Managerial Grid, concern for production is represented on a scale of 1 to 9 on the x axis (horizontal axis). Concern for people is represented on a scale of 1 to 9 on the y axis (vertical axis). So a score of 1 on the x axis and 9 on the y axis would be designated by the co-ordinates 1,9 and indicates someone with a low concern for people and a high concern for task completion. The managerial grid argues strongly for a 9/9 management style. The team builder approach in most cases, it is argued, will result in superior performance.

Motivation is the third dimension, running from negative (motivated by fear) to the positive (motivated by desire). This is indicated by a + or − sign. By focusing on the three measurable dimensions that have the greatest effect on the ways people work, their concern for productivity, their concern for people, and their motivation, Blake and Mouton sought to fine-tune their classification of managerial personality and style.

According to Blake: 'The third dimension is critical: it's motivation. It's a bipolar scale, running from a minus motivation (below the Grid) through neutral to a plus motivation (above the Grid). The negative motivations are driven by fear, the positive ones by desire. The 9,1 corner, for instance, is down to the lower right, a very high on concern for production, little or no concern for people. At that corner, 9,1+ illustrates the desire for control and mastery. At the same corner, 9,1- represents a fear of failure. These two work together. If I need control I rely to the most limited degree possible on you, because you're liable to screw up and the failure will reflect on me.'

What the third dimension does is clarify the emotional driver underlying the grid style. So, for example, 1,9+ describes a 'people-pleaser' who cares little for production, and operates wholly from a desire to be loved. On the other hand, 9,1- describes a whip-cracker who cares little about people, and operates in fear of something going wrong.

More sophisticated analysis using the Grid also takes account of the reaction of subordinates. Blake and Mouton identified additional management styles that combine various Grid positions. The 'paternalist' style combines the whip cracking (1,9) and the people pleasing (9,1) depending on the response of the subordinate. A subordinate cooperates, for example, is rewarded with a 'people-pleasing' relationship; one that doesn't is subjected to the whip. The 'opportunist' manager on the other hand, is a chameleon, taking on whatever Grid style seems appropriate for the interaction of the moment, never revealing his or her own true feelings.

Concern for production is represented on a scale of 1 to 9 on the x axis (horizontal axis).Concern for people is represented on a scale of 1 to 9 on the y axis (vertical axis). So a score of 1 on the x-axis and 9 on the y-axis would be designated by the co-ordinates 1,9, and indicates someone with a low concern for people and a high concern for task completion. Using this system, Blake and Mouton identified five key manager styles:

1,1 Do Nothing Manager. The manager exerts a minimum of effort to get the work done with very little concern for people or production.

1,9 Country Club Manager. The manager gives considerable attention to the needs of people, but minimum concern for task accomplishment (production). This style is often found in small firms that have cornered the market, and in public-sector organizations where work outputs and goals or outcomes are hard to measure.

9,1 Production Pusher. The manager achieves efficiency in operations by creating systems that ensure minimal human interference.

5,5 Organization Person. The manager maintains adequate organizational performance (production) and (concern for people). Mediocrity is perpetuated, but the wheels keep turning. Many public and private sector managers either consciously or unconsciously pursue this management style.

9,9 Team Builder. The manager is able to elicit high productivity from a committed group of subordinates. Goals of the organization (production) are achieved and people are successfully integrated, with morale being high.

The Grid system provides a framework for exploring what happens when, say, a 9,1+ needs something from a 1,1-. It offers a lens through which people can see themselves and their organizations more clearly. Like many other management concepts, the Managerial Grid has also spawned a consulting business. Most managers, Blake argues, are not self-aware enough to be able to place themselves on the Grid.

CAREER ADVENTURER

JOHN REESE *on office politics*
Title/Position: Business Services Visionary
Company: In transition

'Don't ignore politics. You have to understand that they really exist, but try not to use them as an excuse for not doing your best possible work. That doesn't mean being naïve about politics, integrate it into your understanding of your environment, but focus on getting the right job done well.'

'To advance up the corporate ladder, it's important to work at corporate headquarters. If you're working at a satellite office, you're not going to grow in the same way. You can't get the opportunities to fully understand the business without being able to walk the halls and get the corporate sense. So as you grow in an organization, try to get back to corporate headquarters. That's a kind of middle-management question. It's not so essential when you're getting started, but at a later stage it's important.'

'For younger individuals, make sure that as you grow you try to understand how what you are doing fits into the bigger picture. If you work in a magazine (for example), try to learn what the business is about over time. Obviously, you will not understand all of the facets of the business when you are just starting out, but strive to understand the context, not just the content, of your job.'

Getting along with your co-workers (and everyone else)

Getting along with the boss is important but so, too, is getting along with everyone else. There will be times when you need the support of your co-workers. If your personal stock is low you will receive short shrift when you turn to colleagues for help.

A few simple pointers can help maintain a good *esprit de corps.*

◆ Be cheerful. If you smile, others will smile with you. If you're cheerful people surrounding you are likely to be cheerful. Don't complain, don't frown, be upbeat, be optimistic. No one likes a miserable person.

◆ Be a listener. Talkers are a dime a dozen, good listeners are scarce. Try to balance talking and listening. When people talk to you, make a point of listening to what they say. Don't spend the time while they are talking thinking about what you want to say. Instead learn to listen and think ahead at the same time. Don't feel the need to always be the center of attention, allow others their moment of glory.

◆ Think once, think twice. Acting impulsively can be extremely damaging to your career. You hear on the grapevine that that you are about to receive a promotion. The drawback is it's on the other side of the country. Furious, you storm in to confront your boss. It's a human reaction. Human beings are equipped with a 'fight or flight' response, a neurological vestige from the prehistoric past, when some surprise necessitated immediate action to survive. This response is often inappropriate in the modern world.

If you take no immediate action upon hearing about your promotion, you will not be eaten by a predator, nor will you be bashed over the head by a Neanderthal with a club. (OK, so that depends on the company you work for). Instead you will have time to draw up a measured response. A response which will almost certainly be more effective, if less passionate, than your immediate instinctive response.

◆ Be open-minded. Popular people are invariably open-minded rather than dogmatic and stubborn. This is not to be confused with muddle-headed. Having passionately held beliefs is admirable; cogently arguing your case is commendable. Refusing to admit you are wrong or acknowledge that anyone else might hold a worthwhile opinion is pigheaded. Met many popular know-it-alls?

Emotional skills

Skills are not just about turning lathes or writing spreadsheets. There are other so-called soft skills, to which experts are beginning to attribute equal if not greater importance. You are unlikely to find conventional college courses, few if any, for these kinds of skills. Nonetheless, a study of some soft skills is essential for the serious career adventurer.

An important example of this type of skill is emotional intelligence, a concept brought to the fore by the psychologist Daniel Goleman. In his 1995 book *Emotional Intelligence*, Goleman concluded that human competencies such as self-awareness, self-discipline, persistence and empathy are of greater consequence than IQ in much of life. Goleman asserted that we ignore the emotional competencies at our peril, and that children can and should be taught these abilities at school.

Goleman has gone on to explore the issue of personal and professional effectiveness. His 1998 book, *Working with Emotional Intelligence*, argues that workplace competencies based on emotional intelligence play a far greater role in star performance than do intellect or technical skill, and that both individuals and companies will benefit from cultivating these capabilities.

In particular, he claims, that the emotional dimension is critical in determining the effectiveness of leaders, arguing that in demanding jobs where above-average IQ is a given, superior emotional capability gives leaders an edge. At senior levels, emotional, rather than rational intelligence, marks out the true leader. According to Goleman, studies of outstanding performers in organizations show that about two-thirds of the abilities that set star performers apart in the leadership stakes are based on emotional intelligence; only one-third of the skills that matter relate to raw intelligence (as measured by IQ) and technical expertise.

'Our emotions are hardwired into our being', he explains. 'The very architecture of the brain gives feelings priority over thought.' In reality, it is impossible to entirely separate thought from emotion. 'We can be effective only when the two systems – our emotional brain and our thinking brain, work together. That working relationship, which encompasses most of what we do in life, is the essence of emotional intelligence.'

The good news is that, according to Goleman, emotional intelligence can be learned. There are five dimensions to this, he says. These are:

◆ Self-awareness. We seldom pay attention to what we feel. A stream of moods runs in parallel to our thoughts. This, and previous emotional experiences, provide a context for our decision-making.

◆ Managing emotions. All effective leaders learn to manage their emotions, especially the big three: anger, anxiety and sadness. This is a decisive life skill.

◆ Motivating others. The root meaning of 'motive' is the same as the root of emotion: to move.

◆ Showing empathy. The flip side of self-awareness is the ability to read emotions in others.

◆ Staying connected. Emotions are contagious. There is an unseen transaction that passes between us in every interaction that makes us feel either a little better or a little worse. Goleman calls this a 'secret economy'. It holds the key to motivating the people we work with.

5. PERFORMANCE APPRAISALS

Remember the dreaded report card from school? For the fortunate few it was a time for smug satisfaction and parental praise. For the masses it was yet another 'could do better' or worse. It would be nice to think that as so-called mature adults, who have left the carefree days of college for the responsibility of work, that the days of the report card were long past.

Unfortunately for the 'could do betters' that is not the case. For report card read 'employee appraisal' or 'review'. In many ways the employee review is more of an ordeal than the student report. In place of the teacher, the role of judge and jury is taken by your boss, your peers, or even your subordinates. And while you may escape the wrath of your parents, any pleasure derived from this thought is sure to be short-lived when you realize that you will have to face the music in person, rather than vicariously through your parents.

Yes, you think, the under-performers at work have much to worry about at review time. But not you. Your career is, you think, progressing well. You have mastered new skills, acquired new knowledge, met performance targets and ultimately improved your company's bottom line.

So why is it that every time you come out of your appraisal you get that same old feeling? Somehow your boss isn't looking at the same picture that you are. How can the idyllic white cottage that you see, with the roses hanging around the doorway and the warm summer sun glinting off the roof tiles, be the same rundown ramshackle cabin with peeling paint and an overgrown garden that your boss sees. How can your boss overlook your tremendous achievements, yet highlight all the things you have failed to do?

It is the same old story – 'could do better'. Good bosses perform fair reviews, based on full information about your performance that they have obtained in the time between appraisals, or since you joined the company. They do this because they view a job review as: a means of providing employees with feedback on their performance; an opportunity to identify and discuss career development needs; a way of clarifying the role of the employee; a process of collecting information to be used in decisions about promotion and pay.

A bad boss, however, sees employees' reviews as: an opportunity to keep the organization's expense ratio down by handing out the smallest pay rise they can get away with; a forum for putting 'upstart' employees in their place; a means of pointing out all of an employee's failings.

Even good bosses have their work cut out. Despite conducting employee reviews for the right reasons they can only do an employee justice if they have the systems in place to collect and collate information about employee performance. To conduct the best review possible they need help from the organization and most importantly from you, the employee being reviewed undertaking the review.

Help yourself

If a good employee appraisal is about better communication, identifying areas of possible improvement, fostering teamwork and clarifying expectations then it is up to the employee to try and ensure this is what happens. How? By taking a proactive approach.

Instead of sitting back waiting for praise, and being disappointed when it fails to materialize, go to your employee review prepared to make your case. Treat it as a law trial, where you are the defendant, counsel for the defense (and in preparation, counsel for the prosecution). Take an honest and critical look at your performance and write down areas where you fall short or could improve. Equally, write down where your performance is above average and collect supporting evidence. Ask a trusted colleague, or your mentor if you have one, what they think your strengths and weaknesses are.

When you have your review make your case and support your argument with the documentary evidence you have gathered. When your appraiser makes critical comments, hopefully you will be prepared to counter. In the case of adverse comment do not let it pass uncontested. Make sure your objections are noted. If you are lucky you may be able to steer the review in the direction you wish especially if the reviewer is disinterested in the review process.

A proactive approach is the key to a good appraisal. Passivity is self-defeating. It's time for a tuneful rendition of your own praises. Don't rely on others to sing them for you.

Choose your weapon

Traditionally an employee review is conducted as a 'top down' exercise. The employee's immediate manager conducts the review with the emphasis on skills and performance, and with performance indicators being quantitative rather than qualitative. The trouble with such an approach is that focusing on the numbers obscures the story behind the numbers. If an employee fails to hit targets, what does this tell the reviewer other than the fact that they failed to hit targets. If the employee hits their targets the manager is still none the wiser as to the employee's qualitative performance. What is their relationship with customers like? What are their communications skills like? Etc., etc.

It is no surprise to learn that, according to a Society for Human Resource Management study, only 61 percent of HR managers are satisfied with their overall evaluation systems. As a result, organizations are re-evaluating their employee reviewing techniques. The result is raft of alternative techniques.

Coming at you from all angles

In a police investigation, how do the police investigate criminal suspects? Do they interview the suspect and then take everything they say at face value? No, they interview everyone connected with the suspect so they can build up a complete profile of the suspect.

It's the same with the 360-degree performance review. Immediate managers, the employee's colleagues, even customers and suppliers; in the 360 review, opinions of an individual's performance are taken from a multitude of sources.

This is competency-based performance management. Under scrutiny are the employee's personal characteristics, traits and skills as well as quantitative criteria.

An example of how this might work is as follows. A list of possible reviewers is drawn up and then the employee is allowed to have some influence over the list possibly vetoing selected reviewers in a similar way to jury selection. Next the reviewers provide a ranking from 1 to 10 on a range of performance criteria. Finally the employee is confronted with the results.

This type of appraisal tends to be more accepted by employees because of the element of peer review. It is this same element of peer review however, that leaves the 360 review open to criticism. The review of colleagues by their peers can become something of a popularity contest, a beauty parade. But popularity does not necessarily equate with high performance. In fact, some of the greatest CEOs of all time were unpopular or at least not universally loved.

A generally held opinion by HR directors is that to be effective, 360-degree reviews should only be conducted in organizations with over 100 employees and that they should be an anonymous process from the perspective of the reviewed employee. In smaller groups personal bias threatens to negate the findings of the review. Even within large employee populations employers must be careful to smooth out bias.

The question of bias is even more contentious in another type of employee review, the ranking. In this method of review managers are required to rank their subordinates. The result is a forced distribution of employees as high, middle or low ranking. Also known as 'rank-and-yank' the review method was famously used at General Electric. The unfortunate low rankers often found themselves on the way out of the company. Other well-known companies who have used ranking review techniques include Microsoft, Hewlett-Packard and Ford. Advocates argue that ranking reflects the market-forces reality of entrepreneurial America. In a Darwinian world, the bottom ten per cent of performers deserve to be ejected in this corporate version of natural selection. Critics counter that it victimizes certain classes of employee, be it on the grounds of ethnicity, age or sex. Hence the class-action lawsuits bought against several Fortune 500 companies including Microsoft, Conoco and Ford, alleging discrimination during ranking.

At the other end of the scale is the 'bottom up' approach of the employee-driven appraisal. In this review the employee conducts their own research, identifies their own training needs, conducts their own round of performance interviews with whoever they think appropriate and presents their report to their boss. Virtually unheard of, this type of employee review is only likely to be encountered in the most forward-thinking organizations where there is an emphasis on employee empowerment. Organizations such as Semco in Brazil, where Ricardo Semler has implemented some of the most progressive and radical management ideas seen in any company worldwide.

Whichever review you receive traditional or alternative, the basic points remain unchanged:

◆ **Prepare**. Do not shirk in your preparation. Make sure you know your job description and what is expected of you right from the first few weeks you start work. Collect information to support your claims about your performance throughout your career. Keep a portfolio of your achievements just like a journalist keeps their press cuttings, or a model builds a modeling portfolio of photographs. Find out what type of review to expect and who will be conducting it. Make sure the venue is on neutral ground if possible, away from distractions and your colleagues.

◆ **Be proactive.** Take to the battle to the reviewer. Take control of the review by suggesting your own agenda. Take notes. Let the reviewer know that you have done your homework, explored training and education possibilities, know where you fit in to the organization and how you are contributing to the bottom line. Be confident and assertive. Don't agree to anything you don't agree with. Don't sign anything you don't agree with. Make sure your objections are noted if you have any.

◆ **Be honest with yourself.** If you were honest with yourself in the research phase you will know your weaknesses. It is never pleasant to have someone point out your deficiencies but clever career adventurers learn to accept constructive criticism where it is deserved. Take as much as you can from the appraisal, assess any criticism honestly and resolve to deal with it then move on.

◆ **Agreed outcomes.** Reviews are conducted for various reasons, identifying training and education needs, determining pay rises and assessing promotion prospects, are three of the main reasons as well as the obvious general performance assessment. Whatever the reason for your review you should try to come away with agreed actions and a timeframe for those actions. If does not happen at the appraisal then you should submit your own suggestions for agreement as soon after the appraisal as possible.

Plan ahead –once one appraisal is done it is time to start planning for the next.

EMPLOYEE REVIEWS RESOURCES

Reading
Tornow, W. (Editor), *Maximizing the Value of 360-Degree Feedback: A Process for Successful Individual and Organizational Development* (Jossey-Bass, 1998).

6. BALANCING LIFE AND WORK

It's been a long hard day at work and it's about to get longer. Here comes your boss with the usual 'I wonder if you could just do this before you go'. Of course, you would like to say 'No way, I'm going home', but you don't. You can't because whether it's a fiction or not the perception is that the days of a job for life are gone. You've got a goodish career and you're not about to throw it all up in the air. Besides, Jones, your rival for promotion, is always working late and crawling to the boss. So you bite your lip and watch as the clock ticks on to 19.30 . . . 21.00 . . . 22.00.

Long hours aren't just the price for being an investment banker, management consultant or corporate lawyer. Yes, they do work late nights and weekends; they also get rewarded handsomely for their dedication. Today, the toll of long hours can affect anyone from a bartender to a schoolteacher. As the media is fond of telling everyone, we live and work in a global market. The global economy, increased competition, the demands of consumers, deregulated labor market, information technology; all adds up to one thing, the company's need to squeeze more out of their workforce to stay in business. Bad news.

Beware burnout

In the United States, the phenomenon of career burnout has long been recognized. Employees who work too hard, for too long, can become demotivated, depressed and in extreme cases suffer nervous breakdowns or worse. Comparative figures are hard to come by, but anecdotal evidence suggests that the problem may be getting worse in the UK. The situation in the US is so bad that almost one-third of the workforce feels overworked or overwhelmed by the amount of work they have to do.

'Feeling Overworked: When Work Becomes Too Much' is a survey conducted by the non-profit Families and Work Institute, supported by international accountancy firm PriceWaterhouseCoopers[7]. 'Overworked' was defined by the authors of the study as 'a psychological state that has the potential to affect attitudes, behavior, social relationships, and health both on and off the job.'

The study looked at a sample of 1,003 adults who performed paid work for an employer (as opposed to being self-employed). When asked how often they felt overworked and/or overwhelmed by work over a period of three months, over half said that they felt overworked and overwhelmed sometimes, and a significant number said they felt that way most of the time.

Corporate restructuring has added to job insecurity, reduced the number of employees and heaped higher workloads on those who remain. Some workers pay the ultimate price for their loyalty. In Japan, a small number of managers are believed to die from work-related stress each year.

The authors of a book on the subject claim that companies can no longer afford to ignore the problem. 'Burnout is the outcome of a mismatch between workers and the workplace', say Michael P. Leiter and Christina Maslach, authors of *The Truth About Burnout*. 'A critical point about burnout which is often missed is that it is a management problem, not simply an individual one. Too often, managers side-step the issue as being either outside of their mandate or impossible to address.'

Professor Andrew Kakabadse at the UK's Cranfield School of Management, has also investigated the phenomenon of burnout as part of a worldwide study of top executive performance. His data, based on a detailed survey of 6,500 managers from ten countries, suggests all leaders are prone to burnout, but their organizations are often embarrassed by the phenomenon and don't know what to do about it.

'Corporate life requires deadlines to be met and inevitably workloads are unevenly shared, meaning that organizations generate their share of workaholics irrespective of the wishes of the individual', he says. 'In addition, organizational chaos is rife, yet most workplaces still implicitly demand employees be 'corporate people', living and dreaming about attaining success in organizational life.'

Serious attention, Professor Kakabadse says, should be given to how burnout happens, how to recognize and cope with it and how to combat it. The symptoms include:

◆ increasing fatigue;
◆ not listening effectively;
◆ feeling saturated with work;
◆ feeling unable to participate in routine operational conversations.

What make the telltale signs hard to spot, however, is that declining morale and feelings of personal vulnerability usually emerge slowly and insidiously.

'Increases in stress, job pressure, competition, higher work complexity, faster pace of life and the greater likelihood of redundancy all make for an inevitable drip, drip of negativity which leads many top managers to burnout', says Professor Kakabadse.

Some of the causes of burnout can be linked to the removal of middle-management tiers in many organizations, with more senior managers being required to undertake a greater volume of repetitive, detailed and often tedious tasks.

The move to flatter management structures inevitably means that the spans of control are increasing, with managers having direct responsibility for a larger number of employees. In many cases, the traditional reporting spans have altered without sufficient support being provided, for managers who have to adapt to the new way of operating.

According to Dr Barrie Brown, a consultant psychologist: 'The traditional view was that the optimal span for reporting lines was seven.

Older managers, people aged 40 and over, were taught that directing the work of more than seven people makes it very difficult to remain in control. But some companies now have reporting spans of up to 150 people. If you double the number of people a manager is overseeing, then unless the manager delegates authority the workload will automatically double too.'

The problem is compounded in companies where a macho 'can do' culture means that delegating authority is viewed as a sign of weakness. Ambitious young managers can become obsessed with keeping their plates spinning to the detriment of their health. Flatter organization mean fewer promotions, with people stuck in the same job for longer periods.

'Prolonged demotivation leads to an emotional deterioration which is worsened by a realization that to some extent current lifestyle traps us in our jobs', says Professor Kakabadse. 'Age, difficulty in matching remuneration packages and the continuity needed to support family life contribute to a sense of being trapped.'

It is often worse for those further down the organization. Evidence suggests that stress is more pronounced among those who are not in control of their own destiny.

Employees who are suffering burn out and feeling overworked and overwhelmed by work are detrimental to an organization. According to the Families and Work Institute study overworked employees are more likely to:

◆ make mistakes at work;
◆ resent their employers for expecting them to do so much;
◆ resent co-workers who do not work as hard as they do;
◆ look for a new job.

While these effects are bad for the employers, it gets worse for the employer. The study also found that employees who feel overworked:

◆ are more likely to suffer from sleep loss;
◆ are more likely to neglect themselves;
◆ are less likely to report very good or excellent health;
◆ feel less successful in personal relationships;
◆ experience more work-life conflict;
◆ have higher stress levels;
◆ are less able to cope with everyday life.

If you recognize these symptoms, if you suffer from significant overwork or feel constantly overwhelmed by work then it's time to start thinking about a change before you become ill or worse. It doesn't have to mean a new employer. It might mean negotiating new hours, new workloads or a different job within the same organization. But it might also mean it is time for a new employer, or a new career.

Burnout is a good reason to change your job or your career, but it's not the only one. Insufficient career development, impeding redundancy, the realization that you are in the wrong career. These are all equally valid reasons for charting a new course.

WORKED TO DEATH...

The raising of wages leads to overwork among the workers. The more they want to earn, the more they must sacrifice their time and perform slave labor in which their freedom is totally alienated . . . In so doing they shorten their lives . . . Thus, even in the state of society which is the most favorable to the worker, the inevitable result for the worker is overwork and premature death, reduction to a machine, enslavement to capital. — Karl Marx[8]

At 8.30 a.m. on 24 October 1988, Satoshi Nagayama, aged 28, climbed out onto the rooftop of the Kawasaki Steel Corp. building in Tokyo, walked over to the edge and threw himself to his death.

In April of that year Nagayama, a Kawasaki Steel employee with a promising career ahead of him, was asked to take on the development and implementation of an experimental plan.

These duties were outside his normal responsibilities. Nagayama worked diligently on his new task. Too diligently. Almost every day he worked until midnight. He worked weekends. He worked holidays — including public holidays. He even stayed at the office overnight. His overtime for the month of October 1988 amounted to 85.5 hours not including the overnight periods from midnight to 8.00 a.m.

The night before Nagayama hurled himself from the building to his death, he telephoned his mother. He had stayed over two nights in the previous week and told his mother he was exhausted and couldn't go on.

In some ways Nagayama's death wasn't in vain because in a groundbreaking decision his death was found to be occupational by the Tokyo Central Labor Standards Inspection Offices (LSIO) one of the main local authorities that promote occupational safety and health.

Why did they come to this decision? For three main reasons: 1) he was mentally overstressed because he had almost sole responsibility for completing the planning experiment. Plus repeated modifications in the plan increased his workload; 2) from July 1988 onwards he exhibited the symptoms typical of reactive depression. The increased workload is believed to have aggravated the depression; 3) There was an absence of other factors that might have caused mental stress; it was therefore concluded that the depression which led to his untimely and tragic death was solely due to significantly heavy mental stress because of work. Nagayama's death and the resulting LSIO decision bought the issue of overwork in Japan into sharp focus.

The Japanese have a word for it: they call it *karoshi*, death by overwork. Karoshi became a social problem in the late 1980s. As the country's economic miracle ran out of steam, the number of hours put in by workers increased. As unemployment became a growing concern, the pressures on overworked salary men intensified. Used to a job for life, the social stigma attached to redundancy means that workers are often unwilling to complain even when their workload has become unbearable. The Japanese government officially recognized karoshi as an occupational hazard in 1994, and figures released by the Japanese labor ministry indicate that 90 people died from overwork in 1998 alone.

In June 2000, the Japanese advertising company Dentsu made legal history by admitting responsibility for the karoshi of an employee who committed suicide in 1991. Ichori Oshima worked an average of 80 hours a week, on grueling shifts, sometimes toiling from 9.00 am to 6.00 am the following morning. The case against Mr Oshima's employer was pursued by his parents for eight years. The company belatedly demonstrated its remorse to the tune of Y168 million ($1.65 million). Sadly, however, Mr Oshima is not an isolated case. The inevitable corporate restructuring of recent years has piled more work onto those who survived the job cuts. 'Service overtime' or working beyond normal hours without payment is a growing problem. In May 2000, for example, Karoshi 100, the *karoshi* hotline that offers counseling to overworked salary men, received more than 200 calls.

BURNOUT RESOURCES

Reading
Maslach, C & M. Leiter, *The Truth About Burnout* (Jossey-Bass, 1997).
Demarco, T., *Slack: Getting Past Burnout, Busywork, and the Myth of Total Efficiency* (Broadway Books, 2001).
Berglas, S., *Reclaiming the Fire: How Successful People Overcome Burnout* (Random House, 2001).

Changing expectations

The good news is that the expectations of the workforce are changing. Not long ago in the employer-employee relationship the power was all on one side, that of the employer. Today it is more difficult to pinpoint who has more power, the employer or the employee. On the one hand the nature of work has shifted so that knowledge and skills are a vital competitive resource for an organization. Ergo, talented, mobile employees should in theory wield considerable power and so be able to determine how, when and where they work.

This new generation want to strike a new balance between work and family. They don't see it as an either/or. They want it all. In one survey of final year MBA students 45 percent said that a balanced lifestyle was a priority in a future career. Ninety percent saw the work-life balance as key factor in determining commitment to their employer[9]. 'When I'm old, looking back, I want to be able to say I have led an extraordinary life', says a young MBA currently working for a credit card company. 'My goal is to have been extremely happy. To squeeze life for everything it can offer. Work will play a big part ... but it isn't everything. There are so many things I want to do, to climb mountains, to travel, to learn to sail, to give something back to others, to spend time with my friends and family and to slow down frequently enough to keep healthy and balanced. How can I fit everything in?'

It's an attitude towards work-life balance that is percolating upwards through the generations. In Gemini Consulting's International Workforce Management study, a survey of 10,000 managers in Europe, the US, Russia and Japan the statement 'Balance the needs of work and family or personal life' was selected to describe the most or second-most important attribute about a job[10]. It ranked higher than remuneration in almost every country.
Creating the right work-life balance for employees makes good economic sense. A high turnover of staff costs an organization money. Accountants Ernst & Young has calculated that the cost of losing an employee is the equivalent to four times the salary of that employee. According to research by the Hay group, high labor turnover results in a 40 percent reduction in annual profits[11].

As well as impacting on profits, a high staff turnover impacts on the morale of the existing employees. Over one-third third of managers cite staff turnover as a principal cause of workload pressure[12]. It is the start of a chain reaction. Poor work-life balance leads to dissatisfaction at work and workplace stress. In turn, this lead to illness and absenteeism. Absenteeism causes stress to co-workers, and costs industry a substantial sum of money. The evidence is unequivocal:

'70% of respondents cite a lack of balance between work and personal life as a major factor in occupational stress.'
Industrial Society, *Managing Best Practice Research Summaries No. 83: Occupational Stress* (Industrial Society, 2001).

'Workplace stress is the main cause of longer-term absence among non-manual staff.'
Chartered Institute of Personnel and Development, *Employee Absence: a survey of management policy and practice* (CIPD, 2001).

'6.5million sick days are taken every year as a result of stress.'
Briner R et al, *A critical review of psychosocial hazard measures* (HSE, 2001).

'Employers believe that general sickness represents the most common cause of absence but home and family responsibilities, personal problems and poor workplace morale are also significant.'

'Absenteeism costs £10 billion to UK business as a whole in 2000 or £434 per employee per year.'
Confederation of British Industry, *Pulling Together: 2001 absence and labor turnover survey* (CBI, 2001).

'94% of organizations report that sickness absence constitutes a "significant" or "very significant" business burden.'
Chartered Institute of Personnel and Development, *Employee Absence: a survey of management policy and practice* (CIPD, 2001).

CAREER ADVENTURER

FRANZ LANDSBERGER *on work/life balance*

Title/Position:	VP Human Resources, Bioscience Division
Company:	Baxter, Europe
Industry:	Pharmaceuticals

'I guess there have been a couple of big changes in the German culture. Now people who join a company at least have an understanding that they may not retire from that same company. That has changed.

The other thing that has changed a lot is that younger workers, those in the 25 to 35 age group, are looking more for work-life balance. They are relatively well off economically, and they question whether they want to run around like crazy in a $200K/year senior management position. They can make a good living with less income, why stretch to earn $200K/year?

You will find some people who are engaged and want to do more. But more and more you have to work with people who don't want to build a career. Not everyone wants to become a CEO. Ensure that they have appropriate job levels, content, authority, autonomy, and accountability and treat them well; they are your internal business partners.'

Happy campers

In the light of the facts you would expect that employers were addressing the issue of work-life balance wholeheartedly and that the working life of the average employee was a happy and contented one. Regrettably it seems that this is not the case. Like the mythical village of Brigadoon, a perfect work-life balance remains an elusive concept, shrouded in a mist of conflicting needs and desires.

People talk a great deal about achieving a balance in their lives. They talk of what they really want to do. Often, however, work takes over. The route to personal fulfillment and an 'interesting life' is blocked by meetings with venture capitalists.

One obvious measure of this is working hours. 'I personally work long hours, but not as long as I used to', Bill Gates observed recently. 'I certainly haven't expected other people to work as hard as I did. Most days I don't work more than 12 hours. On weekends I rarely work more than 8 hours. There are weekends I take off and I take vacations.' Not much room for a life, then.

When it comes to working hours, Americans work the longest hours in the industrialized world. The average American worker clocks up nearly 2,000 hours at work every year. Despite the heady speed of technological innovation, American working hours have actually increased by 4 percent since 1980. The United States fares badly compared to a wide range of nations. Norwegian workers work an average of 1,399 hours per year, while Japanese workers work nearly two weeks less than their American counterparts. The general trend is downwards. German hours have fallen from 1,742 to 1,560 between the 1980s and the late 1990s. At the same time as workers in Europe have been working fewer hours, productivity has actually been rising. Indeed, productivity growth of 22 percent in Western Europe since 1980 exceeds that experienced in the United States. 'Americans have more money because they have less leisure,' MIT's Lester Thurow has noted simply.

Wealth has increased. A recent study found that over 3.5 million US households have a net worth of $1 million or above. Yet, over 17 million Americans suffer from depression and over 22 million take 'mood-lifting drugs'. In the study of US workers between 25 and 30 percent of employees claimed that their work-life balance had a negative effect on their personal life often or very often[13]. 'People are reaching the top, using all of their means to get money, power and glory and then self-destructing,' Harriet Rubin writes. 'Perhaps they never wanted success in the first place, or didn't like what they saw when they finally achieved it.'

This is not just an American thing. A five-year tracking study by the UK's Institute of Management and the University of Manchester Institute of Science and Technology found that the work and home life balance was still a pipe dream. Over 80 percent of executives worked over 40 hours a week and one in ten worked over 60 hours. A resounding, though depressing 86 percent said that the long hours had an affect on their relationship with their children and 71 percent said that it damaged their health[14].

'We want to have it all: More money and more time. More success and a more satisfying family life. More creature comforts and more sanity. We can work hard, we can find love and have a family, and we can enjoy the fruits of our success,' concludes a survey in Fast Company. Equilibrium is proving elusive.

Some pull it off. Equilibrium, when found, comes in many shapes and forms. The quest for balance leads the new generation in a variety of directions. Not all rush out and start their own business while busily cutting the corporate umbilical cord. Dual careering, an ugly phrase, we know, is increasingly common as people try to crowd entrepreneurial activities into already busy executive lives.

Flexible working practices

'Two-thirds of families in the UK are dual career,' says Professor Cary Cooper BUPA Professor of Organizational Psychology and Health at UMIST. 'UK employees work the longest hours in Europe, second only to America in the developed world and new technology has erased the barriers between work and personal time. The challenge is to design a future, using technology to our advantage, allowing our workers the flexibility they require to perform efficiently and deliver the productivity that our businesses need.'

One way of addressing work-life balance issues is through flexible working. The majority of our grandfathers will have worked regular fixed hours, whether it was down a mine, in a factory or in an office, whether it was five, six or seven days a week. Our parents may have been afforded a greater degree of latitude with their working hours, but not much. Nine-to-five office hours were still standard, as was a fixed working week. Today, however, the working week has been shattered into myriad of different permutations. Flexi-time, job-share, part-time, full-time, shift time, home-working, staggering hours, annual hours; take your pick. At a time when the consumer is king and consumer choice paramount, employees have never had such a great choice of how to work their hours.

Reasons for wanting to work flexi-time vary. They include:

Childcare – wanting to spend more time with your children, needing to be at home to take care of your child;

Study – gaining more skills and qualifications;

Caring – needing time to care for family or friends;

Health – when health problems place limitations on your ability to work;

Travel – when geographical location makes it difficult to travel to work;

Leisure – taking time off to pursue leisure activities such as competitive sports;

Voluntary work – giving your time to others on an unpaid basis; retirement -taking time to prepare for a retirement, winding down;

Quality of life – it may just be that you don't want to work the many hours you do and, like a third of the women and a quarter of the men in one work-life study, would definitely trade pay for time[15].

SO WHAT TYPE OF FLEXIBLE WORKING IS AVAILABLE?

Don't think that flexible working is confined to flexi-time. There are many different options as highlighted by a recent report:[16]

Flexi-time
Flexi-time, as the name suggests, offers a degree of flexibility to employees regarding their working hours. Normally there are agreed core hours, outside of these core hours workers start and finish when they wish. Most flexi-time systems allow the individual to build up extra hours which they can then carry forward, and if enough are accumulated take the appropriate amount of time off. The downside of this being that if the number of hours they have worked falls short of the prescribed minimum they will have to make up the time. As the system requires keeping a record of the number of hours worked, employees will usually have to clock in and out, or complete a record sheet.

Time off in lieu
Less formal than flexi-time, the employee takes time off by arrangement with management. The time off is to compensate for extra hours worked.

Staggered hours
Starting, finishing and break times are staggered. This is usually to ensure that the employer can cover the opening hours. Can be useful for employees, however, who can gain flexibility through swapping work times with co-workers.

Shift working
When an employer needs to open for extended hours, for example running a 24-hour manufacturing facility, they will usually introduce shift working. Shift working may fit in with some individual's needs, however, shifts are normally rigidly structured and the opportunities for part-time working may be limited. Shift swapping, where workers negotiate working times and are able to rearrange and swap shifts, may be available.

Self-rostering

In self-rostering workers put forward times when they are able to work and when they don't wish to work. Management then compiles shift patterns taking this information into account, and trying to satisfy the wishes of as many employees as possible. Self-rostering provides the opportunity for flexible working but it will usually be a trade-off with each employee's needs weighed against those of the other co-workers.

Annual hours

The amount of hours worked is calculated on a yearly basis rather than weekly or monthly. This system provides considerable flexibility for both employer and employee. The downside is that as working hours are scheduled to meet demand whenever it arises, an employee may be called upon to work long or late hours at short notice. On the plus side it should theoretically be easier to arrange time off in quiet periods. However, it is worth determining in advance exactly how flexible the employer is, and in particular what is its attitude towards taking blocks of time off in practice.

Part-time work

Once associated with menial, low-grade low status jobs, part-time working is an increasing fact of modern working life. Today, part-time working encompasses a range of jobs, anything from professional such as doctors and accountants to short-order chefs. The status of part-time workers has changed accordingly and they are often, in Europe for example, afforded the same rights as their full-time counterparts. The hours worked can vary from a few hours a week to only a little less than those worked by full-time employees. For career adventurers, who are happy to trade less income for more time, part-time working may offer the perfect solution, particularly if combining several part-time jobs. Potential pitfalls include pressure to work extra hours, and a reduction in job satisfaction due to the amount of time devoted to a particular job.

Job sharing

With job sharing two people perform the same job part-time, which together amounts to one full-time job. Thus one individual might perform the job in the morning and the other in the afternoon. Pay, benefits and holiday entitlement are divided up pro rata. The logistics of dividing up work in this way can be complicated, it requires close cooperation between the job sharers, and therefore a job sharer's personality must be suited to this type of working for it to succeed. However, where permitted, job sharing provides extremely flexible working arrangements providing the individual job sharer is happy to forgo a full-time pay packet.

Home working

Like part-time work, home working was once the province of poorly paid piece-workers. With the advances in information and communications technology over the last 15 years, home working or tele working as it is also known, has gradually become accepted practice for more senior, better paid workers. Whether it is occasional work from home, or the individual is based at home and occasionally comes into the company's offices, many jobs offer the opportunity to work at home for some of the time. Home working is not for everyone. It may sound but the ideal solution, but for the wrong person it can turn out to be a nightmare. Home working requires the ability to work despite distractions and to separate personal from working life.

Temping

Working short stretches at a time for a variety of different companies can suit some people. The advantages are that you can meet many different people and do a range of different jobs. Potential downsides include lacking a clear career path and being unable to obtain regular work. Temping can be a good way to bridge gaps between longer term employment or to get cash when studying.

If the idea of flexible working hours appeals to you, then you will need to plan ahead before taking your next job. And if you are already in a job but would prefer different working arrangements to your existing ones don't despair, you may be able to negotiate a preferable system of working.

Job applicants must consider carefully what kind of working arrangements suit them best. Maybe you would to like job share. Perhaps to go home later and to come in later. Or would annual hours give you the flexibility you need? Next, find out what, if any, flexible working arrangements the prospective employer offers. The organization may offer work-life balance policies, existing employees may be working flexible hours – find out. If it is essential to you that the job you eventually take offers flexible working practices and you're unable to find out whether your prospective employer offers this opportunity, make enquiries directly. If you have the skills and experience the recruiter is looking for, if you are clearly the right candidate, the company may be willing to discuss working-hours flexibility with you and accommodate your needs.

Alternatively, apply in the usual manner without mentioning your preference regarding working hours and if you get the job you can discuss the matter at this point. Don't bank on getting the hours you want this way, though.

If you are already in work and wish to change your working arrangements, you should already have a good idea of the feasibility of what you are proposing. Any change in your existing arrangements will have to benefit the employer, as well as yourself, if you are to overcome your employer's probable resistance to changing the status quo. Remember also that changing your own working hours may have wider implications. If you decide to job share, then who will be doing the sharing with you? What if others want to follow your example?

If you work for a large organization, there may be a set procedure to follow. This is often the case with matters such as returning to work after pregnancy. In the absence of a set procedure you have to be creative. First try and establish if someone else, either in the past or the present, has already done what you are proposing. Someone in the personnel department is most likely to know.

Before you approach your manager with your proposal, cover the bases. Prepare for any questions or objections that are likely to arise. Consider how your proposal will affect the areas you cover. How will you ensure there is no decline in service? If you are proposing to work from home how will you keep in contact? Can you demonstrate to your boss that your new working arrangements will increase your efficiency and productivity? If you work closely with others it may be worth discussing your proposal with them, especially if they are happy to fit in with your plans.

And if you are refused?

◆ **Find out why.** Essential if you are to take any further action.

◆ **Go over your boss's head?** Risky, depending on the boss's power base. And if you get your way, for how long is your boss going to resent you for bypassing him?

◆ **Take it on the chin and keep going.** A good strategy if you think further negotiating may pay dividends later on.

◆ **Take independent advice.** Union membership has its advantages. A union will be able to advise whether your employer has infringed your rights. Even if not, the union may be able to negotiate on your behalf. Be pragmatic though. Involving the union is unlikely to endear you to your employer and is likely to up the stakes.

◆ **Leave.** Only if it is essential for you to change your working arrangements or you want to leave for other reasons.

WORK-LIFE BALANCE

Reading
Berman Fortgang, L., *Living Your Best Life: Work, Home, Balance, Destiny: Ten Strategies for Getting from Where You Are to Where You're Meant to Be* (J P Tarcher, 2001).
Harvard Business Review on Work and Life Balance (Harvard Business School Press, 2000).
Pearsall , P *The Pleasure Prescription : To Love, to Work, to Play Life in the Balance* (Hunter House, 1996).

Notes

1. Phillips-Jones, L., *Mentors and protégés*, (Arbor House, 1982).
2. Zey, M., *A mentor for all, Personnel Journal* p.46. January 1988.
3. Bell, C., *Managers As Mentors: Building Partnerships for Learning* 1996.
4. Shaw, E., *Mentoring goes modern,* The Arizona Republic, 7 July 1998.
5. Hill, L., *Developing the star performer in leader to leader:* Number 8. Spring 1998 (pp. 30-37) Drucker Foundation.
6. Peddy, Dr S., *The Art of Mentoring: Lead, Follow and Get Out of the Way* (Bullion Books, 1998).
7. Galinsky, E. and S Kim and J Bond, *Feeling Overworked: When Work Becomes Too Much.* Families and Work Institute, 2001.
8. Bottomore, T B (Editor) *Early Writings* (McGraw-Hill, 1964).
9. *International Student Survey Report.* (Coopers & Lybrand, 1997).
10. Gemini Consulting, *International Workforce Management Study: Capitalizing on the Workforce* (Yankelovitch Partners Inc, 1998).
11. *The Retention Dilemma,* (Hay Group, 2001).
12. *Work/Life Balance: Whose Move is it Next?* (Ceridian Performance Partners, 2001).
13. *The 1997 National Study of the Changing Workforce* by Bond J, Galinsky E, Swanberg J. (Families and Work Institute, 1997).
14. Surveys have found that employees believe working continually long hours affects their health. *The Family Friendly Workplace: An investigation into long hours cultures and family friendly employment practices,* (Austin Knight, 1995). Kodz J, Kersley B, Strebler M T, O'Regan S, *Breaking the Long Hours Culture* (IES, 1998).
15. *Work/Life Balance: Whose Move is it Next?* (Ceridian Performance Partners, 2001).
16. *Work/Life Balance.* Dti. 2001.

"Comes over one an absolute necessity to move. And what is more, to move in some particular direction. A double necessity then: to get on the move, and to know whither. "

D.H. Lawrence, *Sea and Sardinia*

"And the days went by like paper in the wind Everything changed, then changed again."

Tom Petty, *To Find a Friend*

FIVE

MOVING UP, MOVING ON
KNOWING WHEN TO STAY
AND WHEN TO SAY GOODBYE

For career adventurers, change is a given.
Learning to take control is the key to navigating a successful career
change. In this chapter you will learn to:

■

Assess your prospects in your organization

■

Anticipate change

■

Recognize when it's time to move on

■

Cope with downsizing and other setbacks.

1. ALL CHANGE

Change. It happens in all of our lives; a new house, a new relationship, a new wardrobe, a new job, a new career.

Change can be voluntary or involuntary, welcome or unwelcome. People tend to be distrustful of change at work, hence the huge amount of literature on how to manage change within organizations, change consultants and a whole industry built on change management.

Like other forms of change, career change can be exhilarating, but it can also be traumatic, frightening, unsettling and difficult to deal with. But when you've gotta go, you've gotta go. At one end of the scale is career change imposed on you by your employer or other circumstances beyond your control. One moment you may be the golden boy, or girl, and can do no wrong. One pay rise follows another, one promotion after the next. Smart house, fast car, great lifestyle; all yours. The next moment, wham, pink slip or P45, clear the desk and you are out of a job.

It would be nice to think that career adventurers don't get pink slips or P45s; that they only experience the positive aspects of a modern career. But that is not the case. Along with the career highs come the inevitable lows. The reality today is that most, if not all, of us will experience the pain of being let go from a job at some point. So when it happens to you, remember you are not alone. Being forced to leave a job or change career can really knock your confidence. It can happen for a variety of reasons such as being laid off, being fired, ill health or personal circumstances. No matter how grim things look, don't give up. Never give up.

At the other end of the scale is voluntary career change; you decide to change career, move job, apply for promotion, or give it all up and live on a desert island. Although some people deal easily with change they tend to be the minority. For everyone else successfully coping with change is about adopting the right strategies to get through it. These include:

- ◆ **Predicting change** – if the change is a surprise its effect is usually worse than if it is expected. Learn to read the tell-tale signs and predict change, and you can plan your response.
- ◆ **Being proactive** – if you know an event is going to happen don't wait for the fallout to hit you, make plans to ease the pain.
- ◆ **Taking control** – it's often easier to be a victim than a survivor. Being a victim means being passive and doing nothing, surviving requires you to take action, to follow your plans through.
- ◆ **Confronting change** – if you meet change head on, instead of shrinking from it, you will get through it OK.

CAREER ADVENTURER

JOHN BROOKS *on changing careers*

Title/Position: Senior VP and Manager – Media Practice
Company: Silicon Valley Bank
Industry: Commercial Banking

'A lot of career people and job experts tell you that you have to reinvent yourself. That's probably good advice, but it's a lot easier said than done. In order to do that you have to be willing to either re-educate yourself, which is not practical for a lot of people, or to start at the bottom in a different industry. Try going from low-tech to high-tech at 40 years old, and convincing a 25-year-old hiring manager that you are going to be happy working in an entry level job where your peers are 25 years old. That's not to say that it can't be done. It's just a really tough transition to make.

I found that in good times if you have the right skill set or credentials, you should have no problem getting a job. In any other time or place you have to think of yourself in terms of how you will help improve someone else's bottom line, either by increasing revenue or reducing expense. People look at you as an expense, and they have to be able to justify you as an expense. So you either have to have some special skill or credential that's in very high demand, or you have to be able to convince them of how bringing you into their organization is going to improve their bottom line.'

2. TAKING STOCK

◆ **Who am I?**
◆ **Where am I?**
◆ **Where do I want to go?**

If you suspect that is time to change jobs and/or careers, or someone else has decided for you, then now is the time to take stock. The first thing to do is to establish if your ambition, aims, drives and desires have changed since you first embarked on your career. You may have already taken a variety of self-knowledge tests to determine what kind of personality you have, what kind of values you hold, what kind skills you possess and so what kind of career will suit you best. If not, then reread Section One and take some action. Even if you have already gone through this process before, it is worth retaking the tests to see if you have changed your outlook on life since you first took them.

Now might be the time to think about making use of professional career change services. Sylvia Milne, partner at Catalyst Career Strategies, recommends turning to professionals 'in the very early stages of identifying what is lacking in the current job. Is it the environment? The tasks? Have your values changed? Don't wait until your boss is unhappy or until after you have left your current position.'

When companies need to define their direction, or reset the compass, they use a mission statement. Try writing your own personal mission statement, setting out your objectives and aims. This should help to clarify exactly what it is you expect to get out of your career. Another way of doing this is to create a 'to do' list for life. Write down all the things you would like to do in your life and haven't yet accomplished (see Adventure 14 at the end of this section).

In 1987 Ted Leonsis, president of America Online Interactive Properties, was flying from Miami to Atlanta. It was a routine flight. Routine, that is, until the passengers were told that the plane had lost its flaps and landing gear. Leonsis and his fellow passengers had 30 minutes to contemplate their fate before the pilot attempted a landing.

'That's a long time,' said Leonsis. 'I was nervous, frankly. I didn't want to die. I just said if I live, I'm going to play offense for the rest of my life. About a week later, over the weekend, I wrote down 101 things to do before I die, and I try to do two or three a year.' An ardent sports fan, the first 25 items on his list were to do with sports: playing Augusta National golf course, catching a foul ball, making a hole in one, meeting baseball legend Mickey Mantle, buying a sports team, winning an NBA championship and winning a Stanley Cup.

Non-sports items included: meeting the US president, publishing a novel, making a movie, doing a standup comedy routine and traveling to outer space. Leonsis, who is now the owner of the ice hockey team the Washington Capitals, has ticked off about 70 items from his list. 'I've been clipping them off,' he says, 'so it really has been a way to coalesce my thinking, goals I want to achieve.'¹

Not everyone will be able to list and accomplish buying a sports team as an aim, but compiling a list like Leonsis did will help you focus on what you really want to achieve in your life.

Adventure 11

Every six months at least you should ask yourself some tough questions and give some honest answers to see if it's time to pack up the rucksack and hit the road again.

How safe is your job?
1. Is your job connected to delivering a product or service that has performed poorly recently (the sales graph looks like Sir Edmund Hilary's route down Mount Everest, the television ads have been pulled, stores are selling the product at a discount because it can't get rid of the stuff)?
2. Would the organization suffer if your job didn't exist?
3. Could someone less experienced (i.e. cheaper) do your job? Or could the job be shifted elsewhere within your organization or outsourced?

4. Are you middle management? A manager of managers? (Of managers etc.)?

5. Is your job concerned with data gathering, assimilation, ordering or a repetitive admin job (i.e. can you be replaced with a machine)?

6. Are you the work equivalent of the invisible man? Are you in a low-profile job and will anyone notice when you're gone?

7. Is your performance below average, below targets, worse than your principal co-workers?

8. Could the company relocate the premises where you work to somewhere cheaper without adversely affecting business?

9. Are you located in an area that is suffering economically?

10. Do you know where the bodies are buried? It could be your saving grace.

1. Yes 2. No 3. Yes 4. Yes 5. Yes 6. Yes 7. Yes 8. Yes 9. Yes 10. No
More than four or five of the above answers and things are looking dicey.

How safe is your company?

1. Is your company heavily dependent on one or two clients?

2. Is your company's cash flow in good shape (are customers and other debtors paying up on time)? If you don't know, check the financial reports if published or have a quiet word with the people in accounts.

3. Have you heard any bad rumors about the company (in the media, from friends at other companies, from suppliers or customers, from the boss)?

4. Is your company tightening the purse strings (expenses cut, office parties downgraded or scrapped, travel suspended, executive box at Ascot dispensed with, company car downsized)?

5. Does the company serve a saturated, mature or declining market?

6. Is the competition increasing? Are your competitors becoming more successful?

7. Does your company operate in a cyclical market or is your company characterized by periods of contraction and expansion (they hire them, they fire them, they hire them, they fire them)?

8. Is your company's business heavily reliant on the fortunes of other industries or companies?

1. Yes 2. No 3. Yes 4. Yes 5. Yes 6. Yes 7. Yes 8. Yes
More than three or four of the above and it's not the time to make a major financial commitment.

And finally. Are you being short-changed in the career stakes?

1. Does your job challenge you?
2. Do you have opportunities to increase your skills base (to avoid becoming a one-trick pony)?
3. Do you hate your job/dread going to work in the morning/feel ill when you think about your job?
4. Do you feel stressed at work more than 50 percent of the time?

1. No 2. No 3. Yes 4. Yes

If your answer to 3 is Yes, whatever your other answers are to the rest of these questions then it is definitely time to reread this book and think about a career change. Otherwise, two or more out of four and the winds of change are blowing.

Career change

In a survey conducted in the UK in November 2001 by career consultants Penna Sanders & Sidney, four out of every ten respondents said they would change their career the next day given the opportunity. Only one in every ten respondents would definitely stay in their existing job.

Greed appears to be a prime motivator for change. Most people wanted to move to increase their earnings, although reasons such as taking up a new challenge, doing something more fulfilling, making a dream come true or having a better quality of life were also cited.

Barriers to career change were primarily concerned with fear that earnings levels couldn't be assured in another career. Respondents were also unclear about what else they would be able to do. A perception that they were too old to change was also cited as a reason to stay.

Penna Sanders & Sidney drew a number of important lessons for employees:

◆ Think very carefully about what you are best at. You are likely to be happier in work doing something you are good at.
◆ Think over your day and write down the interesting, fun and exciting bits as well as the uninteresting and dull bits. This will help you to assess you strengths and weaknesses and allow you to focus on the type of work you find most satisfying.
◆ Sit down with your boss, or employers and map out a career path that suits you both.

◆ If dissatisfaction at work is causing you to consider resigning, discuss the matter with your employer. Employers like to keep talented staff; they may not realize you are unhappy. Alerted to the fact they may try to find you new opportunities.

◆ Push yourself beyond the comfort zone.

◆ Try and maintain a good work-life balance. If you have a satisfying life outside work it will help if you are becoming unhappy within the workplace.

Tips for taking stock:

1. Take professional career advice while still in work.
2. Retread the path of self-evaluation.
3. Write your own personal mission statement.
4. Make a list of 101 personal goals.
5. Keep a diary (a career chronicle, if you will).
6. Take time out if you can afford to.

Thinking time

If you think it's time to move on, then it probably is. But don't rush yourself. Sometimes the urge to move is no more than a subconscious desire to avoid a bigger issue. We all feel like running away some times. Most of us don't act on the impulse. Take time to reflect on what it is that's really unsettling you. Perhaps you are frustrated in your current job. Maybe you feel threatened, or inadequate. Don't jump to hasty conclusions. Think before you leap.

Consider what happened to a young man called Welch from Peabody, Massachusetts. Let's call him Jack. He grew up in Salem, Massachusetts, where his father worked as a railroad conductor. As a boy he suffered from a stutter that continued to bother him for much of his life. It might have badly affected his confidence had it not been for his mother's imaginative explanation. 'She told me I didn't have a speech impediment, Welch explained, '[it was] just that my brain worked too fast.'

Jack joined General Electric at the age of 25. A year later, in 1961, he decided that a career at GE was not for him. Sick of the cumbersome bureaucratic systems, Jack quit. And that might have been the end of it. But fortunately for Jack (and GE) his boss at the time persuaded him to stay, tempting him with the offer of a higher salary and a better position.

In 1963 Jack was put in charge of chemical development, and in 1968 at the age 33 he became GE's youngest ever general manager. By 1972 Welch had risen to the position of divisional vice-president, and had set his sights on rising even higher. On his employee evaluation form Jack was asked to state his long-term ambitions, to become CEO he wrote. By 1979 he was vice-chairman and executive officer. Along the way he built GE's plastics division into a formidable $2bn business; turned around the medical diagnostics business; and began the development of GE Capital. In December 1980 Jack was appointed as the new CEO and chairman of GE, at 45 the youngest chief the company had ever had.

Jack Welch went on to become one of the most renowned corporate leaders of the twentieth century. Throughout his 20 year reign, he maintained GE's reputation as world beater. He presided over a 600 percent increase in profits; 80 consecutive quarters of increased earnings. Under Welch, GE moved into new business areas and reached new heights. In 1999, John Francis Welch Jr, was named as *Fortune* magazine's 'manager of the century'. He finally stepped down as CEO in September 2001.

None of this would have happened if Jack Welch had changed jobs in 1961. True, his autobiography reveals a man who was driven to succeed and would probably have had a successful career elsewhere. But GE fitted him like a glove. Over time, he shaped the company in his own likeness. He was the right man in the right place at the right time.

Jack Welch personifies some key issues for the career adventurer. Namely he consistently demonstrated:

◆ a voracious appetite for knowledge (life-long learning);
◆ a willingness to make bold, and sometimes tough decisions;
◆ an ability to channel energy in one direction, without ever losing sight of the bigger picture;
◆ dogged determination.

These traits are all vital for a successful career adventure. But there is another lesson from Welch's career: don't quit just because you're bored.

Ambition can sometimes make us rush decisions. It needs to be tempered with reflection. Anyone who has read the famous diarist Samuel Pepys will have been amazed at how little work Pepys had to do despite his rapid career progression in the Admiralty. They might also have noticed how the man's naked ambition is laid bare in his extensive musings. (Reading the autobiographies of successful career adventurers can also be inspiring and illuminating.) Keeping a diary is an excellent way to articulate your hopes and fears. It requires effort and discipline, but this is no bad thing. So why not take a leaf out of Pepys' book and join the ranks of famous diarists such as Anne Frank, Marco Polo and Captain Cook? The great thing about keeping a diary is that it allows you to trace the evolution of your own thinking and aspirations. Think of it as your career chronicle. It will help you reach a balanced view about whether it is time to move on.

Talking to other people can also help. Changing jobs or careers is a major decision and as such can place a considerable burden on you while you decide what to do. There is no need to shoulder this burden alone, as there are plenty of people with whom you can share it, both professional and personal.

Friends and family may provide some wise words to help you. Then there is your mentor, if you have one, who can be invaluable at such a time. If you are a spiritual person then seek advice from your priest,or other trusted person connected with your belief. Professional services abound. Career consultants and advisors, headhunters, personal coaches, will all provide you with advice of varying quality and usefulness for a fee. You can even take a course in career and life change. At Marylhurst University in Oregon, for example, there is the Life Planning and Career Development Program.

Before jumping back on the treadmill, why not take some time out. Depending on your financial means you might want to try some 'work' in the voluntary sector. Volunteer work comes in all shapes and sizes ranging from a brief encounter with a local non-profit to travels abroad. The Peace Corps for example, established by John F. Kennedy has over 7,000 volunteers working in over 70 countries. The Corps offers a range of work from agribusiness to teaching in such far flung locations as Moldova and Vanuatu.

Or take the vacation of a lifetime. If you've always wanted to travel around the world, off you go. Of course, family commitments may make this impossible, in which case you might have to settle for reading Jack Kerouc's *On the Road*.

Whatever you decide to do before you get back on track, whether it's volunteering, traveling, going back to school or just chilling out, make sure that when you make your next career decision that it's the right one.

CAREER ADVENTURER

LESLIE L. KOSSOFF *on moving on*
Title/Position: Chief Executive Officer
Company: Menton Productions LLC

'My advice is, when taking a job; don't look at it from the perspective of staying a particular number of years. You don't know what the job will have to offer or how your needs and desires might change. Move into a position, giving it all you have to give, and getting everything from the organization that it has to give. Only when you have exhausted all possibilities for yourself and knowing that you have given the enterprise your best, should you consider moving on.'

CAREER ADVENTURER

ELAINE SOLOWAY *on moving on*
Title/Position: Owner
Company: Elaine Soloway Public Relations
Industry: Public Relations

'I don't think there's ever the right or perfect time for your next career step. Whatever path you take, you're going to make the best of it and do your best. There aren't any "wrong decisions". You have to trust your instincts more and not worry about what other people say. When we ask someone for advice, we really know what we want them to answer. We just want a cheering section. We know what we want to do, but we're afraid of what people will say. We have to have enough faith in ourselves that we move ahead. I rarely regret anything I've done in life.'

'I guess the advice that I give to many people is not to think of it as a permanent move. People get stuck because they're afraid of making the wrong decision. I tell them that they can always leave, that they should try it, and if it doesn't work out they can move on. The thought that you're going to be in a new career for the rest of your life is paralyzing. If it doesn't work out, people should feel courageous enough to move. The worst thing is to be in a job that you hate. No amount of money or security is worth that. Figure you'll be there 6 to 12 months and if it doesn't work out you'll leave.'

TAKING STOCK RESOURCES

VOLUNTEERING

On the web

UK volunteering website – www.volunteering.org.uk

volunteer match – US-oriented volunteering site that lists thousands of non-profit groups seeking volunteers. www.volunteermatch.org
International volunteering programs – www.globalvolunteers.org

The US Government run Peace Corps – volunteering throughout the world
www.peacecorps.gov

Reading

Banerjee, Dillon *So You Want to Join the Peace Corps: What to Know Before You Go* (Ten Speed Press, 2000).
Landes, M., *The Back Door Guide to Short-Term Job Adventures: Internships, Extraordinary Experiences, Seasonal Jobs, Volunteering, Work Abroad* (Ten Speed Press, 2001).
McMillon, Bill and Edward Asner, *Volunteer Vacations : Short-Term Adventures That Will Benefit You and Others, Volunteer Vacations, 7th Ed* (Chicago Review Press, 1999).

CHILL OUT

On the web

Kick back and spend some quality thinking time. Where better than at a retreat. Retreats across the globe listed at www.retreatsintl.org and www.retreatsonline.com.

Reading

For retreats in the US try reading Sanctuaries: *The Complete United States – A Guide to Lodgings in Monasteries, Abbeys, and Retreats* by Jack Kelly, Marcia Kelly (Bell Tower, 1996).
or for Europe: *Europe's Monastery and Convent Guesthouses: A Pilgrim's Travel Guide* by Kevin J. Wright (Liguori Publications, 2000).

TRAVEL

On the web

Instead of rushing straight into the next job, take the holiday of lifetime
www.whereintheworld.co.uk
www.adventureandexotictravel.com/companies.html

Reading

Read about some thought provoking travel experiences of others
Twain, M., *Following the Equator: A Journey around the World* (Dover
Publications, 1989).
Hessler, P *River Town: Two Years on the Yangtze* (Harperperennial Library, 2001).

Or plan your own
Lederman, E., *Vacations That Can Change Your Life: Adventures, Retreats and
Workshops for the Mind, Body and Spirit* (Sourcebooks, 1998).

UNORTHODOX WORK

Reading

Try something out of the ordinary for your next job.

Rosen, Jaime (Editor), Nicholas Corman, Chuck Kapelke and Jake Brooks
(Contributor), *Nice Job: The Guide to Cool, Odd, Risky, and Gruesome Ways to
Make a Living* (Ten Speed Press, 1999).
Smye, M., *Is It Too Late to Run Away and Join the Circus? An Updated Guide to
Your Second Life* (Hungry Minds, 2001).

3. LIFE-LONG LEARNING

Learning is an ornament in prosperity, a refuge in adversity, and a provision in old age.

Aristotle

Sir John Hawkwood was born in 1320 at Sible Hadingham near Colchester, Essex, England. Hawkwood understood the value of life-long learning and transferable skills. Left only £20 and a quantity of corn in his father's estate Hawkwood turned to the trade at which he was most proficient at, fighting. He fought with Edward III in France, and then after the peace between England and France joined a 'free company' – an army for hire – fighting in France for the Pope. Later he traveled to Italy with the notorious band of mercenaries, the White Company, where he fought for the Pope, for the city state of Florence, and for anyone else who paid well.

Hawkwood's success in his field brought him riches and fame. He was the owner of extensive property in Italy and accumulated hundreds of thousands of florins; he was feted by Italian nobility and favored by the Pope. He was one of the greatest *condottiere* (mercenaries) of his time.

Why did Hawkwood prosper? Because he was continually learning. He started as longbow man, but became an excellent swordsman, great horseman and astute military tactician. He pioneered the use of artillery in the field, as well as devising mobile raiding parties, equipping his forces with lightweight armor specifically for that purpose.

In the twenty first century we are all mercenaries; work mercenaries hiring ourselves out to the employer that suits us best. Knowledge and skills are the measure of our value in the market. In place of the longbow and the sword, field artillery and armor, are the laptop, computer software, networking and the mobile phone.

When you get to work you might think that your learning days are over. Not if you want a rewarding career. Even if you have seen the inside of a classroom or lecture hall for the last time, as student at least, there is plenty more learning to be done. As far as work is concerned the buzzword of the 1990s was 'knowledge',

knowledge workers, knowledge management etc. To further your career successfully you will need to acquire new knowledge and skills continuously. Hopefully, your employer will provide you with learning opportunities. If not, you must provide them yourself. Only by embracing continual learning will your career prosper as did Sir John Hawkwood over 500 years ago.

Training and education

Human resource specialists differentiate between training and education. If you wish to arrange for the acquisition of new knowledge or skills with the aid of your employer you need understand the difference between the two.

Education

- ◆ Education is about acquiring information.
- ◆ The content of education is usually principles, knowledge and ideas.
- ◆ The educator is usually an expert or specialist in their field.
- ◆ Education normally takes place over a long period with long-term objectives.
- ◆ Education draws from the past and present, building a body of knowledge.
- ◆ Effectiveness of education is usually judged by ranking or marking.

Training

- ◆ Training is about acquiring the ability to perform some action with information provided.
- ◆ Training usually consists of skills and techniques.
- ◆ In training, the instructor normally adopts the role of coach, facilitator or mentor.
- ◆ Training is usually short-term with short-term goals.
- ◆ Training looks at the future, how the skills to be acquired will affect the behavior and performance of the person undertaking the training.
- ◆ Effectiveness of training is assessed by judging how the trainee is able to undertake the actions they are being trained to perform in the future.

To determine whether it is education or training you require, ask yourself: What do I wish to accomplish? How best can I achieve this outcome? What resources do I need?

Back to school

Mid-life can be a difficult time for career adventurers. It is often the time when the career journey is most at risk of disruption. Internally there may be self-doubt. Are you in the right career? Is your career heading in the right direction?

External forces also appear to conspire against the mid-life career adventurer. Physical performance begins to wane, making you more vulnerable to replacement by younger, stronger employees. Downsizing and redundancy seems to scythe down the mid-lifers in disproportionate numbers. Age discrimination insidiously creeps in. Technology continues its rampant progress leaving mid-lifers in its wake.

A college course is one way of combating the threats to the mid-life career adventurer. Not everyone is able to study full time, but with the plethora of part-time courses now available for adults there is little excuse not to study for some type of additional qualification.

Money and time are the two principal objections. Yes, courses can be expensive but think of the pay-off. Try and calculate where you will stand in the job market with your newly acquired knowledge and/or skills. If money is an issue, make sure the cost-benefit equation has a favorable outcome. As for time, when is there ever a good time to do anything? If continuous learning is something you must provide for yourself rather than the company providing it for you, then it will always be easier to put off the decision. Stop procrastinating and get on with studying. Ultimately you cannot afford to avoid it. If you do not embrace learning the world will leave *you* behind.

There are distinct benefits to be gained from study at any age. The obvious benefit is monetary. You should be able to parley new skills and knowledge into additional pay and benefit. The average increase in salary is measurable in the case of some postgraduate degrees such as the MBA. For others it is a question of market worth, use a salary checker such as that at http://jobstar.org/tools/salary.

Learning provides more than the possibility of greater financial reward. It offers the opportunity to change career direction for example. A more circumspect attitude would be that it provides the opportunity to stay in your existing position as opposed to being laid off.

Problems encountered in mid-life are often connected with self-doubt and a drop in self-esteem. Study can boost confidence by showing you that you are still capable of achieving great things. And you will not be alone, statistics suggest that approaching 50 percent of college students are non-traditional, i.e. straight from school. Expect to find fellow mid-lifers studying alongside you.

Nor should you think that going back to college full time or part time, online or in person, is the sole preserve of the mid-lifer. Life-long learning is what it sounds like, learning throughout your life, from cradle to grave. A message that Italy's oldest woman, Maria Grazia Broccolo, understood. Broccolo returned to school to take her exams aged 108.

For certain occupations or professions a graduate degree or postgraduate professional qualification is an integral part of the professional training e.g. law, medicine, the advice to individuals pursuing this course is think very carefully about whether you are certain that you want to enter the particular occupation. If you are reading this, then the chances are you are having second thoughts. A year at law school to find out that you don't want to become a solicitor is an expensive and time-consuming lesson.

Hard skills or soft skills, computer programming or emotional intelligence, the important thing is to keep learning. Learning keeps you in tip-top career condition. Learning enriches your soul and your bank balance. Start learning and keep learning – you can't afford not to.

LIFE-LONG LEARNING RESOURCES

ON THE WEB

Autodidactic Press – this site is Charles D. Hayes' labor of love for the promotion of life-long self-education. Autodidactic means self-educated, and 'self-education is the essence of genuine learning. Self-education provides the vitality that enables us to turn information into knowledge and to use it in such a way that it adds meaning to life. Indeed, without the dynamism of self-education, we fail to develop our own interests to the degree that they become driving forces in their own right. When our motivation arises from internal sources the value of life-long learning becomes readily apparent to us' (www.autodidactic.com). In addition to extensive links to distance learning and online training resources, this helpful website provides links to educational resources in 32 categories ranging from archaeology and architecture to technology and training under its 'Self-University Campus.' Visitors may also subscribe to the free Self-University Newsletter.

Center for Lifelong Learning – this was established during 1993 to facilitate the introduction of non-formal programs at the Technikon of Southern Africa. The 15 South African technikons (www.studysa.co.za/tech.html) offer career-oriented educational programs designed to meet the needs of industry and commerce in a hi-tech global economic environment. The website provides a diverse array of international links to online colleges and course resources, and sources of information for study and research, including education, technology, business, non-profit and recreation journals, magazines and newspapers that are available in whole or part online, as well as links to job search and project management sites. **http://pgw.org/cll**

Globewide Network Academy (GNA) – this links to information on thousands of online courses and programs available from academic and training institutions around the world. GNA has been in existence since 1993 and is an educational non-profit organization in Texas, USA. Its purpose is to promote access to educational opportunities for anybody, anywhere. GNA pioneers and develops distance-learning relationships and facilities for the worldwide public to use. Its tools are created under the open-source philosophy and others are encouraged to copy GNA's products and build upon them in the spirit of the open source community. The website also includes resources and forums for distance learners and teachers. **http://confucius.gnacademy.org:8001**

Lifelong Learning – for one-stop shopping on information and resources on life-long learning in the UK and beyond, look no further than this outstanding website, supported by the Access to Learning for Adults Division of the UK Department for Education and Skills. Scroll to the bottom of the home page to find links to categories of resources helpfully arranged according to key learning themes. There's something here for everyone, including people of all ages and levels of education, small businesses, government agencies, community service providers, educators and media. Themes include: promoting learning, financing learning, older learners, young people, post-16 learning, family learning, for work, communities, equal opportunities, basic skills, online learning, further education and more. From money to motivation, this comprehensive knowledge portal has links to just about everything you need.
http://www.lifelonglearning.co.uk/index.htm

Learndirect – in its Green Paper, *The Learning Age* (full text available online at www.lifelonglearning.co.uk/greenpaper/index.htm),'the British Government details its vision for 'a learning society in which everyone, from whatever background, routinely expects to learn and upgrade their skills throughout life.' Learndirect is an innovative online learning center, supported by the government, and established to help realize that vision. Now UK residents can enjoy life-long learning, for business and/or pleasure, on the Internet, free! Courses are flexibly designed to enable you to choose what, when, where and how fast to learn. Courses last from 15 minutes to several hours, and offer instruction in everything from computer and Internet-related skills to various management topics. You may enroll online from home or work, or at one of the increasing number of learning centers throughout the UK, purposefully located in easy access places like sports clubs, leisure and community centers, churches, libraries, university campuses and even in railway stations! Now UK residents truly can learn anywhere, anytime. **www.learndirect.co.uk**

TRAINING
US Department of Labor – Education and training – www.doleta.gov
British Council – Education and training – www.britishcouncil.org/education
UK Government Department for Education and Skills –
www.dfes.gov.uk/index.htm
TrainingPages – the UK's largest independent directory of training on the web.
www.trainingpages.co.uk

3. EXIT STAGE LEFT

'Parting is such sweet sorrow', Shakespeare noted. Deciding when to exit from a job can also be a bitter-sweet experience.

On a bad day, a change of jobs seems appealing. But the next day, when the sun is shining and the gloom has lifted, it doesn't seem such a bad place after all. Better the devil you know, and all that.

It is difficult to overcome human nature and the tendency to hang on just a little bit longer. The risk is that people will remember failures at the end of your career rather than the triumphs of your glory years. Think of the number of boxers who insisted on having just one fight too many. Boxing aficionados would rather remember the 'rope-a-dope' Muhammad Ali of Ali v Foreman than the Ali who was battered around the ring by Leon Spinks or Trevor Berbick. Think of the countless number of sports stars who have finished their careers in relative obscurity, scratching a living in the lower reaches of their profession. It is better to choose the moment and manner of your own departure. Think of Margaret Thatcher, ousted in a most undignified way and forever burdened with the image of a leader who outstayed her welcome.

Knowing the right time to go is a matter of personal judgment. But there are some tips that can help you decide the timing and manner of your exit:

◆ Keep a weather eye on the outside world. Things have a habit of changing very quickly. One minute the economy is booming, companies that have been on their feet for matter a few months are valued at millions of dollars, recruiters welcome employees with welcome bonuses and contracts for stock options and you have just been awarded a substantial pay rise. The next minute the Western world is at war with terrorism, economies have suffered a crisis of confidence; the downsizing word has reared its ugly head. And your pay rise has been replaced by a pink slip of paper or P45.

◆ Think before you leap. Before you jump, think about your priorities. If the financial security and money is very important to you, it may be worth waiting until you are pushed. It may be worth grimly hanging on until you are finally eased out. Balance the ignominy of redundancy with the financial rewards of a fully paid pension, large redundancy package or vested share options.

◆ Attitude is important. You may not want to go, you may dread the moment of departure, you may feel resentment towards the company, you may be glum and dissatisfied, unhappy and miserable. Don't let it show. Grit your teeth and try to stay upbeat. Put a positive spin on your exit. Say you received an offer you couldn't refuse. Or you were headhunted. Say that you are seeking new challenges, becoming self-employed, signing up to the 'free agent' philosophy, rather than signing on to the dole queue. Recruiters don't hire glum, they hire happy and positive.

◆ Don't burn your bridges. Everyone has, at one at time or another, considered flouncing into the office and telling a few home truths before letting the boss know where they can stick their job. Yes, it's dramatic and yes, there is probably a good deal your boss doesn't know that he should. It may be tempting, but such impulsive behavior is unlikely to help you in the long run. Why? Because you poison your career trail. Your colleague probably does not want it known that he takes Friday afternoons off. Your boss may have already figured out who the white powder in the staff toilet belongs to. All you succeed in doing is reducing your list of potential referees and networking contacts. Cut the whining, and stick to wining and dining. Treat your co-workers to a farewell drink. Their memories will be much kinder for it. They may be able to help you in the future.

The specter of downsizing

Many workers do not have the luxury of deciding when to change jobs or careers. For hundreds of thousands of employees every year that decision is taken for them by their employer. Redundancy is a specter that hangs over the heads of workers even in what are apparently the most secure jobs.

'The analogy that I think of is a bit like myself and others who are a little bit overweight, who need to shed 15 percent to 20 percent of our body weight by our eating habits and by physical exercise.' This was how Geoff Boisi, chief executive of the JP Morgan Chase investment-banking, referred to a cost-cutting exercise that was likely to lead to in excess of 6,000 job losses worldwide[2].

Quite how cutting out some calories and visiting a gym a couple of times a week equates with losing your livelihood is hard to see. But the comment reflects the attitude of some senior managers towards their staff. (If you ever reach the boardroom, remember this.) Downsizing, headcount reduction and rightsizing, these are the euphemisms applied to the act of shattering employees' career dreams. At the height of the downsizing era during the recession of the early 1990s, a wholesale reduction in staffing levels was advocated as the key to greater efficiency and improved financial performance. Downsizing was very much in keeping with other changes taking place in the business world in the late 1980s and early 1990s, especially the trend towards delayering. Much of the restructuring involved cutting out layers of middle management to create lean, mean management machines.

Although originally intended as the antidote to the ballooning bureaucracy within large organizations, downsizing became a flag of convenience for many companies looking to boost profits by cutting headcount. In many cases where companies downsized, corporate income rose significantly while conditions for many working families continued to stagnate or decline. The corporations, on the other hand, saw aggregate profits rise to near-record levels, a 10 percent increase in 1994 after a 13 percent increase in 1993. In the twelve months ending June 1995, one half of the major US corporations eliminated jobs, averaging eight percent of the company workforce.

Downsizers of the brutal kind included Albert J. Dunlap. With his white hair and dapper suit, Dunlap was the very picture of benevolence. Yet, his management of companies such as Scott Paper and Sunbeam earned him the nickname 'Chainsaw Al'. His book was called *Mean Business*. Interviewed on ABC's Nightline, Dunlap explained his narrowly focused business philosophy: 'The reason to be in business is to make money for your shareholders. The shareholders own the company. They take all the risk.'

From a shareholder's perspective, Dunlap's business record was impressive. His resumé boasts eight turnarounds. The most notable of these was at Scott Paper where the stock price rose 220 percent in the first 19 months under Dunlap's control. At Sunbeam, merely appointing Dunlap as CEO produced an overnight rise of 59 percent in the stock price. Dunlap's managerial mantra was simple cost cutting. He could be relied upon to strip an organization to its bare bones. At Sunbeam, it took Dunlap a year to reduce the company's factories from 26 to eight, and to cut costs by $225 million.

In a poignant post-script, Dunlap was himself downsized in June 1998 when Sunbeam ditched him, the company was making a loss and its share price was plummeting. Dunlap now treads the boards as a conference speaker. Sunbeam Corporation went into bankruptcy early in 2001.

By the mid-1990s, public anger at seemingly unnecessary corporate blood-letting led to downsizing being reinvented in the more politically correct guise of 'rightsizing'. No one was fooled. The corporate world had overplayed its hand, generating a backlash. Much of the damage, however, had already been done. Many companies lost some of their most experienced middle managers and, as they walked through the doors for the last time, so also did the corporate memory. Companies suffered memory loss.

Expectations have now changed on both sides. Employers no longer wish to make commitments even implicit ones to long-term employment. The emphasis is on flexibility. On the other side, employees are keen to develop their skills and take charge of their own careers. Their emphasis is on employability.

Living with uncertainty

In the current economic climate, living with uncertainty is a fact of life. Recent events, including the global economic slowdown and the knock on effects of 11 September 2001, have fuelled uncertainty. Companies have reacted by cutting jobs. Downsizing, the scourge of the early 1990s, is back and back with a vengeance. In the US in 2001, layoffs reached levels last seen in the late 1980s and early 1990s. Many companies are in the spasm of a knee-jerk reaction that will kick many talented people out of their jobs. It will also convince many others that whatever loyalty they have to their employers is misplaced. The course of action that many companies are now embarking on will come back to haunt them in the years ahead.

Downsizing is the *bête noire* of management thinking. Of all the management remedies prescribed, it is perhaps the most drastic, demoralizing and inhumane. Few in the medical world would advocate amputation as the answer to a famine, yet the logic of the current bout of downsizing resides in hacking away the corporate flesh in response to falling orders.

Along with the predictable rash of dot.com staff casualties, those wielding the knife are household-name companies such as Motorola and Charles Schwab. The speed and ferocity of the cull suggests that little has been learned from previous downsizing experiences.

Today, however, companies have a more pragmatic attitude to layoffs than in Chainsaw Al's heyday. The changing attitude of companies faced with the tough decision of whether to lay off large swathes of their workforces reflect the expensive and time-consuming process of having to subsequently rehire employees when trading conditions take a turn for the better.

Avoiding the axe

The limitations imposed on employers by redundancy regulations present an opportunity for employees threatened with redundancy to avoid being made redundant. To begin with, those employees who have actively developed their brand and increased their skills and knowledge base throughout their employment, as suggested in Section Four of this book, should be at an advantage. An objective evaluation of skills and qualifications should show career adventurers in a positive light.

If you think that the redundancies are a direct result of an economic downturn, and that the downturn is likely to be temporary, then you can offer to take a pay cut or unpaid leave for period, hoping that the economy and therefore the company's fortunes will recover sufficiently to re-employ you, or restore your wage to its original level. Often, when a company engages in a large-scale clear out of employees, the subsequent reduction of costs enables it to stage a recovery. If you are happy with your company, and happy with your career, it may well be worth putting considerable effort into negotiating an alternative solution to redundancy for yourself in the hope that the company, post-redundancy, will be an even better place for you to further your career ambitions.

Mind the gap

The practice of an 'executive gap year' is becoming more common. 'Faced with slowing revenues we would be foolish to do anything silly like axe a third of our staff and then rehire the next year when things pick up. But in the meantime we have no work for them. So long as they don't go and work for our competitors, we really don't mind what they do,' said one human-resources director.

It was an attempt to avoid the situation that faced Merrill Lynch when it let 3,400 staff go during a Russian financial squeeze in 1998, and then had to rehire when the economy picked up again. In the aftermath of the terrorist outrage of the World Trade Center, airlines around the world were forced to scale back their operations. Yet rather than make wholesale redundancies some adopted a more forward-looking approach. Virgin, for example offered several alternatives to straight redundancy to its airline pilots. Pilots at BMI, the United Kingdom's second largest carrier, were asked if they would take a cut in hours and pay to help save jobs.

In the US, some law firms have offered sabbaticals that include 25 percent of the annual salary. Remember a switched-on firm wants to keep its most talented staff. 'Because it is often the most talented people who leave first, this is rather perverse way of ensuring they stay because by letting people go, we've found a great way of retaining them', is how one partner of a management consultancy puts it. Global management consultancy Accenture introduced a FlexLeave scheme. Under the scheme, executives are able to take a six to 12 month sabbatical and still bank 20 percent of their salary, as well as their employee benefits. Ultimately it may be impossible to avoid redundancy. But before you resign yourself to your fate make sure you explore all the alternatives.

Dealing with downsizing

Whether you are a City high-flyer who expects to pocket thousands of pounds or an administrative office worker who is likely to receive the statutory bare minimum, the impact and the effects of redundancy can be equally distressing.

Losing your job no longer has the stigma attached that it once had. In an age of downsizing, many of us can expect to lose our job at some time or another. But being fired is still undoubtedly a traumatic business. How is it that some terminated managers make the best of it while others fall apart? What is it that differentiates them?

One answer, according Maryanne Peabody and Laurence J. Stybel, authors of an authoritative article on the subject in the Harvard Business Review are co-founders of US outplacement and career management consultancy Stybel Peabody Lincolnshire, is mind-set[3]. Many workers, they say, unconsciously hold a 'tenure mind-set', believing in the promise of employment security. In fact, this idea has long been dead, though companies are unwilling to admit it openly.

By contrast, other workers hold an 'assignment mentality'. They view their job as no more than just one of a series of transient, career-building stepping-stones. Perhaps just as well, because most corporate board members and CEOs have this mind-set. They see their executives, even the best performers, as filling an assignment. When it's over for strategic or financial reasons so is the executive's tenure with the company. People who possess this mentality usually rebound swiftly when fired.

However, the authors argue that those who hold a tenure mind-set and are suddenly fired or laid off can fall into three common traps.

First there is the 'lost identity' trap. The people most susceptible to this are likely to have been with a company for some time. They may include founders and senior executives who have achieved positions of power through promotion. They may have come to nurture the belief that they are indispensable. Confronted with sudden job loss they fall apart and often lash out against their former company now rife with what they see as 'enemies'.

In the 'lost family' trap, employees possess tight-knit, emotional bonds with co-workers. This trap is most prevalent among people working in fields such as marketing, magazine publishing, or start-ups, environments with high emotional intensity. On termination, executives in such fields feel grief as they are separated from 'the old gang'. They feel as if friendships have been severed and they've been rejected. They sink into bitterness and depression.

Finally, some introverted executives fall into the 'lost ego' trap; they quietly retreat without negotiating fair termination packages, and may settle for less satisfying work the next time around. Such people tend to work very effectively in areas such as accounting and finance, R&D, manufacturing or engineering, which don't demand high levels of socialization with other constituencies.

To prepare for the eventuality of termination, Peabody and Stybel suggest that we all adopt the assignment mind-set at all times. We should keep our social networks alive, include a termination clause in employment contracts, and consider hiring an agent. If warning signs warrant, we might even volunteer to be terminated.

Terminations are among the most predictable crises in business. With an assignment mind-set, termination becomes predictable on a personal level, too. Then, even a negative experience such as being fired can become empowering. Once you assume control over the way you are fired, you gain control over your career.

Redundancy survival tips

Employees who have recently been made redundant are especially vulnerable and are more likely to make poor financial decisions. And there are plenty of companies in the financial-services industry who view redundancy as an opportunity to make money. In some cases, the behavior of such firms can be astonishingly tactless and offensive. In the mid-1990s, when a cider brewery made a number of staff redundant the police had to be called in to remove advisers and insurance salesman from the factory gate, who were unceremoniously foisting their business cards on the unlucky employees.

Fortunately for employees who are made redundant, companies increasingly offer comprehensive redundancy packages that include financial advice, advice on retraining and looking for work, and counseling. Larger financial advisers may also have specialist departments providing similar services.

The consensus of opinion seems to be that recipients of decently sized lump sums, as a result of redundancy, should take their time deciding what to do with their money. Making long-term investments is a bad idea when you don't know what the short-term holds. Redundancy and financial advisers also recommend keeping organizations such as your bank, mortgage lender, credit-card company and hire-purchase firms informed of your position. This way debts may be rescheduled and payment holidays instituted if necessary.

If you're not an employee of a firm that offers these kinds of redundancy services, do not lose hope. Trade unions offer a range of services to their members, many of which are useful to employees who are laid off. If you are already a member of union fine, if you are not, it is well worth considering joining, especially if you sense trouble ahead.

Failing the services of specialized redundancy advisers or a trade union, if you are resident in the UK you might wish to consult the Citizens Advice Bureau (CAB). The CAB can provide legal and financial advice for free. The legal advice is especially useful if you are unsure about whether your employer has complied with the various statutory regulations when making you redundant. Employers were often unaware of their rights regarding such issues as holiday pay entitlement and the right to take days off to seek work, the CAB will be able to explain these and other rights accruing to workers who are laid off.

Keeping your head above water

◆ **Keep your resume up-to-date.** You should periodically re-evaluate your resume and update it. If you have not done this recently, now is the time. Your resume is a vital part of your job-search armory. Make sure it is the best it can possibly be, by consulting the career adventurer's guide to resume writing as well as other resources.

◆ **Keep your chin up.** The job market is rarely as bad as the media paints it. Even in the worst job market companies are always looking for talented and skilled employees. Sylvia Milne, partner in Career Change specialists Catalyst Career Strategies says 'Evaluate your past successes and don't focus on your weaknesses. Look to your support network of friends and family to keep your spirits up.'

◆ **Re-evaluate.** Now is the time to take a fresh look at your career. Read Section One of this book. Take some of the personality and values tests and see if the results correspond with your own perception of yourself. It may be that your talents and skills – your personality traits characteristics – are suited to an entirely different type of career journey.

◆ **Network**. There is no substitute for networking. If you read this more than once in the pages of this book it is because it is simply one of the most essential skills the career adventurer can master. Continually cultivate your personal and professional contacts. Attend as many industry functions as you are able to.

◆ **Affordability**. You may have ideas of disappearing into the sunset and living on a desert island for a year or so. Or your philanthropic alter ego may fancy a spot of volunteering. Your bank manager may have other ideas. Sit down and assess your finances, only then will you know what you can and can't afford to do.

◆ **Life-long learning.** The more you learn, the more skills you have, the more employable you are. From learning the piano, to building your own website, unless you are renaissance man/woman reborn there should be hundreds of new things you can learn to do. If you can tailor learning towards your chosen career even better.

◆ **History lessons.** You must know yourself and your employment history inside out. Learn every line, every nuance of your resume of by heart. Rehearse why you took jobs, what you achieved there, what you learn there. It is this kind of preparation that saves you embarrassment and humiliation when it comes to interview time.

◆ **Research the market.** Hopefully you can avoid spending hours in the library by using the Internet. In the age of the Internet, research has never been easier. On the Net you can find out about the industries intend to work in, and the companies you intend to work for.

◆ **Keep up-to-date.** Sign up for industry specific e-mail newsletters, read the newspaper, read the trade press, tune into and watch the news on television and radio. If necessary, take a refresher course to keep up-to-date in your chosen field.

◆ **Feedback**. Always be polite and thank those who help you. If appropriate ask for feedback. For example, in the case of rejection following an interview, don't be afraid to ask why. You may not get a straight answer but if you do you may avoid making the same mistake twice.

Networking: your best bet

Despite your best efforts, you may still find yourself out of a job. What to do next? The standard response is to send out a mass of carefully crafted job applications together with updated resume. The result of this frenetic activity is usually no more than a handful of acknowledgements. Chances are that other companies in your industry are also laying people off.

The mass-mailing approach is a waste of time (see Part Two). Your best route back into work is through networking. The majority of clients who turn to outplacement specialists eventually find jobs through networking. This is confirmed by other practitioners in the field. According to Oliver West, global relationship manager at recruitment group Bernard Hodes: 'Knowing people who know people always comes top of every recruiter's poll. As a tool, it is the best route to finding the right sort of job.'[4]

But before you go back and reread the passage on networking in Section Two there are other options. It might not necessarily be the best course of action to plunge straight back into the deep and often muddy waters of the world of work. It may be time to consider a change of direction.

Adventure 12

It took a close brush with death to focus Ted Leonis' thought on what exactly it was he wanted to achieve in life. His hit list ran to 101 items. Try starting here on a less ambitious scale. Write down the 20 things you most want to do while you still can. Let your imagination run riot. If you have always wanted to conquer Everest and stand on top of the world then write it down, it's do-able. Sure, if your life's ambition is to travel to Mars you might be out of luck, so a degree of realism is required, however, this is the time to write down your dreams. It's a great way to crystallize priorities. And hopefully you will get to check most of them off.

Use this list as a foundation for a longer list of lifetime ambitions, say 50 or 100.

THINGS I WANT TO DO WHILE I STILL CAN

1.	11.
2.	12.
3.	13.
4.	14.
5.	15.
6.	16.
7.	17.
8.	18.
9.	19.
10.	20.

CAREER ADVENTURER

JOYCE E. BARRIE *on career advancement*

Title/Position: Founder, President, CFO (Chief Fun Officer)
Company: Joymarc Enterprises, Inc.
Industries: Consulting/Coaching, Professional Speaker, Seminar Leader, TV & Radio Personality

If you're already in a career and want to advance within it, ask yourself:

1. What have you done to get where you are, and what haven't you done?

2. How far have you advanced since you took the position, in both financial and promotion terms? Are you merely getting cost-of-living increases, or rewards based on results that you produce? If it's more based on results, what areas do you have to work on so that you can get noticed and receive the rewards that you want?

3. Are you willing to do what it takes to climb the ladder? What do you think that is? (Chances are if you knew what it is, you would have done it!) The reason people don't know is because they don't focus on the 'what it takes' part. The other reason is that they don't step out of their comfort zones. What it would take is to step out of your comfort zone and make a quantum leap into another dimension to reach the higher level position and greater rewards that you seek. Most people find that really uncomfortable. You have to work harder and/or smarter. The person you've been being will get you the results that you've been getting, so you have to reinvent yourself if you want to get more than a cost of living increase. You have to strengthen both your weak and strong points.

CAREER ADVENTURER

FRANZ LANDSBERGER *on redundancy*

Title/Position: VP Human Resources, Bioscience Division

Company: Baxter, Europe

Industry: Pharmaceuticals

Franz Landsberger started at Baxter, the healthcare company, in April 1990 as the Compensation and Benefits Manager for Baxter Germany. After a year and a half he became the overall HR Director for Baxter Germany, and then HR Director for the BioScience division.

Here Franz talks about redundancy from an HR Director's perspective:
'I am engaged in acquisitions on a European and global level, with a main focus as the HR integration leader for Europe. Industry often makes the quick assumption that a lot of positions automatically become redundant as a result of an acquisition, which is a big mistake. It is very important for everyone involved to have the complete picture of why this acquisition has happened and what the strategic and operational goals are. That clarity in mind will help everyone make the best decisions with regard to organization and people.

You will only be successful with the people you have, because that's all you have. It's very difficult these days to find the 'right' people. Before you treat someone the wrong way you should be sure that this individual is someone that you want to lose. Before looking at redundancy, consider those individuals in terms of their competencies, enthusiasm, etc., and maybe find another place for them.

Many companies talk about people being their greatest asset, but underneath the surface they do not really help them to be successful. Walk the talk. Running a company is very simple. Really. Believe in what you're doing, show respect for individuals, be clear in your expectations, and include people in your decision-making. There are many books that talk about all of that, perhaps number one being All I Really Need to Know I Learned in Kindergarten *by Robert Fulghum (Ivy Books, 1993).*

CAREER ADVENTURER

DONNA MARTIN *on redundancy*

Title/Position: Senior Vice-President, Human Resources
Company: Faulding Pharmaceuticals
Industry: Pharmaceuticals

'Ask questions about why you are being made redundant, so that you clearly understand. Take the opportunity to gain any feedback, counsel and advice from your management. Seek counseling, be it through an outplacement group, or through human resources, to work through your feelings, because you will certainly have a lot of feelings come up during that process. Then take a step back and say, ok, this is an opportunity to really think about what you would most like to do. What kinds of things do you excel at, what are you passionate about? Think about and focus on those things, and you are much more likely to find yourself in a next role in which you can be successful. Think of it as an opportunity to assess yourself and move on, as an opportunity for change.

Be very proactive in networking. Reach out to people. The more you talk to people, the more you find out that lots of people have been through this. You can then get beyond the feeling of 'what's wrong with me', which happens quickly, and realize that it's something that happens to a lot of people, and that you can move through this and learn from it.'

REDUNDANCY RESOURCES

1st UK Redundancy Network – is an offshoot of Business and Professional Partners, Ltd, (www.bppartners.co.uk), an executive search firm and management consultancy. Thus it is not a free service, but based on membership (12 months for £85 plus VAT). It enables those who have or are experiencing redundancy to network with others in similar situations, share feelings (perhaps including anger over the hefty online membership fee when so many other free bulletin boards and chat forums exist), a suite of tools, techniques, templates and processes, and links to relevant information including books, articles, websites and other resources. One-on-one consultations are also available in 1.5 hour increments. **www.1stukredundancynetwork.co.uk**

Redundancy Help – is a free site with links to information on redundancy in the UK for both management and employees, including definitions of voluntary and compulsory redundancy, and various reasons for redundancy. The management section essentially provides a crash course on communicating and executing a redundancy program. It includes suggested alternatives to redundancy, communication plans, sample letters, selection criteria and guidance on the provision of aftercare. Resources for employees facing redundancy include information and advice on job hunting, legal and financial concerns, jobseeker's allowance (UK unemployment benefits), books on related topics, and links to commercial resources. **www.redundancyhelp.co.uk**

Her Mentor Center – Career changes and choices are often interwoven with other significant life transitions involving family, health, emotional and psychological needs, and so on particularly in mid-life. Her Mentor Center is designed to help partner women through these significant mid-life transitions. The site offers a free Q&A with a panel of mentors, subscription to a free newsletter and archives of past newsletter issues, links to online resources and books, guidance on finding and effectively using support, mentoring and more. Fee-based services include mentoring on an individual or group basis. **www.hermentorcenter.com**

North Pole Memo – perhaps the greatest aid through redundancy, outplacement, downsizing, rightsizing, or just plain getting fired, is a well-developed sense of humor. Still, it can be hard to find humor in the grim corporate slash-and-burn routine. If misery loves company, than you may love to know that even Santa's workshop is cutting back considerably this year. For a wry look at the inside scoop, go to **http://www.thehumorarchives.com/humor/0000140.html**

Catalyst Career Strategies, Inc. – Based in Toronto, Canada, this consulting firm provides strategic career guidance to executives and professionals, and a career support program for employers. This helpful website offers eight steps to follow in the first stressful weeks after being fired, guidance on job-search strategies and on changing jobs or careers, a short career quiz and other useful information. **www.catalystcs.on.ca**

Notes

1. 'New owners have some Capital ideas to sell hockey', *Slam! Hockey Online,* Sunday, 13 June, 1999.
2. 16 August 2001, *The Sunday Times* business section.
3. The right way to be fired *Harvard Business Review* July/August 2001 Maryanne Peabody and Laurence J. Stybel.
4. 21 October 2001, *The Sunday Times*

"Two roads diverged in a wood, and I –
I took the one less traveled by,
And that has made all the difference."

Robert Frost

SIX

THE ROAD LESS TRAVELLED

LIVING THE LIFE OF THE FREE AGENT

You don't have to rely on an employer, you can blaze your own career trail as a free agent. Working for yourself requires special skills:

What will you sell?

Who will your customers be?

Will you be able to pay your bills?

What work should you take on and how much?

Who will you turn to for support?

1. FREE ENTERPRISE

Growing numbers of people are throwing off their corporate chains to work for themselves.

Freed from their work cubicles, these free agents decide when and where they will work and for whom. The road less traveled is fast becoming a super-highway.

Is the life of a free agent for you? There are thousands of businesses you could start. From florist to farmer, from potter to psychologist, from sound studio to ski school. You may have visions of building the next General Electric or simply going it alone as a freelance or free agent. The range of possibilities for budding entrepreneurs is as wide as their imaginations. Whatever your aspiration, the opportunities for starting a business are probably greater now than at any previous point in history. But all free agents face some of the same challenges. The ones who succeed share certain characteristics. Talk to some free agents and you will quickly discover that the world they live in is very different to that of the employee. Only you can decide if you've got what it takes.

The rise of the free agent

The role of entrepreneurs in successful economies has long been recognized. Without them there would have been no industrial revolution, and no Silicon Valley. In recent years, however, entrepreneurs have increasingly come under the spotlight. In part this reflects fundamental changes in the landscape of work. More and more people now work for themselves. Whereas in the past entrepreneurs typically created organizations, today they are able to make a living in some cases a very good living on their own or in very small groups.

Entrepreneurial units of one or two are increasingly common. In the 1990s an unprecedented range of people took control of their own work, liberating themselves from the daily grind of nine-to-five jobs. For them, singing the company song lost its appeal. Under their breath, many were already humming Frank Sinatra's refrain 'My Way'.

In the United States, tens of millions of people have now freed themselves from corporate control. According to Daniel Pink, formerly Al

Gore's chief speechwriter, and now fast becoming the guru of free agency, there are more than 14 million self-employed Americans. There are 8.3 million independent contractors; and a further 2.3 million who work for temporary agencies. This adds up to around 25 million free agents, he says, 'People who move from project to project and who work on their own, sometimes for months, sometimes for days'.

Many of those who have left the corporate fold actually find greater security in self-employment. The redundancies of recent years mean that being on your own no longer holds the fear it once did. Attitudes are changing. A marketing consultant recounts how a bank was dubious about giving a loan to someone without a real job. 'If one of my clients goes away, I'm still going to make my payments,' she explained. 'But if I'm employed by Apple and they let me go, I'm out on the street.' That's free-agent logic.

A similar pattern is unfolding in cities around the world. In London, independents working in design, fashion, broadcasting and the Internet, for example, now make up ten percent of the workforce and generate £50 billion ($82.5 billion) per year in the UK as a whole. That figure is set to rise to £80 billion ($132 billion) in the next decade (six percent of the country's GDP.)[1] It's a global movement.

'The economics of free agency relate to a basic psychological shift, a tremendous San Andreas Fault between employee and employer', says futurist Stan Davis. Earthquakes are inevitable.

SoHo, So You?

SoHo (small office/home office) describes companies with one to 20 employees. It is the fastest growing segment of the business community. What are the characteristics of the typical US small business? A Dun & Bradstreet survey of companies with fewer than 100 employees found that the average small business has three employees, generates between $150,000 and $200,000 in revenue each year, operates from 1.3 locations, is privately owned, not franchised, and has an owner who puts in a 50.4 hour week. Doesn't sound too bad does it?

The notion of free agency is integral to the way a new generation of workers thinks. More than a statistic, it's a state of mind. Many remain inside, or on the periphery of companies, but their mental software is different to previous generations. They think for themselves. They think differently. Twenty years ago it couldn't have happened. Work has changed.

There are two forces at work. Push and pull.

◆ The push is the destruction of the notion of a job as a permanent fixture.
◆ The pull is the move to new organizations and business models as the principal drivers in the creation of wealth.

Together these two forces have accelerated the rise of individualism. Together they represent a potential double whammy to the notion of working for a large corporation.

New attitudes and new technology are now converging to create the environment where free agents can thrive. These new footloose career adventurers have evolved to fit this new environment. Technology, including the Internet, plays a part in that. But it's only an enabler. Equally important is their perception of, and relationship towards, employment.

Free agents have grasped the fundamental work reality: if they don't create value either for themselves or for someone else then they won't have a job. No amount of corporate cocooning can change that fact of economic life. Being entrepreneurial is an economic necessity. Survival depends on it. The question, then, is do you want to do it for yourself, for a company, or for some other organization?

For a growing number of people, it's a no-brainer. Why, after all, would they want to line someone else's pockets? Why would they trust their skills to someone else? Why take that chance?

These people are entering the workplace with their own agenda and are not prepared to stick around if their needs are not being met. Companies had the chance to earn the loyalty and respect of their knowledge workers. But companies blew it. It didn't happen overnight. It took time. Shifts in the employment market during the 1980s and 1990s have had a profound influence on the way people think about work and their relationship to employers.

In no small part this has been made possible by the arrival new technology, which has allowed individuals to greatly expand their markets. Thanks to the marvels of information technology, a computer programmer in Bangalore, India, or Phoenix, Arizona, can do business with clients anywhere in the world. For many people, especially those with specialized skills, geographical location no longer limits their work catchment areas.

Entrepreneurial role models

Entrepreneurs are the new heroes. There is growing interest in entrepreneurship at the level of the individual. A fundamental shift in aspirations appears to be taking place. Growing numbers of people now want to work for themselves, and run their own businesses.

The entrepreneurial urge crosses all age groups. The so-called new economy spawned an array of youthful entrepreneurs. Simultaneously, it also re-ignited the entrepreneurial urge among the older generation. Many of the youthful entrepreneurial endeavors were encouraged by older investors and mentors. The dot.com gold rush bears a significant responsibility for the flight to freedom and entrepreneurship. And while the deflating of the dot-com bubble may have cooled the entrepreneurial ardor, there is evidence that the underlying trend remains strong.

'ePeople', a study carried out in the summer of 2000, offered a much-needed perspective on the post dot.com crash career landscape. The report explored the views of early career professionals towards the opportunities offered by start-ups. It was the second major study by the Career Innovation Group (Ci Group) an international alliance of 18 major employers, created to try to understand the new generation of talented young workers. The findings indicate that far from being over, the real entrepreneurial revolution may be just beginning.

Based on an international survey of 1200 high-flyers in 63 countries, the study confirmed that today's generation are far more entrepreneurial in their aspirations than their predecessors. If correct, then this is significant. It suggests that the dot.com phenomenon was symptomatic of an underlying trend.

According to the report's authors, Colin Graham of the Robert Gordon University in Scotland and Professor Charles Jackson of Kingston Business School, the advent of the Internet simply accelerated a process that was already underway. 'The dot.com boom, it seems, was just a skirmish in a much greater revolution,' they say, 'in which the Internet has allowed the growing army of free agents and small ventures to communicate and collaborate.'

CAREER ADVENTURER

Dr PETER NEVILLE *on self-employment*

Title/Position: Animal Behaviorist
Location: Salisbury, Wiltshire, UK
Website: www.pets.f9.co.uk

'When you're self-employed you have a great fear of being self-unemployed. You work hard and don't say no to things that perhaps you should. So it can be a bit all-consuming, though I'm not sure it's different from anyone else who works for themselves. But I wouldn't swap it for being middle management in a corporation that can go bust because some idiot didn't get the marketing right. I know a few colleagues who've been laid off because their company was taken over, merged, etc. They're in their early to mid-40s with nowhere to go and a lot of responsibilities. I wouldn't want to be in that position. They're not in control of they're own destiny.

I've been going long enough that I'm not worried if the phone doesn't ring for a few days. In fact I enjoy it. And I get up late if I feel like it. The other side of that coin is my very good friend and partner in our education business looked at me and said 'You're *!#$ unemployable!' I'm forty-three and haven't worked for anyone in fifteen years.'

Keeping good company

The fact is that entrepreneurship has been gaining momentum since the late 1960s. Since the 1950s, the growth in new firm creation in the US in particular has been striking. In the 1950s around 200,000 new US firms were created every year. By the mid-1970s that number had trebled to 600,000 start-ups per annum. By 1994, it had reached 1.2 million, and by 1996 it had soared to around 3.5 million.

The entrepreneurial trend is not confined to the United States. Outside of the US, the countries with the highest per capita levels of entrepreneurial start-up activity include Brazil, Australia, Canada, Argentina, Norway and South Korea.

The dot.com gold rush didn't start in earnest until after 1996. Fuelling it was a huge growth in the venture capital industry, another significant factor in the new found interest in entrepreneurs. The rise of the venture capital industry itself is based on traditional capitalist principles. Superior return on investment has ensured a plentiful supply of capital. But entrepreneurial activity is no longer confined to making money. A new breed of so-called social entrepreneurs is applying entrepreneurial practices to addressing social issues. They are moving the provision of support for the socially disadvantaged away from the begging-bowl approach to one that pays its way.

2. HAVE YOU GOT THE RIGHT STUFF?

Can you learn to be an entrepreneur or is there something in the genes that creates a Richard Branson (the Virgin boss), Sam (Wal-Mart) Walton or (the recently departed razor magnate) Victor Kiam?

According to a study of young entrepreneurs, there do seem to be some in-built traits or typical profiles recognized in the average thrusting business maker.

A study commissioned by the McQuaig Institute in Canada, in November 2000, investigated 1,509 members of the Young Entrepreneurs Organization (YEO). Those studied all ran businesses worth at least $1 million and were under 38 years of age. Each of the 239 women and 1,270 men in the study were given the well-established psychometric test, the McQuaig Word Survey.

The results are pretty clear: a huge majority (nearly 80 per cent) had strong innate leadership traits. They are born leaders. The sample showed a strong level of what McQuaig calls, "Dominance" people who by nature are competitive, goal-oriented, ambitious and decisive. Many also exhibited a noticeable level of aggression. 'These are natural traits, not ones that people

While you can teach yourself business via the airport book shop, or by putting in the time to gain an MBA, the most successful business people are those who are natural born entrepreneurs.

have learned', says Roger Summerfield, Principal Associate with The Holst Group and an expert on the MacQuaig Word Survey. 'The study shows us that entrepreneurs have a natural ability to make decisions over a wide area, they can make things happen, they are independent and restless'.

Summerfield also points to the findings that most entrepreneurs have a high 'Sociability' rating, that means they are good 'people people' are willing to empathize, 'and know how to fire you with a smile'. According to the study, there is a small difference between female and male entrepreneurs: males scored higher on the Dominance rating, females scored higher on Sociability than males. The one surprising result of the study is that male entrepreneurs scored higher than females on 'Relaxation' a trait that focuses on patience and steadiness. Does that mean that female entrepreneurs are less 'cool and laid back' than their male counterparts? The jury is out on that contentious issue. Many believe, however, that there is something in the DNA that marks out entrepreneurs.

The nature over nurture position is firmly held by Taylor Edgar, of the telecom and Internet group, Iomart. 'While you can teach yourself business via the airport book shop, or by putting in the time to gain an MBA, the most successful business people are those who are natural born entrepreneurs', he says. Edgar is sure that commercial heroes possess an inherent flair and single-mindedness that is second nature and cannot be taught. 'This is what sets them so starkly apart from the rest of the herd. This gut instinct, charisma and nose for business is invariably allied to an uncanny knack for surrounding themselves with the best team possible and having a vast network of information sources. Of course, this inbuilt business ability may not always be apparent at start-up, but these people are very quick learners and are soon distinguishing themselves by what becomes very swiftly a trademark: their rapid and unrelenting progress in building and growing businesses', he says.

This view is echoed by John Farmer, co-founder of the SMS text messaging organization, Carbon Partners. He is one of the new generation of buzzing entrepreneurs that have emerged from Cambridge. Farmer completed his MBA at the University's Judge Management Institute in 1999 and had his eye on starting up his own company after years of working for others. A business school education helps, he says, but it only gets you so far. 'The MBA was a great opportunity to see what opportunities were out there', recalls Farmer. He feels that entrepreneurship is definitely in the blood (he is after all son of Sir Tom Farmer, the founder of Kwik Fit). 'When I was a kid I never thought, "I want to be entrepreneur when I grow up", but I read a lot of business books and through the family came into contact with many great business people, good role models.'

Larry Page, co-founder of the Internet search engine company Google, had this advice to people who want to run a business one day:

'I'd tell them that it's not that great a job. There's a lot of stress and a lot of responsibility, and you never know if you're doing the right thing. It's not a job for everybody.'

What kind of attributes do people need?
'The ability to get people to do things, even in informal situations, is really important. Stanford was a great training ground for that, because I had to convince people that they should work on Google. I didn't actually have any employees. Four people were working on Google off and on for three years [before we launched]. The reason they did it was because I motivated them and convinced them this was a good thing to work on.'

His year at Cambridge convinced Farmer that there was gold in the text messaging business. 'Back in 1999, that's what I could see really taking off especially among young consumers'. Farmer is about to launch a new product for this market, one which will enable mobile phone users to use SMS chat rooms, download games and even make a blind date. 'At school I didn't have the stereotypical entrepreneur's urge to run a sweet stall or play the stock market but I am very enthusiastic and energetic in everything I do. My main drive is to build something worthwhile and being part of a new dynamic sector is very exciting. I love being with people and sharing my enthusiasm for the new technologies.'

Farmer also runs a web-site for actual and would-be entrepreneurs called Click2Think.com. Here you can find a study on Cambridge entrepreneurship by another Judge Institute MBA graduate, Iain Edmonson. Over a period of two years, Edmonson talked to business starters in the cauldron of Silicon Fen, young entrepreneurs like Adam Twiss and Damian Reeves, who turned Zeus Technology, a classic student-bedroom business, into a £30 million plus company. Edmonson concludes that entrepreneurs do indeed have specific traits; 'Self belief is the biggest factor that helps them to speak with authority and persuade would-be investors. The real entrepreneurs can take knocks, if their ideas are rejected, they say that "It's your fault, you're not understanding me". They are usually pretty evangelical about their projects and develop a thick skin'.

No one can really be sure whether entrepreneurs are born or develop. Edmonson believes that we all have entrepreneurial traits but it's a matter of how we develop them. A study by Krueger and Brazeal in 1994 suggested that environment plays a key role in encouraging and nurturing entrepreneurial behavior. They found that where an environment encouraged innovation and change, where mentors and role models were held up, then entre-preneurialism would be more likely to flourish. This would support Edmonson's view that innovative clusters such as those in Silicon Valley (and the Cambridgeshire Fens) are most likely to spawn the next generation of great entrepreneurs. The conclusion seems to be that the enterprise debate ultimately comes down to nature *and* nurture.

If you are considering becoming an entrepreneur, a word of warning. It's tough. For every Pierre Omidyar (eBay), Julian Richer (Richer Sounds) and Richard Branson (Virgin) there are thousands of would-be entrepreneurs who crash and burn, many before the first year is out. For a number of years, Scott Birnbaum has been global chief of the private equity practice at Mercer Management. Birnbaum, who's a vice-president with the consulting firm, leads Mercer's interface with both venture capitalists and entrepreneurs. He talks with one or the other every day. In fact, over the last two years, Mercer has been directly involved in over 150 entrepreneurial deals spread over eight different industries with a total value exceeding $27 billion.

'The number of entrepreneurial ideas each year is anyone's guess,' Birnbaum says, 'there are millions.' However, he notes, it's not the number of would-be entrepreneurs that's significant: it's how long they last. 'When it comes to entrepreneurs, there's a 99 percent failure rate. Only one percent of the entrepreneurs who make it to the marketplace last five years or longer.' (There is some disagreement about the level of small-business failures depending on how 'failure' is classified, what type of businesses are counted and other criteria but the general consensus seems to be that a high proportion of small businesses to cease trading in the first five years.)

There is no blueprint for the perfect entrepreneur, but research and experience suggest that entrepreneurs share a number of common characteristics.

There are a profusion of wish lists of the traits required by entrepreneurs. Tim Waterstone, founder of the eponymous book chain and a successful entrepreneur, observes that great entrepreneurs share the following characteristics. They:

◆ are inspirational leaders;
◆ believe their vision is right and don't falter in their belief;
◆ derive energy from being the underdog;
◆ are driven by a strong desire to beat the competition and to defeat the enemy;
◆ combine enormous energy with fortitude and tenacity;
◆ demonstrate courage by taking risks;
◆ have a deep respect for the people in their team, and value team building;
◆ understand how money works. Not necessarily in a technical way, but in an intuitive way.

Recent research by the Hay Group identified nine competencies essential to entrepreneurial success:

◆ Integrity   ◆ Confidence
◆ Initiative   ◆ Self-direction
◆ Commitment   ◆ Selling
◆ Drive and determination ◆ Leadership.
◆ Directiveness

There are a host of other lists, rankings and profiles. Distill down their essence and these six attributes appear essential:

Energy and enthusiasm

Entrepreneurs are dynamic, restless creators. They buzz. 'I always run through the office', says Amazon's Jeff Bezos. 'I mean physically I'm a little bit hyper kinetic. That's why I like this environment.'

High energy levels are vital for entrepreneurial success. There aren't many lazy success stories out there. Energy is a prerequisite for the job.

There is a difference between possessing energy and being a seriously hard worker. Maximizing entrepreneurial energy is more than running fast or working harder. Anyone can work 16 hours a day. For entrepreneurs, how they spend their time, how they enthuse others is more important than the hours they work.

'Entrepreneurs are particularly strong in their ability to align their own needs and priorities with the needs of the business, and generally put the business before their personal and family concerns,' says Chris Dyson, director of the Hay Group.

The energy characteristic of entrepreneurs leads them to question what others assume. Their belief and desire to change things gives them energy and inspires others. They discover energy from the mundane, from the routine. They extract ideas to generate enthusiasm. They invent different approaches and try new things. They generate energy from themselves and stimulate energy out of those they work with. They attract people with energy.

More than money

To top off energy, entrepreneurs are natural enthusiasts. Not for nothing does a major US auto manufacturer carry out training in enthusiasm. 'Some people think enthusiasm at work is childish. We reject that notion. Emotion, enthusiasm, energy, passion, whatever you call it, is the lifeblood of entrepreneurial activity,' say Matt Kingdon, Dave Allan, Kris Murrin and Daz Rudkin, the founders of the innovation consultancy ?What If!. 'Too many managers have erected barriers to protect themselves from these very emotions. We believe that in time, creative revolutionaries will swarm over this barricade. They will demand to know why emotions are excluded from a large proportion of people's lives. They will throw off the chains traditional managers have shackled themselves and others with. Yes, we are passionate about this.'

For entrepreneurs, the job itself provides a reservoir of motivation. Their motivation is rarely purely financial. In the Hay Group research, Robin Saxby of ARM Holdings observes: 'Although many of us at ARM have now achieved a position of personal financial security, it is the non-financial achievements that are most motivating and satisfying.'

Entrepreneurs who succeed rarely start off with the sole intention of making money. They want to change the world, solve a problem or maximize the potential of their brilliant idea. Money is a welcome by-product of success.

Communicating the essence

The next characteristic of entrepreneurs is an ability to focus energy and thinking on the issues, trends and people that really matter. They channel energy into the essence of what is important.

The ability to cut out the dross, the distracting stuff, has never been more important. Choice and complexity can overwhelm. The supply of information and opinions that business leaders receive is incredibly complex. Despite the flood of calls, the letters, faxes and e-mail, entrepreneurs make sense of it and extract the important details from the vast bulk of paper and input from a wide variety of sources. No matter what, they keep communication as simple as possible.

Entrepreneurs understand the importance of precise communication. 'Say you have a meeting and someone goes home at night and the next day there's a ten-page memo that's crisp in evaluating the ideas, that's a smart piece of work. In software, it's not like ditch-digging where the best is two or three times faster than the average. The best software writer is the one who can make the program small, make it clever,' says Bill Gates. At one company executives giving presentations are restricted to no more than three overheads.

The need for considered brevity also applies to entrepreneurs at the earliest stages of their business. Their presentation must cover the length of an elevator journey. David Ishag of the Internet investment firm, Idealab, observed: 'Plans have to be light as a feather. You have to be able to make your case in an elevator – and I'm talking about an elevator in a very low building.'

Entrepreneurs communicate, distil, communicate and then distill some more.

Maximizing technology

When it comes to new technology entrepreneurs get it in a way most big companies can only dream of. 'The nerds have won,' management guru Tom Peters proclaimed when the market valuation of Microsoft exceeded that of General Motors. Nerds, geeks, techies – we've invented labels for them, but the reality is that increasingly, they are the people who call the tune.

Many in business still regard technology with suspicion. It is powerful but prone to gimmickry; it has potential but they're not sure for what. (At the other extreme there are those who see it as the cure for all known organizational ills.)

Entrepreneurs regard technology as a tool. It is a tool to make money, have a better quality of life and a tool to enjoy yourself. Technology is seen by them in an entirely practical light.

Failing persistently

Failure is increasingly recognized as an essential part of personal and professional development because, simply, it provides learning. 'Because many professionals are almost always successful at what they do, they rarely experience failure. And because they have rarely failed, they have never learned how to learn from failure,' says Harvard Business School's Chris Argyris. Entrepreneurs have mastered the art of failing. They fail, then fail again. Along the way they learn.

Failure is inextricably linked to risk. 'Share, understand and confront then risks, even if they fail, can become learning,' advise leadership theorists Randall White and Philip Hodgson, authors of *Relax, it's Only Uncertainty*. 'Fear of failure has to give way to respect for failure and learning from failure. Executives need to toughen up. They are going to be tested and tested again in ways they never previously contemplated. This takes humility and bravura. Building from failure tests executive resilience. Our work with derailed executives found, not surprisingly, that all executives make mistakes. At senior levels these mistakes could be costly, capital intensive ones. The crucial thing was that when the successful executives make mistakes they acknowledged and accepted them. The derailed, however, rejected them, often blaming others. The resilient executive takes in experiences, particularly failures, and incorporates them into a structure of concepts that is used to evaluate future experience and guide future actions. Resilient executives learn from experiences, both good and bad.'

Entrepreneurs recognize that, though painful, failure is good for you. When life gives you lemons, make lemonade.

Constant learning

More than ever before, education equals money. In the new economy, it pays to have an education. Where once entrepreneurs pooh-poohed a formal business education, they are now trained to the max.

Business schools are now falling over themselves to prepare entrepreneurs rather than corporate administrators. From being a peripheral subject, entrepreneurialism is moving to the heart of the world's MBA programs. Like other schools, INSEAD, the international business school based just outside Paris, has beefed up its entrepreneurial courses in recent years. This is a clear response to student demand. 'Thirty years ago MBA students dreamed of running General Motors; ten years ago they dreamed of working at Goldman Sachs; five years ago it was McKinsey. Now they dream about running their own company,' observes Antonio Borges, who recently stepped down as dean.

Many students go to business school with the express intention of starting a business. Between 30 percent and 40 percent of Harvard MBAs do something entrepreneurial at some point in their careers. But since the mid-1990s there has been a significant change: students now start companies within four to six years of graduation, rather than the 10 to 15 years previously. More than one-third of INSEAD MBAs now end up running their own company five to ten years after graduating. The problem is that the world is hardly awash with academics with specialist e-commerce or entrepreneurial knowledge.

The human touch

The final important element in entrepreneurial DNA is that they value the human dimension. They ooze empathy, easily and effortlessly. Previous generations just paid lip-service to the idea. Entrepreneurs know that people make the difference. Their greatest commitment is to their immediate colleagues and staff. Entrepreneurs are people people.

CAREER ADVENTURER

JOHN HUDDY *on running your own business*

Interviewee: John Huddy
Title/Position: Owner
Company: The Illustration Cupboard
Location: London
Website: www.illustrationcupboard.com

How would you describe your job?

'I refer to myself as an art dealer. This is not just for my own satisfaction. Part of the task I have undertaken is to raise the status of original picture book art and place it on a commercial level with other fine and applied art forms.'

How did you get in to your present business?

'The progress has been evolutionary. I never planned it nor did I ever expect to be doing what I am currently pursuing. Having started at St Andrews University in History, I changed mid-degree to History of Art, and found a subject that I truly enjoyed. This impromptu change has been one of the more influential of my life. I was determined to make use of the degree and subsequently went to work in the auction houses, firstly at Bonham's in Knightsbridge as a porter for a few months, where I met a number of people my age all setting off for careers in the art world. Some are still very good friends. I was subsequently taken on by Christies St James and worked there for two years until the beginning of 1995. I then left to work for myself as a dealer in Italian and French old-master drawings. The ensuing shift in to Picture Book Art was largely due to a family connection in the children's book field.'

What particular skills does it require?

'Working for myself in a commercial enterprise requires the ability to engage in, albeit at a relative simple level, all the tasks one would find in a large company. I find myself everyday at different points working in managerial, administrative, accounting, manual and technical roles. It is the ability to learn these skills efficiently and switch between them that makes the business run. I hope in time to delegate as much of this as possible.

Communication is the main skill in working with artists and catering to the interests of collectors. It also requires the ability to communicate to and handle staff and service suppliers. All of these relationships are different, but overall it is important to be clear, decisive and confident.'

What are the good and bad things about working for yourself?

'One of the main reasons I left corporate life to work for myself was to stop commuting. I had through school and work been doing this on and off for about 20 years. This is just an example of the main advantage of working for yourself. I believe most people do it for the lifestyle. The opportunity to do things as you want when you want and to be responsible for the actions you take. The hours, the work and the security are neither greater nor less. Being able to chart one's own course is the important factor.

Acting as a dealer is an individual business as everyone is your competition, and coupled with working for oneself can mean that this is one of the worse elements as it can seem a bit lonely at times. The absence of daily social interaction with office colleagues, although sometimes a blessing, is a loss. However I have found an interesting camaraderie amongst the self employed which goes some way towards redressing this balance.

The highlights and lowlights of running my business:

It is a business of extremes. One has to push through the lows to reach the highs, and sadly vice versa too. I remember 1 March 2000 particularly well. After two winter months without an exhibition and very slow sales I woke up truly believing that I had to come to an end of what I was doing. That was until the telephone rang and I was told that the arts pages of The Times had published a large article about my work. Within minutes my course had once again changed direction, and although I was not any the less happy about my circumstances I knew this was an important break. It gave me the confidence to believe what I was doing was right and that people were interested. I knew I had to continue. It was a morning I will not forget as it taught me that things can always change.'

What advice can you give to those contemplating casting off the shackles of wage-slavery?

'**Personality:** Working for oneself requires a certain mentality. It is not for everyone, and requires sacrifice on levels material, personal and with those close to you, emotional. To consider one's expectations and needs before starting is vital.

Drive: It is important to identify the reason why you are doing it. What is the engine that is going to drive the motor? There should be a good enduring reason for working for oneself.

Skills: Make sure that one has the physical skills to do it. Typing, pc skills, IT knowledge, financial and accounting skills, physical strength. (I have realized in these years that one has to be physically much stronger working for yourself than in corporate life as there is nobody to carry and lift for you.)

Resources: *Check one has the resources, and think to whom one can turn when those run out, as they are sure to do.'*

CAREER ADVENTURER

JULIAN RICHER Founder and CEO of Richer Sounds, *on life as an entrepreneur.*

Entrepreneurship modules are very popular on MBA programs but do you think you can be taught to be an entrepreneur?

'You can teach basic stuff like understanding a balance sheet, writing cash flows, IT skills. But buying and selling, which is at the root of every business, negotiating, getting on with people, handling oneself in meetings, these are things which it's very difficult to teach formally. They're the product of experience. If schools could find teachers who had been there and done that, it would be very useful. The problem is that entrepreneurs are a pretty impatient lot, not good at sitting around in classrooms; plus the fact that while they're doing that, opportunities are passing them by or so they feel. I don't deny that I might have learned a good deal if I'd gone to a business school, but I wouldn't have had my first Rolls-Royce at 23 either.'

So where did you learn about being an entrepreneur?

'My parents both worked for Marks & Spencer while I was growing up, so it came with the morning milk, as it were. M&S in the 1960s was caring and socially aware, but very demanding and I think that's stayed with me. The other big influence on my life was a socialist housemaster at school. In a small way I was starting to become active as an entrepreneur by the time I was 14. He didn't mind that, but he did teach me how important it was to care about people if you went into business. Later on, when I was 19, I learned a lot from the man who backed me when I started my first shop. He was a successful photographic discount retailer. Apart from that I just picked up things along the way.'

Did you have any kind of grand plan when you started?
'Not at all. I just started buying and selling and hoping to get more customers
through word of mouth about our products and our service. Initially I was very
grateful that I could pay our suppliers at the end of the month. I think what drives
an entrepreneur forward is energy and enthusiasm, not a plan or even a vision.
At least that's been true in my case. I was just happy to be in business and
getting on with it. Still am.'

They say mistakes are a great teacher. What did you learn from yours?
'When I was 21 and had been in business for a couple of years, things went
wrong. My overheads were too high, I thought turnover was profit, I had a lousy
bookkeeper and my auditors on the outside weren't keeping a proper eye on
things. I just wasn't important enough to them. I lost a lot of money at that point
but I also learned very quickly, the hard way, that it's a great mistake ever to lean
back and think you've made it.'

So what sort of things do you need to monitor?
'Well the cash is the big one. Is the cash that's coming in going into the bank? It's
like water going into a bucket, you'll never fill it if there's a hole in the bottom. In
retail you know your cost price and your selling price. What you don't know is
how much is going out through the backdoor through pilfering and such like. The
money going into the bank is crucial.'

Do you think handling growth is a problem for entrepreneurs?
'I haven't found it to be so. The mechanics are just the same, it's just that the
numbers have extra noughts on them.'

How hard do you personally have to work?
'I have a loose, but pretty full working week which includes weekends, though
sometimes I take a day off during the week. Work and fun are pretty
indistinguishable for me, though I tend to do stuff I like doing because that's
what I do best. On the other hand, there has to be some discipline in the week.
There are boring bits in your work that can't be avoided and people need to be
able to see you on a regular basis. You can't just swan off whenever you want,
though I have a lot of outside meetings which I find much more stimulating and
just as effective as sitting in the office all day.'

GREAT ENTREPRENEURS

FRANK WINFIELD, Woolworth

A pioneer of price-driven retail, Frank Winfield Woolworth (1852-1919) laid down the tradition of value-for-money merchandising followed by companies such as Wal-Mart. On the way to success Woolworth endured considerable personal hardships, working for little or no money, suffering long periods of illness and watching three of his first five stores fail. Others would have given up. Woolworth persisted with his retailing vision, building his 'five and dime' empire from a single store in 1879 to one thousand by 1911.

Woolworth's concept of a business based on bargain goods survived until 1977, when the Woolworth corporation announced that it was to close its last 400 F.W. Woolworth five-and-dime stores in the US. Modestly, Woolworth attributed his success not to his own genius but to delegation and the ability of others. 'So long as I was obsessed with the idea that I must attend personally to everything,' he observed, 'large-scale success was impossible. A man must select able lieutenants and or associates and give them power and responsibility.'

3. BUILDING YOUR BUSINESS

There are seven steps to becoming self-employed:

1. THINKING
What?
How?
Why?
Where?
Who?
When?

2. QUESTIONING
Yourself
Potential customers
Family
Friends

3. WHAT'S THE BIG IDEA?
New or old
Quality or quantity
Think differently

4. TESTING
Does it work?
Market research
Learning about the market

5. TIMING
Now
Later
Getting the time right

6. CREATING
Sole-trader
In partnership
Franchise
Limited company

7. STARTING
The first sale

The development of a business often follows this pattern:

Stage One: Survival

This can last for up to two years and is the most testing time for the business and all those involved in it. At the beginning merely surviving from one week to the next is an achievement. Every new customer is a cause for celebration and every week of business a triumph.

Stage Two: Settling down

During this stage, concerns with merely surviving become secondary, though they linger at the back of your mind. Preoccupations with simply keeping afloat are replaced with an emphasis on consolidation and consideration of where to go next. The way forward can seem fraught with decisions and difficulties.

Stage Three: Development

Having weighed up the possibilities, the business now moves forward, seeking development in new markets or investing in new technology or buildings. This is the growth period. The business achieves a certain status.

Stage Four: Building the business and its people

A business that develops its products and services alone is liable to encounter problems. People, too, need to be continually developed. The emphasis during this stage, therefore, should be on building and developing new skills within employees and yourself. You may, for example, have to develop team working skills or improve your technological or mechanical skills.

But, bear in mind the crucial don'ts.

◆ **Don't move too fast.** Impatience is sometimes necessary but, in the early stages of building a business, it is more likely to cost you money than make it. Companies often go bust by moving too fast and trying to develop too quickly, without adequate financing or back up.

◆ **Don't lose control.** Subcontracting or passing jobs on to someone else runs the risk of damaging the fragile fabric of your reputation if it goes wrong. You have to keep control, while still being flexible, responsive and quick.

◆ **Don't respond too slowly.** If a customer enquiry yields the response 'Our sales representative will be around to see you soon' your demise may be more imminent than you think. You need to respond with a firm date. No sales support means no sale.

Adventure 13

Ask yourself the following questions. These are not optional - any business needs to know the answers if it is to develop.

◆ What do your customers expect from your business?
◆ Do you consistently deliver what they want?

◆ How do you know?

◆ What do your employees expect and receive from the business?

◆ What do your suppliers expect and receive from the business?

CAREER ADVENTURER

SUSI RICHARDS

Interviewee: Susi Richards
Title/Position: Product Developer
Company: Safeway
Location: UK

'Basically a product developer's job is to come up with new ideas for fantastic new food for our customers. As I work in chocolate this involves eating loads of chocolate from all over Europe to find the best, I then work with suppliers to produce our own version.

At university I studied French but have always been a real foodie, which is really the most important thing, you need to love food and eating! I got into the job through Marks & Spencer, joining their graduate program in stores. Then moving into Head Office to retrain as a Product Developer.

The recruitment process normally entails talking about food and innovation, packaging, answering food-related questions etc. Most people would come from a food background, perhaps having trained as chefs or having worked in the industry, I was a bit of an exception to the rule.

The most important attributes are to be passionate about food although other skills such as teamwork, negotiation, leadership, communication, self-starter, visionary come in handy.'

What are the best and worst parts of your job?
'Best aspect of job is coming up with ideas and seeing them become reality and selling on a shelf. Worst aspect is dealing with company politics. Good career structure with lots of companies now looking for people with these skills.'

CAREER ADVENTURER

BETTY BIANCIONI *on freelancing*

'You get a lot of variety and different challenges. For example, once a company had an artist who had drawn all of these pictures for a black-and-white ad that they were doing, and they wanted recipes that went with all of these black-and-white line drawings. So I had to come up with a variety of recipes for them to choose from, based on what shapes were in the drawings, and if a shape had a glop on it in the picture, what kind of sauce that might be.

You never know what kind of job you're going to get; you never know who it's going to be when the phone rings, what company may be calling. You always get to meet new people, work with different personalities, and see how different people do things and run their companies. You get to work your own schedule. And no one says 'boo' about dress code.

Another major advantage is there's no traveling on a daily basis. You can listen to the traffic reports and laugh. In terms of everyday work, there's less stress. I always do my best for the client, but I don't have to get caught in the corporate politics. I can just come in, do a great job, and not be worried about whose foot I may be stepping on, or any of the politics that go on in the corporate world.

The biggest downside is that you're not guaranteed a regular paycheck. There is a lot of scrambling to do when the phone doesn't ring. Another downside is when your biggest client decides that they no longer have the budget. It's hard to plan financially as a freelancer, because you never know what your finances are going to be. If you plan vacations and you get a call for a big huge job, you have to decide what you're going to do: take the job or vacation.

Another downside is that you don't have contact with people on a regular basis. Sometimes you're kind of just by yourself at home. And with phones, faxes and emails, sometimes you don't even get to see the client until the actual photo shoot. I edited four books for Time-Life, and I never physically met the people that I worked with. The graphic artist who designed the book lived on Cape Cod, and the editor was down in Maryland.

You really have to be disciplined. If there's a time slot when you're supposed to do something, you have to make sure you're doing it. There can be a tendency to put things off. You've got to be reliable and meet deadlines without excuses. You need *to be self-motivated and disciplined, and self-policing in not letting things slide and in making sure that your work is well done, not sloppy or incomplete. You have to have a good presentation. You have to be good with people because you're promoting yourself. You also have to be someone who can kind of flow with things, and give people what they want. That's what they are paying you for. Rely on your ego to get the job, but then let your ego go once you're doing it. You have to know that this is not about you; it's not personal. There are times you don't get the job. They may not hire you because the sound of your voice reminds them of someone they don't like. Whether you get the job or not, it's not about you.'*

CAREER ADVENTURER

BETTY BIANCONI *on work-life balance*

'Work-life balancing was easier when I worked at home and my daughter was young. I could spend the time that I wanted to with her, and then work when she was in school, taking a nap, etc. So I could work without my having to be 'away'. The freedom to plan my own schedule really helped.

Making long-terms plans for financial security can be challenging. It may look like you're not making any money for the year then all of a sudden you make more than you have for the past two years. You can't rely on pay rises that happen when you hang out in a company long enough. Sometimes you're working seven days a week, and sometimes you're off for weeks. You always know that you should be calling people, sending out cards, making contacts. But if you start doing that when you're not busy, people get that you're not busy. And when you're busy you don't have the time to make those contacts. So that's another flow thing. Another is that you can plan things but when a job comes up you may have to let your social plans go. If you don't have understanding friends and family, sometimes it can be a little strained.'

If you're a budding entrepreneur then time is money. In the early stages at least, most entrepreneurs are the jack of many trades and master of quite a few, yet it is unrealistic to expect to master everything from contract drafting to running your own retirement investment portfolio and still have time left over to find clients and do your work.

Unless you are truly an organizational genius and one of those rare people who manages to find time for everything and still remain sane, it is a good idea to outsource some of the essential functions. Yes, it costs money. But hopefully it will leave you free to make enough and more money than necessary to cover the cost. Equally important, outsourcing may help you keep in the right frame of mind to conduct your business in the first place.

Areas where outsourcing is possible include:

Insurance

Your business will require insurance to cover possible litigation and subsequent damages arising from various events. The sources of such litigation might include a secretary injuring themselves in your home (the workplace), libeling someone if you are a writer, or damage caused to a third party by a product sold by you.

Insurance brokers will source competitive insurance premiums, find suitable policies, and arrange insurance on your behalf. They will also help you deal with claims and negotiate on your behalf if necessary with the insurance company. How much do you pay the broker for the service? Normally nothing at all. The broker recoups his remuneration as a commission on the policy from the insurer. Commissions range from five to 20 percent. If you pay large insurance premiums, but your insurance needs in terms of sourcing new policies etc., are minimal, you may be able to arrange a flat rate fee and have the broker pass on the commission to you.

In addition to their normal services insurance brokers occasionally offer added value services such as risk-management advice. This type of service can be particularly useful to 'free agents'. Yes, insurance is there to pay claims if and when they arise but, despite the financial burden being met by the insurer, claims are still costly in terms of time and hassle. Far better to avoid them in the first place. Effective risk management can help you do this.

Law

Lawyers are expensive. Generally they charge by the hour and, in the UK at least, that hourly figure can range from £60 to £500 plus. As you might expect a senior partner in a top-ten law firm in London or New York will cost you more than an assistant solicitor in a small provincial firm.

Contacting a lawyer is a good idea for drafting contracts and general commercial legal advice. In these cases a junior is often a cost-effective route. This is because in routine matters a more senior lawyer partner may pass the task to a junior in any case. Whereas a junior will always refer upwards any matters that are beyond their competence.

Litigation is entirely different proposition. Even minor litigation is likely to prove costly. Cases that have the potential to go to a higher court that requires senior representation or the services of a barrister will probably be prohibitively expensive for any but the richest of free agents. This is where legal expenses insurance comes into play. This type of insurance will cover the cost of defending lawsuits. There are of course policy exceptions and legal insurance doesn't cover all types of litigation. Nonetheless, given the cost of litigation, the insurance is worth purchasing.

IT

Information technology is both a boon and a bane for many 'free agents'. Often IT is the enabler that allows individuals to operate effectively and profitably as free agents in the first place. E-mail and the Internet, mobile phones and the computer, these are the essential tools for many road warriors and home workers. They are also the target of much cursing, and the cause of many wasted hours.

When the computer screen goes dead and the usual checks and measures refuse to bring it back to life; when your home network crashes; when the printer churns out meaningless garbage; when you can't get your favorite word-processing program to work properly, when a virus wipes out your hard disk; screaming, shouting and throwing things or counting to ten may momentarily relieve the stress but is unlikely to get you back to work. Unless you are a technology whiz kid, and even if you are, the solution to your IT problems may well be beyond you. It is at times like these that the services of a technology consultant can be invaluable.

And technology consultants are not just there to fix problems, they can help you set up systems, and provide advice on the latest IT developments. Small, local IT providers, with a reasonably lengthy trading history are often the best source of IT help for the free agent. It may be cheaper to purchase technical equipment from a variety of direct retail sources, but often the best approach is a combination of background knowledge gleaned from a cursory reading of computer magazines combined with the help of your local IT business. If you source your equipment from them, despite it costing a little more, then they are more likely to help you out when your screen goes blank for some unknown reason.

Another important service provided by IT consultants is website building. Although building your own website is always an option depending on your level of HTML proficiency, it can be a time-consuming and frustrating process. Screen resolution, browser idiosyncrasies, graphics optimizing, these are just a few of the things you need to get to grips with if you plan to build your own website. With professional website building services available for only a few hundred pounds or dollars, often including the purchasing of your domain name, and setting up the web hosting, this is often the easiest solution.

Accountancy

As the responsibility for computing taxes is increasingly devolved upon the individual, so the need for an accountant becomes greater. Accountants come in a large variety of shapes and sizes, from the international practices, to the small one-man bands. The scale of charges similarly varies from a small fixed fee to many hundreds of pounds or dollars an hour.

For most independent workers the services of a small local practice will be sufficient. In addition the smaller the accountancy practice, the more likely they are to give attention to your returns. Although an accountant's professional services can be expensive, the independent contractor can go some way to alleviating the costs. The more work you do on your accounts the less work your accountant does, assuming you are doing a competent job. It pays to find out what software package your accountant uses and maintain your own records using the same software. Assiduous record keeping also lessens the accountant's final bill.

Rather than bother your accountant continuously for advice, arrange to see them on a regular basis, and save your queries until then unless they are urgent.

Financial advice

Finances are difficult area for the independent entrepreneur. As a trade-off for the responsibility of freedom that independent work affords, free agents sacrifice the benefits taken for granted by many employees. These include healthcare provision, company cars, mortgage subsidy, business expenses and perhaps most importantly of all, pensions. With no company pension, subsidized or otherwise, the independent worker has a number of difficult choices to make.

At the most fundamental level there is choice of whether to purchase a pension at all. This will often depend on personal circumstances and the tax position of the individual. While pensions were once seen as de rigueur because of the tax incentives they offered, today a wide range of other savings vehicles with tax benefits are available.

Attitudes towards finances vary from the financially indifferent who know, and wish to know, nothing about investment practice and those who wish to know every detail. For the former, the decision to go to an independent financial adviser is an easy one. For the latter, the decision is a lot more difficult. Either way, is important to remember that what is at stake is a comfortable retirement. Handing over your financial affairs completely to an independent financial adviser may seem attractive, but no matter how uninterested in financial matters you are, it is essential to have some background financial knowledge.

This is not say that independent financial advisers are untrustworthy. Or even that, in the light of numerous financial scandals, such as the mis-selling of pensions in the UK, it pays to be cautious although it does. The point is that you need to be equipped to make informed decisions about your finances. To do this it is necessary to have a basic understanding of the options available. After all if you know nothing about finance and three different independent financial advisers offer you different advice how will you know which advice to follow?

Once you have done your homework using one of the many books or magazines available on the subject, then you're ready to visit and to take advice from an independent financial advisers on how to arrange your finances.

PR and marketing

Another time-consuming but essential activity, PR and marketing is often considered an activity only outsourced by large companies. Increasingly however, small to medium agencies are offering services for free agents. Even if it's only the drafting of advertising in the local press, it can often be worth turning to a professional. Guerrilla marketing is also a specialist area relevant to independent contractors. Individuals are unlikely to be running ads on national television to advertise their services. Although no substitute for networking, the professional services of one of a small but growing band of guerrilla marketers, can be invaluable for finding cost-effective means of spreading the gospel about your services.

GREAT ENTREPRENEURS

KING CAMP GILLETTE

The man who shaved a nation, King Camp Gillette (1855-1932), the US safety razor entrepreneur, made a fortune from improving a mundane, everyday product. Before Gillette applied his razor sharp mind to the problem of male grooming, shaving involved cut-throat razors or unsatisfactory stick razors that were as liable to injure as to shave, especially if used on the latest transport technology, the train.

Taking some advice from another entrepreneur who had made a fortune from the cork bottle stopper, Gillette developed a disposable razor that worked. So confident was he in his idea that in 1901 he formed the American Safety Razor company and persuaded investors to back him, before he had a commercial product. The investors were not disappointed. Gillette's savvy marketing skills pushed sales up from 51 razors and 168 blades in his first year, to 250,000 razor sets and 100,000 blade packages by 1905.

Much of Gillette's success was down to pure force of character. He was one of the first businessmen to exploit the cult of personality and the corporate brand.

By printing his reassuring face on the razor blade packaging he became world famous, and his image became a symbol of quality. Unfortunately, the Wall Street Crash of 1929 took its toll, robbing him of his personal fortune. But, although his later entrepreneurial efforts came to nothing, attempts to extract oil from shale for example, his legacy lives on in the company that brought us Right Guard and Mach3 razors.

The road less traveled is not for everyone. It requires distinct personal characteristics and involves a degree of autonomy and risk that many would feel uncomfortable with. There are plenty of potential negatives. Working for yourself can be lonely, it will involve long hours, it carries considerable pressure, the burden of which will weigh heavily on your shoulders. There will be sleepless nights a-plenty for the fledgling entrepreneur and in many cases the considerable investment of time and money will hang in the balance and, unfortunately, for a majority the dream will turn out to be an illusion and end in failure.

If the outlook is really as bleak as this you ask, why would anyone want to work for themselves? The answer lies in the potential rewards for those who succeed, both in monetary terms and in other areas.

Even if the business does eventually cease trading the experience can be a beneficial one. As you have read, one of the qualities needed to become an entrepreneur is the ability to deal with failure, and to come back stronger than before. The great entrepreneurs, Walt Disney, Walter Chrysler, Richard Branson, et al, have encountered both Triumph and Disaster and in Kipling fashion treated those imposters both the same. Early in Walt Disney's career, for example, he lost his first big cartoon character Oswald the rabbit to another studio, as well as some of his artists; but as a result of this setback he was forced to invent another character which turned out to be Mickey Mouse. Chrysler took his new motor car to the national car show only to be refused admittance on the grounds that it was a prototype, he exhibited it in a hotel foyer instead, where it garnered as much, if not more, attention.

If you have the stomach for it, starting your own business is undoubtedly character building, even if it doesn't all go to plan. If it does work out, however the rewards can be tremendous. For some the ability to control their own work, when, how and where they work is sufficient reward, in itself. Even if the financial rewards are average. For the truly successful however the material reward can be staggering. You only need to check out the list of the world's richest individuals to realize the potential upside of starting your own business.

In the Forbes 2001 billionaires list of the top 15 richest people in the world, six founded the business empire on which their wealth is founded: Bill Gates (no.1,

$58.7bn, Microsoft), Warren Buffet (no.2 $32.3bn, Berkshire Hathaway), Paul Allen (no.3, $30.4bn Microsoft), Larry Ellison (no.4, $26bn, Oracle), Karl and Theo Albrecht (no.5, $25, Aldi). One, Sir Kenneth Thomson, (no.14 $16.4bn, Thomson Corp.) continued to build on the empire built by his father.

Few people become fabulously wealthy working for someone else. If serious money and all the trappings that come with it is your career aim then starting your own business is the most likely route for realizing that ambition. The odds of becoming the next Bill Gates are, admittedly, slight, but who knows. Maybe you are that one in a million.

Alternatively, you may make just enough money to survive but rejoice in your new found freedom. Enjoy.

RESOURCES FOR ENTREPRENEURS

eMarketer.com

The marketing budget is often a start-up's biggest spend. Before you start signing cheques, a little information won't go amiss. Marketing advice and statistics are available on the Internet from a variety of sources but to save all that browsing time, pay a visit to eMarketer.com.

eMarketer is recognized as an authority on online marketing. The website provides a comprehensive resource for anyone interested in e-commerce. Information from hundreds of leading research sources is aggregated, filtered, organized and analyzed and put up on the website in easy-to-understand tables, charts and graphs.

Sections include: eReports, in-depth analysis of specific market segments and eNews, up-to-date news and analysis on industry issues. One especially useful section is the statistics section. Here surfers can get the low-down on ecommerce spending figures, demographic trends on the Internet and other information essential for planning an online marketing campaign, or assessing the market when writing a business plan.

An eNewsletter is available. Emailed to over 30,000 market professionals every week, it encapsulates the main points from the website. It is free but visitors need to register before they can receive it.

Entrepreneur.com

The fact that entrepreneur.com is one of the largest and most frequently visited sites on the Internet is a measure of the entrepreneurial spirit at large in the business world. The company's website has over 500,000 unique users and racks up more than 3 million page views a month.

As you might expect, entrepreneur.com's content is aimed at would-be dot.com millionaires. But it's not simply a site for dot.com start-ups. It offers interesting and practical information for anyone thinking of, or in the process of, starting a business.

In April 2000 entrepreneur.com overhauled, redesigned and re-launched its website. Content on the site is both wide-ranging and deep. Business travelers can check out the 'Quick Guide to Business Travel', for example, and learn how to make their travel budget stretch a little further. Executives in unchallenging, comfortable jobs dithering about joining the free agent society can consult a motivation expert to help them take those first steps to relinquishing the company car.

Elsewhere there are areas where you can chat online to other businessmen and experts. Or you can use the onsite search facility to search through a list of Entrepreneur Magazine's 100 best websites for small business. And, should you need to buy anything, then head for the marketplace where you can even locate vacant office space to start the next Microsoft or Amazon.

Links: **www.entrepreneur.com**

Fast Company

Fast Company magazine is widely acknowledged to be the bible of the new economy. Before launching the magazine, in November 1995, Alan Webber and Bill Taylor spent a combined total of eleven years at the *Harvard Business Review*, the bastion of old-economy theorizing.

From their vantage point, Webber and Taylor could see the world was changing quickly. A global revolution, they concluded, was changing business. A new magazine was needed to show how companies were transforming to compete in the new world. The idea clearly struck a chord, and the magazine received the backing of luminaries such as business guru Tom Peters and the esteemed Harvard academic Michael Porter.

In issue no. 1 the co-founders outlined their manifesto: *Fast Company* aims to be the handbook of the business revolution. We will chronicle the changes under way in how companies create and compete, highlight the new practices shaping how work gets done, showcase teams who are inventing the future and reinventing business.'

Fast Company set out not only to report the business revolution, but play a part in shaping it by creating a vocabulary for the new economy. Many issues later, the magazine can justifiably claim a spectacular success. A new generation of entrepreneurs has grown up on its diet of cutting-edge informative reporting. It has won its fair share of awards on the way. In 1999, for example, it was named Magazine of the Year by *Advertising Age* and came top of *Adweek's* hotlist. Possibly the greatest measure of its success, however, is the place Fast Company has found on the shelves of the major players in the new business revolution. Its one great weakness is its US-centric bias, although that may now be changing as the Internet revolution rolls across Europe and the rest of the world.

Links: **www.fastcompany.com**

Inc.com

The online extension of *Inc.* magazine, Inc.com proclaims itself as the website for business builders who are 'long on work and short on time.' The site offers advice, information products and online tools aggregated from many different sources. It is a particularly useful website for small to medium-size businesses and entrepreneurs.

One of the best sections on the site is the advice section, divided up into two principal areas: 'Getting Started' and 'Growing Your Business'. 'Getting Started' provides articles, case studies, research reports and tips on the best way to go about starting up your own business. The business plan is a key element in any start-up's strategy to raise finance and yet it is difficult to find good information on the Internet about what exactly is required in a business plan without having to pay for it. Inc.com, however, in the 'Writing a Business Plan' subsection supplies links to sources on the net where information about business plans is freely available including comprehensive templates if required.

Under 'Growing Your Business' a comprehensive range of subjects is covered. These include those that you would expect to find such as marketing, e-commerce, sales, finance and law, plus more surprising, but no less interesting, categories such as the section on business ethics.

Links: **www.inc.com**

Redherring.com

Redherring.com is the online version of the magazine that provides leading analysis of the companies and trends shaping the technology business. Many regard Red Herring as the new economy investor's bible. The magazine takes its name from Wall Street parlance. Apparently, in the 1920s, American investment bankers called preliminary investment prospectuses red herrings. This was to warn investors that the documents were not finalized. The prospectuses were bound in red covers. The magazine aims to provide early information on up and coming investment opportunities.

The Red Herring website is divided into four different channels. These include: Investor, looking at tech companies from the investor's perspective; Venture Capital, including information about upcoming IPOs, who is being funded and why; and Technology, detailing the impact of technology on different industries. Redherring.com is especially good on the financial aspects of the new economy. It has excellent in-depth coverage on venture capital issues, IPOs and startups, for example.

Links: **www.redherring.com**

Adventure 14

Thinking of starting your own business? Can you answer these questions?

What?

What do you want to make or do? Is it a product or a service? Be clear in your mind what you are offering and don't feel tempted when friends suggest that you should also provide x, y and z. Stay with your original idea and keep it simple.

Come up with a pithy statement of what you are trying to produce or the service you would like to provide. This, in business jargon, is a mission statement.

> **What do you want to make or do?**
> e.g., I want to use my experience in corporate catering to manage catering services for large companies based in the north-west.

What are your skills? Why are you well qualified to start the business? What are you good at doing? What areas of expertise and experience can you use to make the idea work?

What new skills do you need? Obviously running your own business demands different skills than working for an organization. You have to honestly identify areas where you need to improve your skills. It may be you need to go on a computer course or that you need to learn business French or both, but you have to identify any gaps in your knowledge and then attempt to fill them.

What skills?

The following are just a small number of the skills you might already have, will need or would like to have. Some or all might be beneficial to your business. Use these as a starting point to answer the questions which follow.

- ◆ People-management
- ◆ Basic accounting
- ◆ Computing
- ◆ Typing
- ◆ Languages
- ◆ Communication skills
- ◆ HGV license
- ◆ Leadership

- ◆ Motivating others
- ◆ Self-motivation
- ◆ Selling skills
- ◆ Telephone skills
- ◆ Marketing skills
- ◆ Team working skills
- ◆ Working alone
- ◆ Written communication

SKILLS YOU HAVE	SKILLS YOU NEED	SKILLS YOU WOULD LIKE TO HAVE
1		
2		
3		
4		
5		
6		
7		
8		
9		
10		

◆ How?

How will you make the product or provide the service? Think of the basic process of making the product. Will it need a lot of space or a lot of people? If it is a service, think of how you will provide it quickly, on time and to a high quality.

How will you make the product or provide the service?

Will it involve

◆ Just you

◆ You and one or two others

◆ A small number of full-time staff

◆ A large number of staff

◆ Occasional part-time workers

◆ A large amount of machinery and equipment

◆ Minimal machinery and equipment

How do you know it is something which people want? Can you put it down to:

Experience While your experience may have convinced you of a business idea, tread carefully. Is your experience recent or appropriate? Was it formed in a different context? You still have to check that your conclusions are valid.

Intuition Many business people profess to having an innate understanding of what it is that people want. Politicians are also prone to speaking on behalf of the British people, without consulting more than a hand full of like-minded individuals on a particular issue. If you are starting a business, you must back your beliefs with hard evidence.

Advice and opinions of others You should take the protestations of other people that something is a great idea with a pinch of salt. If something is a sure winner, you have to ask why aren't they doing it themselves? Invariably they will retort with an implausible excuse, too little time, too little money, etc.

Research To find out what people really think and the likelihood of them buying your product or service requires research.

◆ Why?

Why do you think the business is a good idea? Write down another short explanation of why you think you and your business idea are viable. Think of why people will buy your particular product or service? Is it a truly new concept? Is it cheaper than the competition, easier to use or simply better quality?

> **Why do you think the business is a good idea?**
> e.g., Because I can supply a reliable, value for money, flexible, nourishing and tasty service on time, every time.

◆ Where?

It is early in the process, but still worth thinking about where you are going to do the work. If you want to open a greengrocer's shop the 'where' seems obvious enough but you have to carefully consider the precise location which will best suit the business. This applies to all businesses. If you want to open a small manufacturing unit, you need to think of the optimal size and location, you will have to consider things like the size of the machines, the space taken by raw materials and stock, and the room needed for deliveries to be made.

> **Where will you carry out the work?**
> **Location**
> An office
> A shop
> A factory
> A workshop
> At home

◆ Who?

Who will buy it? This is the basic question which every business has to focus on, whether it is a giant multinational conglomerate or a corner shop. Without customers there will be no business. Anyone starting a business must have a clear idea of who the potential customers are and where they are.

Do you already know potential customers? If you are confident that there are customers out there you may already know some. This can be vital as you develop your ideas.

The customers

◆ Are they organizations or individuals?

◆ Who actually makes the purchasing decision?

◆ When?

◆ What are their criteria for making the decision?

◆ How do you know what the customers want?

◆ Does the customer know what he or she wants?

Who will be involved in the business? Think of how many people will have to be involved in the business from the outset. These might include family, friends, your bank manager, your accountant, full-time and part-time workers, as well as yourself.

Who will it be necessary to involve?

Person	Status	What skills do they offer?
Accountant	Adviser	Financial advice; accounts; credit control

◆ When?

When do you plan to start? Timescales vary from business to business. It might be feasible to start within a few weeks or it might take months, perhaps years, to get the business off the ground. At the moment, what do you consider to be a realistic timescale?

There is no need to provide instant or comprehensive answers to all of these questions. There are bound to be blind spots or areas which remain very vague, at this stage at least. These questions are not easy, but they need to be answered before you start your business. If you ignore them you increase the risk of missing the mark entirely.

4. THE ENTREPRENEUR WITHIN

Intrapreneuring

If the idea of starting your own business is appealing but you don't feel confident enough to make the commitment some, employers offer an opportunity to sample the entrepreneurial life without all of the associated risk. Occasionally, companies will allow employees to start up their own ventures within the company. This half-way house is known as intrapreneuring.

Gifford and Elizabeth Pinchot were perhaps the first to herald the arrival of the 'intra-corporate entrepreneur' back in 1978, and Gifford is credited with coining the term 'intrapreneur'. His book, *Intrapreneuring: Why You Don't Have to Leave the Corporation to Become an Entrepreneur* came out in 1985; the American Heritage Dictionary added the term 'intrapreneur' in 1992, and the rest, as they say, is history.

History has moved on. Intrapreneuring has grown up and become subsumed within the broader realm of 'corporate venturing.' The Center for Business Incubation in the UK (www.ukbi.co.uk) defines corporate venturing as 'a formal, direct relationship, usually between a larger and an independent smaller company, in which both contribute financial, management or technical resources, sharing risks and rewards equally for mutual growth.' These relationships may take the form of intrapreneurial ventures, as when large companies spin-off new businesses and/or technologies. However, they may also involve the provision of equity and/or non-equity investment to small, independent ventures.

Corporations are increasingly partnering with venture capitalists in financing such ventures, according to Harvard Business School's Henry Chesbrough, in a recent article in the *California Management Review*. There have been several cycles of corporate venturing activity since the 1960s, he says, which typically dissipated during market downturns. He suggests two things distinguish the most recent cycle. First, venture capital structures are being used to encourage internal entrepreneurial activity and risk-taking. And second, the presence and magnitude of the independent venture capital sector, which barely existed during earlier cycles of corporate venturing activity, competes with corporate venturing programs for the same top managerial and technical talent.

There are vital distinctions between independent and corporate ventures, according to Chesbrough, that need be addressed in order to ensure the effectiveness of corporate venturing programs. 'While they may do well to mimic certain VC practices, corporate venture structures ultimately will only work if they can deliver strategic benefits to their sponsoring companies,' he asserts. 'They must leverage the potential advantages of corporate ventures.' Those advantages include corporations' much longer life span, he says, which in turn enables them to support longer-range ventures. Major corporations may also have the ability to finance larger-scale projects that would be beyond the capacity of independent venture funds.

A large company also has the ability to provide its new ventures with physical, technical and knowledge resources that would be difficult, if not impossible, for an independent venture to acquire. Corporations also have a potential advantage, Chesbrough notes, in the development and coordination of complementary technologies that may be needed for the success of certain technology ventures. Finally, corporations may, if they so choose, foster learning from failed internal ventures, which can support the future entrepreneurial activity of their employees, whereas independent ventures tend to disband upon failure and any potential learning scatters to the winds.

These observations highlight a major shift in perspective on intrapreneurial activity. In the past, the talents and characteristics of the intrapreneur have garnered much of the spotlight. That focus is now shifting toward the features of organizational environments that support successful corporate venturing. For example, in a recent issue of *Executive Excellence*, Leo I. Higdon, Jr., president of Babson College and former vice-chairman of Salomon Brothers, says that, 'In entrepreneurial efforts, having the right environment is as important as having the right people.'

His sage advice for developing successful corporate venturing programs is based on his work with major companies, and on the findings of a massive international research effort called 'The Global Entrepreneurship Monitor', co-sponsored by Babson College, The London Business School and the Kauffman Center for Entrepreneurial Leadership. The study, which involved 43,000 surveys and 800 expert interviews in 21 countries over several years, found that differences in entrepreneurial activity accounted for as much as a third of the difference among nations in economic growth, and a significant portion of their differences in new-job creation.

The research findings will no doubt intensify the race to create national and corporate environments that foster both entra- and intra-preneurial venturing. And the demand for entrepreneurial talent should intensify along with it, especially as e-commerce begins to globalize.

So what does all of this mean to your average, everyday, increasingly sought-after intrapreneur? For one thing, the advantages of corporate venturing described above may prove to be more enticing to entrepreneurs during down market cycles, suggests Henry Chesbrough. And the differences in organizational contexts for corporate and independent ventures has a significant impact on the types of resources available to intra- and entre-preneurs and the ways in which they acquire those resources, according to Patricia Green, Candida Brush and Myra Hart, in their 1999 article for *Entrepreneurship Theory and Practice.*

For example, the intrapreneur benefits from the reputation of the corporate parent, these authors say, which may help foster trust in the new corporate venture by resource providers. That heightened trust, rooted in the history and legitimacy of the parent organization, may make it easier for the venture to obtain financing from both internal and external sources. In addition, they say, the longer developmental timeframe associated with corporate ventures provides an extended opportunity for the intrapreneur to develop social capital networks, thereby increasing his or her access to financial, technical and other resources.

Unlike the independent entrepreneur, the intrapreneur has a bank of organizational policies, procedures, systems, and culture to draw upon, the authors note, thereby freeing up time that may be more profitably devoted to core venture activities. However, these potential assets may be disadvantageous if they inhibit the new venture's flexibility and responsiveness.

Clearly, awareness of the impact of contextual factors on the intrapreneur is rapidly increasing. Among Gifford Pinchot's ten enduring commandments for the intrapreneur (www.intrapreneur.com) is 'Honor and educate your sponsors'. vital part of that education may be how to create corporate environments that make intrapreneurial ventures thrive.

CAREER ADVENTURER

GIFFORD PINCHOT *on Intrapreneuring*

In 1985, Gifford Pinchot published *Intrapreneuring*, a book which, through the lens of time, has proved to be seminal. It argued that the core concepts of how to be an entrepreneur could be adapted in creative and unique ways by corporate managers. The book created a wave of introspection inside the corporate world; and, consequently, many companies have relentlessly pursued the creation of an 'intrapreneurial' culture throughout their organization.

In 1999, Pinchot, along with Ron Pellman, wrote *Intrapreneuring In Action: A Handbook For Business Innovation* (Berrett-Koehler). Pinchot did not rely on theoretical ideas in his books. Having been both an entrepreneur and intrapreneur himself, he has helped to launch over 500 new products and new businesses, some now scoring over one billion dollars in sales. He has also been CEO of a successful Silicon Valley software company. Pinchot has consulted to more than half of the Top 100 corporations. He lives and works from Bainbridge Island, just off the Seattle coast.

You invented the concept of intrapreneuring decades ago. Do you see corporate managers more receptive to the concept today?
'Yes. Bureaucracy is no more appropriate to the information age than feudalism was to the industrial era. Alert leaders recognize that to compete in today's dynamic marketplace they must release the intrapreneurial spirit of their employees. The only question is how.'

Are companies, by and large, more innovative? Do they need to be?
'Right, companies are more innovative, because they have to be. The world moves on, leaving the slow-moving in the wake. One can't drive stressed-out employees to be more innovative with traditional techniques. The solution lies in releasing the intrapreneurial talent of the organization to find and implement creative solutions to the challenges it faces. Union Carbide's Specialty Chemical division announced its strategy and called for intrapreneurs. One hundred and fifteen responded and within a few months they launched 14 new products.'

Your latest book talks about a special role that senior managers can play to promote intrapreneurs. What is that?

'Even the best intrapreneurs depend on the support of one or more courageous sponsors. Good sponsors:

◆ Pick out the right intrapreneurs and projects to support;
◆ Bet on people, not just ideas;
◆ Coach without taking over;
◆ Help the intrapreneurs get the resources they need.

Our innovation audits generally show that fewer than 10 percent of managers are good sponsors of innovation. Texas Instruments did something about it by training their top 250 officers to be better innovation sponsors.'

In an earlier book, you advised that true intrapreneurs should go to work 'prepared to be fired'. Is that still your advice?

'Successful intrapreneurs have to manage the fear of authority inherent in every human being. It helps to keep in mind that the bosses really don't have the power to do anything terrible to you. Even the worst thing, firing, is but a major inconvenience. You won't die, you won't starve, and your children can still go to college. Remind yourself, 'I will survive!' Your spine straightens, your gaze steadies and people get out of your way. At the worst, you have practiced the skills you need to be an entrepreneur on someone else's nickel.'

Thoreau talked about people living lives of 'quiet desperation'. You see many employees and managers in that sad state; or do I misread you?

'They've succumbed to fear. They've given up their values and their dreams. (They have agreed to be dominated by a system that gives them little emotional nourishment in return.) It's far better to be an intrapreneur: to have a dream and strive to make it happen. (And if you fail, lick your wounds, rest for a bit and try again.)'

CAREER ADVENTURER

JIM GUSTAFSON *on entrepreneurs*

When one sets out to become an entrepreneur, someone who risks his own capital and career to start a new business or an intrapreneur, someone who does a similar thing, only inside an existing corporation, there are no papers to file, no license to obtain, no oath to take before a civic official.

Instead, he or she must simply convert good intentions and strong passions into determined, focused efforts that yield measurable results, which is what Jim 'Gus' Gustafson did years ago, has been doing ever since, and is doing today. Gustafson has been an entre/intra-preneuer since founding the Student Leadership Association as a university undergraduate in the early 1980s. Now, as Vice-President and General Manager of MECHdata (www.electricjob.com), he leads a Des Moines, Iowa, company experiencing profitable and dramatic growth, while many other dot.coms are fast becoming 'road-kill' on the information superhighway.

You live differently with risk and the anxiety that comes with it, to from those who don't have an entrepreneurial bent. How do you cope?
'To me, one's comfort with taking risks has always gone hand-in-hand with one's comfort with embracing change. That said, if you think of risk in terms of a linear scale with 'risk-averse' on one end and 'risk-inclined' on the other, then I (and most other entre- and intra-preneurs) would be off-the-chart change agents and risk takers. However, temper that with the fact that most entrepreneurs are as intuitive as they are passionate, so they are continually (albeit sub-consciously) minimizing 'real threats' naturally through their actions as they pursue their goals.

As far as the anxiety, I would argue that most entrepreneurs would have far more anxiety by observing the status quo. To an intra- or entrepreneur, not following their heart and passion would be as physically and emotionally damaging as venturing into a crowded theater would be for an agoraphobic.'

What are your personal top three rules for others who aspire to the entrepreneurial life?
'The first (and necessarily in this order) is to follow your passion. All worthwhile intrapreneurial endeavors will come with roadblocks, nay-sayers and ardent challengers. You must be passionate and absolutely driven by your beliefs to be able to navigate the bumpy terrain.

Second is to implicitly trust your intuition, even when everyone else tells you that you're a complete whacko. True entrepreneurs are pioneers, often coming from outside whatever industry they find themselves in, so they are not constrained by the current paradigms that exist. Instead of modifying existing norms, they throw the rule book out entirely and re-draw the picture altogether. This takes tremendous courage and the unwavering ability to trust in your own gut instincts when you are blazing that new trail.

Lastly, it is imperative that you spend time cultivating other intrapreneurial leaders around you. World-class leaders are inevitably world-class teachers (as well as learners) and what better way to ensure that your cause comes to fruition than by inspiring others to a similar level of passion and enthusiasm? This also indirectly helps create an organizational culture that values and breeds innovation.'

Most people think entrepreneurs are just out for the money, to get rich. Has that been your experience? Do you think it should be this way?
'I was recently reading a book both about and by Rob Ryan, who founded Ascend Communications in 1989 with three engineers. The company went public on Friday 13 May 1994 at $13.00 a share. By 1995, the stock jumped 721 percent; if someone had invested in the start-up just two months after the initial public offering, he would have seen a return of 3,223 percent less than two years later. Now, such stories are all over the planet, just waiting to be found. And while I don't know and can't speak for Rob Ryan, here's my own view on entrepreneurs and wealth creation.

Clearly, the opportunity to hit a big payday is an attractive background proposition that comes into play with many entrepreneurs. But my experience has been that the primary driving factor for most entrepreneurs is an absolute passion and desire to create something new or solve some existing problem in an innovative way. In fact, for the entrepreneurs that I know personally that money has always been secondary. They are experts at spotting unmet societal needs and have an absolute fire in their belly to mobilize whatever resources are necessary to meet these needs. They are obsessed with the opportunity to create something new. And if they 'win the lottery'' in the process, that's the icing, not the cake.'

If entre/intrapreneurs aren't in it for the money, such people nonetheless generate wealth. How do you see money, your own, the company's, the investors' capital?
'It has always been my belief that if you follow your heart and do what you love to do, you will ultimately be successful. For some people, the amount of money in their bank account is an indicator of success. For others, it is a chance to create

something new, regardless of the commercial or societal value placed upon it. And for others, it's a chance to make a positive contribution to someone's life or in the world around them.

Most of the entrepreneurs that I know have ultimately become extremely successful, in financial terms. However, most of them have also suffered devastating monetary losses along the way while pursing their passion. I am absolutely convinced that if you stay true to your passion, trust in your intuition and teach others along the way – you will ultimately be successful – in whatever terms are important to you, as well as your company.'

This sounds a little bit too altruistic or dreamy . . .
'While I have been working feverishly to score successes in the marketplace, I have also been pursuing a doctorate in this field. I have been surprised, and reassured, at how much of the current thinking about entrepreneurs is altruistic.

I am studying a very special and growing breed of entrepreneurs that I'm calling Socially Responsible Pioneers (or SRPs). These are the founders and significant contributors of organizations that are making some positive impact on the world around them. They are the visionaries who created organizations like Habitat for Humanity and Up With People, that were established, not to make the founder rich and famous but to truly solve an unmet community or global problem in an innovative and sustainable way. These people to me are our true heroes.

There is also a growing literature base on a broader entrepreneurial subset, called Social Entrepreneurs. Traditionally found in not-for-profit organizations, these innovators are also driven by a social vision or mission, rather than by the pursuit of profits, and are increasingly being found in small and large private-sector companies. There is a swelling global consensus that we need to start looking beyond governments and the voluntary sector for solutions to our social troubles and, as such, there is a growing demand for entrepreneurs who can bridge the gap between social and commercial needs.'

You have also worked inside huge corporations. How would you gauge the level of intrapreneurship?
'Most large organizations fail miserably when it comes to creating widespread cultures that foster and reward entrepreneurial or intrapreneurial activities. Traditionally, most entrepreneurial organizations are small and flat with virtually no bureaucracy. Contrast that with the enormous, hierarchical and incredibly complex global corporations of today, and you can see the inherent structural challenge.

What you will find in most major corporations today are pockets of entrepreneurial brilliance. Typically, this occurs because an intrapreneurial mid-level manager, business-unit director or work-group leader has created an internal subculture that values and rewards out-of-the-box thinking and behavior, regardless of whether or not the parent company does.'

What could be done to make corporations have more of an entrepreneurial feel?
'There needs to be a commitment from the top down that the organization values creativity and innovation. Senior managers need to be open and approachable and create an environment that truly empowers individuals at all levels and rewards risk-taking. These cannot just be empty sentiments on a mission statement posted in the cafeteria, they need to be core values that have permeated and are felt by the entire organization. In the end, companies need to get a whole lot better at trusting the people who are determined to let the organization realize its true potential and who won't sleep easy until it does.'

Notes
1. Leadbeater, Charles, & Oakley, Kate, *The Independents,* Demos/ICA, 1999

Only those who will risk going too far can
possibly find out how far one can go.
T.S. Eliot

You know you're old when the candles cost more than the cake.
Bob Hope

Life is half spent before one knows what it is.
French proverb

SEVEN

WINDING DOWN

With many people now living and working longer, traditional views on retirement are changing. For some, it is a financial necessity, while for others it is a chance to begin a new career adventure.
It is a time to ask yourself some BIG questions:

Is your life's work complete?

Do you want to stop working, and if so what are you going to do instead?

How will you pay for it?

Is it time to give something back to society?

Have you achieved all your ambitions?

1. LAST STOP, ALL OFF PLEASE

You've reached that age. You've said your goodbyes, had the party, pocketed the clock/watch/interesting gift. You may or may not have received a hefty pay off. Hopefully you have a substantial pension plan to cash in.

Ah, retirement: time to hang up the cares of working life and head for the golf course. Time to buy a Winnebago, or caravan, and do some touring, head for the sun, or make mansions out of matchsticks. Time to kick back and take things easy after all those years of hard work. This, at least, is the traditional image of retirement. But it is an image that no longer holds true.

A silver rebellion

There is a silver rebellion under way. Many of those who might once have been expected to be winding down are now getting a second (or third) wind. People are living and working longer. Those past retirement age now represent a significant slice of the world's intellectual capital. In his book *AgePower: How the 21st Century Will Be Ruled By the New Old*, (NY: Penguin Putnam, 1999) Ken Dychtwald, lecturer and consultant in the field of gerontology, looks at how the explosion of 1960s baby boomers hitting their fifties will affect society. With the over fifties in the US owning more than 70 percent of the financial assets and representing 50 percent of all discretionary spending, Dychtwald asserts that the US is becoming a gerontocracy. And it's not just the US. Demographic projections for Germany indicate that within the next 10 years, almost half of the country's population will be over retirement age. Forget the meek, forget the young, it is the old, it seems, who shall inherit the earth.

An increasingly mature population presents a number of challenges as well as opportunities. Dychtwald identifies five dangers to social welfare and suggests some possible solutions. Included in the five are two that evidence suggests are already becoming a reality; that the arbitrary age of 65 be removed as a critical age marker for the purposes of work retirement in many countries; and that opportunities are provided to the grey hairs – or indeed no hairs – who have experience and talents that might otherwise be wasted on less socially productive activities like surfing the Internet, watching television and gardening.

What is clear is that people are working until later in their lives than they used to. There are several reasons for this. A longer lifespan, coupled with falling investment returns and inadequate pension provision, means that many people are unprepared financially for retirement. Individuals whose pensions are unable to support them in the lifestyle to which they have become accustomed face a stark choice: they can cut back and eke out their meager savings; or they can continue to work. For some, this choice may not be such an unpleasant one. Indeed, there are many retirees, even those with adequate financial resources, who choose to work beyond retirement age. They are in good health and have bundles of energy and the experience to use both wisely.

THE GRAY ADVANTAGE

Whether through choice or necessity, working in their old age will be a reality for a growing number of people. It's lucky then that the 'gray hairs', as they have been called, have many advantages over their younger counterparts.

Experience, adaptability, well-developed skills, wisdom; these are all qualities that 'gray hairs' can offer. Yet older workers don't always get a fair crack at the whip. Ageism is a major barrier for retirees. It is, however, possible to improve your chances of obtaining rewarding employment later in your career.

Flexible
Depending on domestic arrangements you may be well placed to offer flexible working hours to your employer. This can provide a distinct advantage over younger workers with family commitments. Similarly, your financial arrangements may make you more flexible when it comes to pay and benefits.

Invaluable
You may be able to play to your strengths by capitalizing on a lifetime of experience. Cast yourself in the role of tutor, guardian or mentor. This is a good way of passing on the knowledge acquired during your career. Mentoring younger workers can be rewarding both for you and for the mentee. It also makes you less dispensable. Alternatively, by negotiating temporary or contract work you aren't a burden on the pay roll, which may make you more attractive.

Up-to-date
One of the popular misconceptions about older workers (see Exploding the Retirement Myths later) is that they are unable to learn new skills and consequently become less useful. Help dispel this myth by signing up to company-sponsored learning programs. If the company can't pay, or won't pay, then pay for yourself. In the long run, the benefits of keeping abreast of technology and work skills justifies the cost. And, as you will find out elsewhere in this section, it may help you live longer.

Shop around
If you fancy a change there has probably never been a better time to try out a new career. Changes in working practices mean that temporary and part-time workers are in demand. Use this trend to your advantage. Try a new career for size.

Going it alone

If you are unable or unwilling to work for another company consider starting your own business. You might be able to turn your skills and knowledge into consultancy work. Alternatively you could try your hand at something completely different. For advice on starting a business try the Service Corps of Retired Executives (SCORE www.score.org) where, appropriately, the advice comes from 'working and retired executives and business owners who donate their time and expertise as volunteer business counselors and provide confidential counseling and mentoring free of charge'.

2. PART-TIME RETIREMENT

So what are the options for seasoned career adventurers (retirees who are not yet ready to take up golf, gardening or travel full-time)?

The first and most obvious answer is to continue working for your existing employer. For those who wish to stick around with their employer a study conducted by human resources consulting firm William M. Mercer Inc., 'Phased Retirement and the Changing Face of Retirement' offers considerable encouragement.

The survey, conducted in 2001, looked at the hiring policy regarding retirees for 232 large US employers. The study discovered that nearly 6 out of every 10 employers had a policy on rehiring retirees. Of the companies with a regional hiring policy, 61 percent were willing to rehire retirees as independent contractors or consultants. This solution has the advantage of providing flexibility for the retiree. (On the downside, however, the retiree acting as an independent contractor, or consultant, is ineligible for employment benefits.)

Another 24 percent of companies who had a retiree rehiring policy said they would be willing to retain retirees on their full-time payroll, after a waiting period.

As the baby boomer generation crawls towards retirement age, the practice of rehiring retirees is likely to become increasingly popular. The alternative is to lose swathes of experienced and knowledgeable staff with key skills, and then struggle to replace them from a dwindling labor force.

This view is supported by Anna Rappaport, a Chicago-based principal of HR consulting firm William M. Mercer Inc[1]. 'Some organizations will have huge drains if they don't do something. We're often talking about people with specific skills that are relevant to their company. If someone has valuable knowledge, companies want to capitalize on that knowledge.'

MIDDLE-AGE SPREADS

Surveys point to rapid growth in the number of part-time retired workers. The baby boom generation, consisting of over 70 million people born between 1946 and 1964, begin to retire in 2010.

One survey conducted by Roper Starch Worldwide Inc. for the American Association of Retired Persons, found that 80 percent of baby-boomers intend to continue working after retirement. Thirty-five percent were going to work part-time for interest or enjoyment, 23 percent for income, and 17 percent planned to go into business for themselves.

Similar findings were reported by a survey conducted by the Gallup Organization for brokerage firm PaineWebber. In the Gallup study, 15 percent planned to work for as long as possible, while another 60 percent said they would look for different work or start their own business.

3. PHASED RETIREMENT

What if you have had enough of the 50-hour week, the tiresome commute, and the constant stress of working life?

What if you really can't stomach the idea of continuing to work full-time? If you fall into this category then there is another solution, phased retirement.

There are several definitions of phased retirement, although the basic idea is generally similar. One definition sees phased retirement as a gradual scaling back of all a worker's hours and responsibility until they retire. Others see it more simply as a return to work by retirees but on a part-time basis. Either way the key feature is that retirees continue to work after retirement but not full-time. Just as there is no single accepted definition of phased retirement few employers acknowledge that they offer a 'phased retirement' program. In practice many do, but do not recognize it as such.

Phased retirement is an arrangement that often suits both employer and retiree better than full-time employment. Large corporates such as General Electric and IBM have operated phased retirement policies for over a decade now. GE's much lauded Golden Opportunity programme allows retirees to work up to a thousand hours a year.

For many retirees phased retirement is the perfect half-way house solution. As Bill Backer, a participant of GE's Golden Opportunity program, and previously a GE employee of 24 years standing, noted: 'It's interesting and challenging and fun to be out in the business world but I wouldn't want to do it full time.' [2]

Not all phased retirement programs are formally structured. In the majority of cases individual arrangements are struck between employer and retiree based on the employer's labor needs, and the skills, knowledge, and experience that the retiree has to offer. The work can take a variety of forms including temporary work, special projects, job sharing, training, mentoring and consulting. Hours can also vary, commonly ranging between 10 and 30 hours a week.

Like continuing in full-time work after retirement, the practice of phased retirement is on the increase. In the survey conducted by Mercer Consulting, of those companies that had a retiree-rehiring policy, 63 percent said they would return retirees to work as part-time or temporary workers, and that these workers would be eligible for benefits if they worked sufficient hours. As for the retirees, a nationwide poll conducted in October 1999 by the *Los Angeles Times* found that 44 percent of the respondents planned to work part-time after reaching retirement age.

RETIREMENT MYTHS

Exploding the retirement myths

The MacArthur Foundation funded a long-term research program to identify key factors in 'successful ageing'. The program started in 1984 and was conducted by a group of researchers drawn from a wide range of disciplines and assembled by ex-Harvard Professor of Gerontology, John Rowe. The group's findings exploded many myths commonly associated with an ageing population. Gloomy preconceptions of declining health and failing intellect, lost libido and dwindling activity were replaced with a far more promising outlook for those of retirement age. The findings of the study were extensively analyzed in the bestselling book *Successful Aging* by Rowe and co-author, Robert Kahn. The book noted six prevalent aging myths dispelled by the study:

Myth 1: To be Old is to be Sick

Dispelling ideas of a failing generation creaking at the knees, spending more time with their doctor than their friends, and clutching a well-thumbed route map of local pharmacies, researchers discovered changes in illness rates had dramatically reduced the disablement of older people. Today's generation of geriatrics are healthier and more robust than ever before. Interviewed in the mid-1990s, 40 percent of over 65s said that they were in excellent or very good health. In the 65 to 74 age bracket, 89 per cent reported no disability at all. In case you're shaking your head skeptically, there is more. What better evidence of continuing health could anyone wish for than that the results of the 2001 Summer National Senior Games, The Senior Olympics, held in July in Baton Rouge, Louisiana? Over 10,000 competitors aged 50-plus gathered to compete in a variety of sports. The results speak for themselves: the Men's 200 metres in the age group 70 to 74 was won by a Bill Melville, Platteville, Wisconsin in a very respectable 28.91 seconds (try it for yourself). Anthony Denardis of Albuquerque won his 200 metres in a time of 59.15 – not so hot you think, well we're talking about the 90 to 94 age group here. It gets better; Jim Selby, Fallbrook, California, won the Men's 800 metres for the 70 to 74 age group in a time of 2:48.37 or an average of a little over 20 seconds for each 100 meters. And finally, congratulations to James Cordell of Houston who cleared a height of 6 feet 1 1/4 inches in the 80-84 age group men's pole vault, yes, pole vaulting in his eighties and he was by no means the only one.

Older people still suffer illness. Illnesses afflicting the aged today include arthritis (50 percent); hypertension and heart disease (33 percent); and hearing and visual impairments. But they suffer them less. Disease arising from high blood pressure, high cholesterol and smoking is dramatically reduced. People are living much longer too. The average life expectancy for women is around 85 while for the men it is a respectable 80 years of age. And these years are unlikely to be spent sitting in an armchair in a nursing home. Research found only 5.2 percent of older people lived in nursing homes designed for highly dependent people down from 6.3 percent in 1982.

Myth 2: You Can't Teach an Old Dog New Tricks

It is a mistake to employ the elderly. Why? Because they find it difficult to pick up new techniques, skills and technologies. It's a commonly held perception and it's wrong. The idea of rapidly declining mental factors associated with old age is based more on fear and prejudice than grounded in reality.

The MacArthur foundation's research discovered that less than 10 percent of the population aged between 65 and 100 were Alzheimer's patients. In another study of individuals aged between 74 and 81, half exhibited no mental decline in a seven-year follow-up study. Additional research has shown that with appropriate training new skills can be developed at any age. For older people to acquire new skills it helps if they are:

◆ Allowed to work at their own pace

◆ Encouraged to repeat and rehearsed the new skill

◆ Not put off or embarrassed by comparisons to faster colleagues

Additionally, the research found that the three most important factors in maintaining intellectual acuity were 1) regular physical activity, 2) a strong social support network of people to interact with,[3]) self-belief particularly related to the ability to handle life's demands. If any other evidence was required to support the findings of the MacArthur foundation's research, just consider how older people are mastering new technology. On the Internet, for example, the so-called Silver Surfers make up 20 to 25 percent of US online users.

Myth 3: The Horse is Out of the Barn

Fond of fried breakfast loaded with unhealthy saturated fats. Prefer to take the car for a spin rather than walk the dog. You've got a filthy temper, always had one, always will.

By the time people get into their fifties they are set in their ways and therefore unable to change habits of a lifetime, or benefit from any change. Untrue. Instead, the research suggests it is never too late to improve your lifestyle. Stop smoking, and smoking-associated risks begin to decrease immediately – both heart disease and lung disease. Similar beneficial effects are obtained through changes to diet, exercise and other lifestyle attitudes.

Myth 4: The Secret to Successful Aging is to Choose Your Parents Wisely

The medical community seem to agree that genes are important in determining longevity. But while genetics are important, your DNA is far from the only thing that determines how long you live. When it comes to developing disease later in life, research has shown that lifestyle and environmental factors are particularly important.

A study of both identical and non-identical twins, in Sweden, demonstrated that the older an individual is, the more important their environment is in determining mental and physical well-being. Equally, factors that point towards maintaining an active engagement in life are less to do with heredity, and more to do with attitudes and circumstances.

Myth 5: The Lights may be on, but the Voltage is Low

Older people don't do it, do they? As the song goes, 'We're talking about sex, baby', or rather in the case of older people, the absence of. Instead of coitus energeticus there is a marked decline in performance, sexual attraction and sexual interest, surely.

On the contrary, while there may be some decline in sexual activity on average in later life, this varies markedly from individual to individual. Better health, lasting longer in life, is prolonging people's sexuality and, coupled with medical discoveries such as Viagra, is helping people to remain sexually active well into their old age. Really it's nothing new. In a sexually repressed America of the 1950s, for example, the Kinsey Report (1953) found that 70 percent of men aged 68 remained sexually active.

Myth 6: The Elderly Don't Pull Their Weight

It's easy to dismiss oldies as unproductive. But this depends on what criteria you use to judge productivity. As the nature of work has shifted from manual-based to more knowledge-intensive, so too the contribution of older workers has increased. Nearly 30 percent of all the over 65s in the United States work in a paid job be it full-time or part-time. And the figure would probably be higher, were it not for age discrimination preventing many willing older workers from taking employment. In addition to paid work, oldies play an important role in society, forming charitable functions, working in schools, hospitals, and other organizations. They also form a large percentage of society's carers.

So, there you have it.

Sources: Study of Aging in America, The MacArthur Foundation.
Rowe, J. and Kahn, Robert, *Successful Aging* (Pantheon, 1998).

Adventure 15

Whether you are planning on sailing around the world, continuing to work or simply putting your feet up, retirement is a time for reflection. Many people find it difficult to come to terms with retirement. To a greater or lesser extent, work defines who we are as people. Without it, many suffer a loss of identity and feelings of dislocation. So, before making a decision about how to spend your retirement, take some time to reflect on your achievements so far.

First, write down what you consider to be your ten greatest achievements in life.

MY 10 GREATEST ACHIEVEMENTS

1.

2.

3.

4.

5.

6.

7.

8.

9.

10.

Next, if you have written a 'Things I want to do while I still can' list like the one suggested in Section 5, this is the time to revisit it and see how many ambitions you have managed to check off.

Now it's time to compile a top 10 'Things I haven't done yet but still want to' list. This should help give you a steer on how you might like to spend your retirement.

10 THINGS I HAVEN'T DONE BUT WANT TO

1.

2.

3.

4.

5.

6.

7.

8.

9.

10.

GENDER, WORK AND RETIREMENT

In a 1999 study into the quality of life following retirement, Cornell University psychologists Jungeen E. Kim and Phyllis Moen studied 534 married men aged between 50 and 744. Their findings showed up an illuminating difference in the attitudes to working in the post-retirement period.

Men who return to work, Moen and Kim discovered, are more satisfied with their lives and marriages than men who retire permanently. The men also enjoyed their marriages if their wives weren't working. Those men who were happy when retired enjoyed the freedom from the pressures of a career, the research suggested.

Life wasn't so rosy for the women however. Women who returned to work did not report similar levels of satisfaction to their male counterparts. Newly retired women were more depressed, and had lower morale, than newly retired men. The situation was worse if the women's husbands were still working.

The conclusion seems to be that, for men at least, continuing to work after retirement age can be very rewarding. The only note of caution is that if there was any bias in the survey it seems to have been that the subjects were predominately career-oriented. Working because you choose to is likely to be more satisfying than working because you are forced to. Unless the work experience is satisfying the associated benefits are unlikely to be forthcoming.

3. GRAY POWER

There is no better ambassador for gray power than renowned management guru Peter Drucker.

Now in his nineties, Drucker has some useful pointers on managing his generation. In 2000 the *McKinsey Quarterly* persuaded Drucker to spend three hours with another, more youthful, business guru Peter Senge, the man who helped popularize the learning organization. 3

Drucker sees managers leaving traditional career jobs much earlier, but continuing to work and, importantly, learn as free agents, full-time well into their seventies. He points to the emergence of a new, wealthy, fit, and active group of workers over 55. No one has experienced such a group before and no one as yet understands them says Drucker.

These changes, Drucker suggests, require an enormous response from organizations that they are not yet making effectively. Both gurus agree that organizations and people need to 'enjoy' what they do, an idea most people reject because of what Drucker calls 'the legacy that work is a curse'. This does not mean enjoying dull routine but accepting it as a necessity for the work that you do enjoy. To illustrate his point, Drucker uses a favourite musical analogy, the gifted piano player who must still practice scales for three hours a day.

Warren Bennis is another business thinker of mature years focusing his attention on generational differences. Based at the University of Southern California where he is the founder of the University's Leadership Institute in Los Angeles, Bennis has made a contribution to an array of subjects and produced a steady stream of books including the best-selling *Leaders*, and more recently, *Organizing Genius: The Secrets of Creative Collaboration*.

In his 70s, Bennis still runs most days before work. His intellectual energy and output remains formidable. He is a humanist with high hopes for humanity. 'I think that every person has to make a genuine contribution in their lives and the institution of work is one of the main vehicles to achieving this', he observes.

The working title of his new book, which he describes as the most urgent and exciting project he's worked on for years, is *Geeks and Geezers*. It's based on interviews with between 15 and 20 leaders who are aged 30 or younger and about the same number of leaders who are 70 and older.

Drucker sees managers leaving traditional career jobs much earlier, but continuing to work and, importantly, learn as free agents, full-time well into their seventies. He points to the emergence of a new, wealthy, fit, and active group of workers over 55.

4. ENJOYING OLD AGE

Whether you intend to work or spend your retirement in some other way, with the prospect of a long life ahead of you, enjoying your old age is vital.

At the age of 78 world-renowned behavioral psychologist B.F. Skinner (1904 – 1990) presented a paper at the annual meeting of the American Psychological Association entitled 'Intellectual Management in Old Age'. Skinner went on to further develop his ideas in his book *Enjoy Old Age: A Program of Self-Management*, which he co-authored with respected gerontologist Margaret Vaughan. The book is Skinner's guide to living well in old age.

At the heart of Skinner's philosophy is his assertion that the secret of a happy retirement depends on creating an environment that the individual finds reinforces positive feelings. So people should focus on what they like or dislike doing, as what we like to do is often related to actions that result in positive experiences.

For Skinner, arranging life to provide positive reinforcement meant doing a number of things. Keeping in touch with the world, for example. Absorbing information through newspapers, magazines or surfing the Internet provides information on how to get more out of life, how to get a better return on our actions. Paying attention to your personal likes and dislikes is vital. This way you can ensure that you avoid situations that annoy you or give you pain, and increase those experiences that give you pleasure.

Construct a pain-pleasure inventory. List the things that irritate you and if possible eradicate them from your life (within the bounds of the law of course). If you hate the picture hanging over the mantelpiece throw it out. Go through your wardrobe and weed out the clothes that no longer please you. If the idea of going to work in the morning fills you with dread, change your job.

Keeping in touch with the world may involve adapting your lifestyle as you grow older. Problems with memory often mean that thought processes need supplementing with physical reminders such as lists and notes. Keeping as active and as fit as possible helps keep your brain from becoming tired. Simplifying your life and removing clutter can also help.

Maintaining a dialogue with others, and talking about subjects that interest you is another important element of keeping in touch with the world. In fact, Skinner suggests that getting along with other people is essential if you are to have a satisfying life as you grow old. To this end he advocates making compromises where necessary to accommodate relationships, and living with other people whether or not they are your partner, by marriage or otherwise. Take on new challenges and learn new skills as a way of maintaining an interest in the world around you. Creativity is not restricted by age. Michelangelo was still painting well into his eighties; the Greek dramatist and statesman Sophocles wrote two of his best plays, *Oedipus at Colonus* and *Philoctetes*, as an octogenarian. While many individuals make their most significant contributions in their thirties and forties others make notable contributions much later on in life, in their sixties, seventies and older.

The name of the game is keeping busy. Pursue activities that are productive and interesting, whether they are paid or unpaid, leisure or work. Interestingly, Skinner also suggested indulging in activities that provide excitement, such as gambling. The point here is that, providing it is done within your means, gambling provides both intellectual challenge – pitting your wits against those of the bookmaker and predicting outcomes – as well as excitement, through uncertainty.

However you manage it, Skinner concluded that the means to an enjoyable retirement is through influencing, controlling and manipulating your environment to create a positive influence on your life. For many people this will mean continuing to work, for others it will be traveling and realizing unfilled dreams.

The answer to the question 'How do I live my life to the maximum during retirement?' will be different for each individual. Such a question deserves a book of its own. Here we look at just a few fundamental issues that affect the lives of seasoned career adventurers who are thinking of folding up the maps, packing up the tent, and putting the fieldbook back on the shelf (don't): health, wealth and legacy.

CAREER ADVENTURER

SERENA WILSON *on retirement*

Title/Position:	Middle Eastern belly dancing instructor; company owner
Company:	Serena Studios, Serena's Closet
Location:	New York
Website:	www.serenastudios.com

'Retirement doesn't make sense in my world. I will continue to teach as long as I am able to, and as long as people want to learn from me. I especially enjoy being a role model for older women, because a lot of women after a certain age almost seem apologetic about their age. I like to show women that when you're over 50 or 55, you don't have to apologize for being alive. I had a very sad conversation today with a woman who wants to come to the studio. She kept referring to herself as a 'klutzy' 50-year-old. I said to her, "Lady, I'm a lot older than you. Stop apologizing for your age and come in and try a class.'

5. HEALTH

Health is one of the biggest issues for retirees and the source of some of the deepest fears.

The common perception of health in old age is of declining physical condition accompanied by failing mental faculties. But, as pointed out elsewhere in this section, this notion of an invalid, aging population is largely grounded in myth. Increasing numbers of retirees are staying healthy well into old age.

The centenarians are one of the fastest growing segments of the US population, if not the fastest. The second fastest growing group is the 85 and over. At the turn of the century only one in every 100,000 people could expect to live until 100 and the average life expectancy was 45. Today that figure is one in every 10,000 with the average life expectancy in the eighties. The oldest living person on verifiable record, Madame Jeanne Calment, died in August 1997 at the incredible age of 122. In the year she was born the game of snooker was invented, Jesse James was robbing trains in Missouri, and Napoleon III was only three years in his grave.

We can't all be healthy in retirement and there are no pat answers to remaining physically active. Wouldn't it be nice if there were? If anyone has the answers, or can provide an insight into how best to prolong health (apart from the scientists that is), it has to be the centenarians. Who better to reveal the secrets of living a long and rewarding life, than those who have made it to 100 years of age and beyond. Admittedly, your DNA may have something to say about how you hold up over the years, but there are plenty of other ingredients that make up the elixir of longevity.

At Harvard University, researchers have conducted a study into the lives of centenarians in a specific region of New England. The study, started in 1998, is still ongoing. It originally included 169 centenarians and was then extended.

The study group was surprisingly varied when it came to race, income, and education. There were no obvious lifestyle patterns. Centenarians were as likely to eat eggs and bacon every day, as they were to eat fruit and vegetables. Equally, while the group was generally described as intellectually active and lively, educational attainment was, on average about tenth grade level.

There were however, some consistent behavioral characteristics and traits among the group. They tended not to be obese and had, on the whole, maintained a steady weight throughout their lives. None of these centenarians smoked, although some had in the past, nor did any drink heavily. One interesting finding was that, although individuals in the group exhibited a wide range of personalities, one common characteristic was that of low neuroticism.

Neuroticism is related to negative emotions such as anger, jealousy, guilt and fear. Individuals who are low in neuroticism tend not to exhibit potentially damaging traits such as depression, anxiety or hostility. As a result, the centenarians' ability to cope with stress was much better than average. Regardless of adversity the centenarians managed to keep their spirits up. Calm and resolute during crises, they were adaptable and emotionally stable. A well-developed sense of humor was another shared characteristic.

Centenarians also tended to be natural networkers. On the whole gregarious, with many friends and social acquaintances, few if any of the group were 'loners'. Over half of the centenarians maintain part of their social life through religion and believed in God. The fact that prayer and religious belief can offer similar health-positive advantages to humor and close social relationships was indicated by research carried out at Harvard Medical School by Herbert Benson (www.mbmi.org/pages/bio1.asp).

CAREER ADVENTURERS

HOWARD AND MARIKA STONE *on health in retirement*

Position/Title: Founders
Company: 2 Young 2 Retire
Location: Weehawken, NJ
Website: www.2young2retire.com

'A healthy mind is the engine for a healthy body. Your mind is healthy when it's about possibility rather than about the past. A healthy mind is a mind that remains curious. The model for this is people in the arts. They never grow old and they never really stop. They are engaged in what they do in an unstoppable way. Every time they get to one plateau there's another one for them beyond it whether in music, the fine arts, film, writing, etc. They tend to live longer because their minds are engaged, and that affects the body.

When he was in his eighties, Pablo Casals, the legendary cellist, would wake up with his body crunched down and stiff. He'd crawl over to the piano and start playing Bach, and after 20 minutes he was able to get up and move. So there is something about healthy mind and healthy body that goes both ways.'

The findings of the MacArthur Foundation Study were examined in depth in the book *Successful Aging: The MacArthur Foundation Study* by John W. Rowe, M.D. and Robert L. Kahn (New York: Dell). In the book, the authors make a number of suggestions based on the research findings for increasing the prospect of living until 100. To prolong mental agility they suggest mental workout – step aerobics for the brain. Chess problems, crossword puzzles, demanding literature, these can all help keep the neurons firing, as can other activities such as playing music, aerobic exercise, art and calisthenics.

In addition to the MacArthur foundation research a 30-year follow-up survey conducted by the Mayo clinic, supports the idea that eradicating negative emotions increases longevity[5]. In the Mayo study 839 patients who received medical care at the Clinic between 1962 and 1965 completed a survey, part of which assessed how optimistic or pessimistic an individual was. The follow-up in 1994 revealed that whereas those with an optimistic approach to life fared well and lived longer than expected, the pessimists were found to have a significantly higher mortality rate.

A healthy retirement, then, is something we can all influence. While we may not live to 122 like the venerable Madame Calment, we can increase our chances of reaching average life expectancy and beyond. It won't always be easy but the rewards appear to merit the effort required.

6. RETIREMENT FINANCIAL PLANNING

Retirement equals vacations, travel, buying things you have always wanted to buy, generosity to the grandchildren, writing that novel.

If this is your idea of retirement you may have a big shock and bitter disappointment awaiting you if you haven't made adequate financial preparation.

For example, if you work in the UK and have a company pension based on final salary, or alternatively work in the US and have an employee-sponsored retirement program, then the outlook is good. In the US a lucky 80 percent of workers in companies with more than 1,000 employees are in company retirement plans. But for smaller companies the figures are less encouraging. In companies with between 25 and 99 employees fewer than 50 percent of workers are in such a plan, between 10 and 24 employees the figure is about 25 percent and below 10 employees a minute 16 percent.[6]

Faced with the facts, it is no surprise that employees are worried. According to a poll commissioned by the Principal Financial Group in 2001, 85 percent of Americans working in growing businesses are 'very concerned' about their financial future. Another 59 percent were unhappy with their financial health, worse still, 27 percent had made no plans whatsoever for retirement.

RETIREMENT FUND

You may have a big shock and bitter disappointment awaiting you if you haven't made adequate financial preparation.

This last figure is reflected in the US Government Accounting Office (GAO) figures that show 50 percent of American retirees are totally reliant on Social Security for income, having no private pension income. And for 21 percent of retirees with no employer-sponsored retirement benefit this means living on or below the poverty line.

In case this doesn't make depressing enough reading then read on. There are some people reading this who are thinking: 'There's no need to worry, I've got equity in my house and the mortgage will be paid off by retirement, plus there are a few savings plans to cash in as well as my ever-increasing salary between now and retirement.' If only things were that easy. Try this for size. How much do you need as an annual income when you retire? Say you had accumulated $200,000, surely that would be sufficient to bring in a reasonably sized retirement income. Hopefully, you will no longer have to find some of the big ticket items such as mortgage, college fees for your kids etc. (Of course, you may want to put yourself through more education.) Now look at the math. Say you decide to invest the money in shares and live off the dividends. In the current climate of low inflation, dividend returns are extremely low, somewhere in the region of 2.0 percent. Even a generous 2.5 percent will give a return of just $5,000 per annum. To bring in $30,000 a year you will need a pot in excess of $1.2 million. Extra funds could be realized if the shares appreciate in value thus giving you capital growth. But as the small print says 'Shares may go down as well as up' and your hard-saved capital could dwindle away to a fraction of its original as many investors found to their cost when the dot.com bubble burst.

Better returns are available from other investments, gilts for example. Interest yields are higher. But gilts offer no capital growth and so are exposed to the effects of inflation. Alternatively, an annuity could be purchased. This will provide a better income but with a catch. When you purchase an annuity you receive a fixed annual income but hand over the pot of money. When you die the annuity provider keeps your hard-earned cash.

It's a bleak prognosis, but don't despair. If you're approaching retirement and have made no provision but still have disposable income then it's never too late to start. If it's still early in your career and you have yet to make provision then now is the time to start. You've probably heard it before but the earlier you start the easier it is, and the more you get on retirement. The wonderful phenomenon of compound interest means that early starters in their twenties gain substantial advantages over those who begin to save in their mid-thirties. Whichever category you are in, the first thing to do is to draw up a retirement plan.

PLANNING FOR RETIREMENT

◆ Step one – What you need

The first step in the retirement-planning process should be to quantify the amount of money you will require annually when you retire. A rough estimate will be of no use to you. You must do your best to arrive at clear objectives requiring quantifiable definable funds. To begin with what are your general living expenses? In a calculation of this kind it is often assumed that a retired person will require somewhere between 75 and 100 percent of their existing salary. But only you will know if this is true in your case.

On top of general living expenses there are all those ambitions you've harbored for retirement. If you plan to take three vacations a year then these need to be costed into your needs calculation. A holiday home? Make provision for this. Sports cars, tuition fees, membership of the golf club, sailing club and gym, regular trips to the opera, eating out, all these need to be factored in.

Remember also that you need to consider the effects of inflation. Even a modest inflation rate running at around four percent will substantially deplete your buying power over time. The sum of $50,000 per annum might seem a very adequate amount to be retiring on. But assuming a four percent inflation rate that $50,000 would need to be over $100,000 in 20 years time just to stand still in terms of purchasing power. The point is that you are planning for a period of time rather than for the moment of retirement.

Consider also when you wish to retire. Are you the kind of person who would be happy to work into their seventies if it were possible? Is this a realistic proposition? Do you have the skills and resources necessary to be employable at this age? Because if you do not you will have to acquire them.

When you finish considering your needs, you should end up with a statement along the lines of: I wish to retire at 55 on an annual income of $30,000/ $40,000/$50, 000. This then, is your goal.

◆ **Step two – What you have**

This step is where you round up all your existing financial resources and project what income, if any, this is likely to provide. If you're in the UK you will be taking into account any savings vehicles you may have such as ISAs, TESSAs, building society accounts and National Savings. Shares, bonds and gilts need to be included. You must also find out the projected value of any occupational pension plans you possess, as well as any personal pensions. If you are in the US you will be assessing the value of your IRA, Roth IRA, company sponsored savings plans (401[k] plan) and similar.

It is also important to assess the value of any other investments or assets you might have, your collection of priceless early Gibson guitars for example, or that first edition of *Harry Potter and the Philosopher's Stone*. It is worth remembering at this point that assets such as paintings, books and other collectables, which you may be planning on selling at a later date to finance your retirement, cannot be relied upon until they are turned into cash. While it is unlikely that your original oil painting of the garden of Giverny by Monet will depreciate substantially, fashions change and there is no guarantee that you will realize the amount you expect to for any of your collectables.

◆ Step three

Once you have assessed your assets and investments you will be able to compare this with the figure arrived at in step one. If you have a greater amount than you require when you retire, congratulations, you are afforded the luxury of deciding how to spend the extra money. If, however, the figure falls short of the amount required upon retirement, you have to take action to rectify the situation if you wish to enjoy your retirement. Proceed to step [4].

◆ Step four

It is time is draw up an action plan. The aim of the plan is to increase your resources to meet the expected needs upon retirement. There's no escaping the fact that financial planning for retirement can be a bewildering and complex process. If you are interested in financial matters, capable of comparing investment products, and have the time, you may wish to research the best methods of financing your retirement yourself. If, however you do not feel comfortable weighing the relative advantages of the Roth IRA and standard IRA, or wading through the tax implications of funding retirement through a personal pension or other means, you will need to seek advice elsewhere.

A good solution is to seek the advice of an independent financial advisor. If you can find an advisor who is willing to give advice on a fee basis this may prove to be a better choice than selecting an advisor who relies on commission on the products they recommend to you for remuneration. Whether in conjunction with a financial advisor or on your own, your plan must set out what investments you intend to make, what payments you will make and when you will make them.

◆ **Step five**

Implement your plan.

◆ **Step six**

Follow up your arrangements. Schedule a regular review of your plan. Make sure you are on track. If not, you will need to consider whether to take further advice, or what other action you can take.

If you follow these steps there is still no guarantee that you will end up in an idyllic retirement. But it will increase your chances.

7. YOU ARE WHAT YOU LEAVE BEHIND

'If a man has wealth, he has to make a choice, because there is the money heaping up. He can keep it together in a bunch, and then leave it for others to administer after he is dead. Or he can get it into action and have fun, while he is still alive. I prefer getting it into action and adapting it to human needs, and making the plan work.'
So said GEORGE EASTMAN, founder of Eastman Kodak.

'The great use of life is to spend it on something that will outlast it',
observed WILLIAM JAMES (1842-1910), psychologist, philosopher and humanist.

Regardless of whether they are at work or leisure, retirees might want to think about the legacy they wish to leave behind them. Do any of us really think about the legacy we bequeath for those who follow? The answer, should be a resounding yes, if future generations are to benefit from the wisdom and experience of those who have gone before them.

Corporate legacy, a term we coined, addresses the issue at a company level.[7] 'You can walk around any country graveyard to remind yourself that you will be under grass eventually', Peter Job, former CEO of Reuters, told us.[8] 'It's sensible, therefore, to say how long do I want my company to go on after me? This company has been going since 1851.'

The notion of corporate legacy concerns the issue of what one generation of management should pass on to the next. In any long-lived company, generations of CEOs will preside over the culture of the organization, inheriting it from their predecessor, passing it on to their successor. This process is an essential one in maintaining the character of the corporation.

Integral to the concept of corporate legacy is the assertion that senior management is the custodian of the values that underpin the culture, conserving them on behalf of and for the benefit of the company in the future. It goes right to the heart and soul of the business: what it exists for and the values it holds most dear.

This idea of passing on values as well as knowledge and experience is equally applicable to individuals on a personal level. The concept of leaving behind your mark on the world is as old as the cave paintings at Lascaux, France.

In the case of the wealthy, substitute 'Institute', 'Foundation', 'Center' and 'Towers' for a hastily etched 'I was here' or a picture of a wooly mammoth. The wealthy indulge in philanthropic large-scale giving, often through trusts set up specifically to administer their largesse. To mere mortals on an average salary, the scale of this do-gooding is staggering. Take the year 2000 for example. Consider the rankings for donations made in that year (yes, such a thing exists http://philanthropy.com/free/articles/v13/i07/07000101.htm suggested by none other than Ted Turner, media mogul, and the man who pledged to give a jaw-dropping $1 billion to the United Nations Foundation). It reveals that Bill and Melinda Gates (no.1) donated $5 billion to their own foundation and the aforementioned Ted Turner (no14) gifted cash and stock to the tune of $50.6 million to the U.N. Foundation.

One of the more useful aspects of the dot.com boom is that it appears to have significantly lowered the average age of philanthropists. Traditionally, wealthy people have turned their attentions to good causes later in life. But a clutch of dot.com millionaires incubated from the Internet madness of the 1990s are leaving their mark on the world earlier. Take vice-president of eBay, Jeff Skoll, Still in his thirties, Skoll is a stripling compared to the great philanthropists of the past such as Andrew Carnegie and John D. Rockefeller. Skoll gave eBay stock worth $39 million to a supporting organization at the Community Foundation Silicon Valley that he created in 1999 with a gift of $33 million in stock.

Leaving a mark on the world doesn't have to mean tall buildings such as the Woolworth building, the Chrysler building, Trump towers or philanthropic institutions like the Carnegie Institute, the Ford Foundation, the Rockefeller Foundation. Neither does it have to involve billions of dollars or the equivalent. Even individuals of the most modest means can hand down something worthwhile to the next-generation. Yes, you can give money to good causes that are suitably in tune with your values and beliefs. But there is something else you can do. The knowledge and experience of a lifetime is one of the most valuable things a retiree possesses. Consider passing it on by acting as a mentor (see Section Three). Helping to guide someone else on their career adventure can be as rewarding as your own.

RESOURCES ON WINDING DOWN

ON THE WEB

The Internet For Retirees – This helpful assemblage of online resources for US retirees is featured on the website for the PBS (US Public Broadcasting) special Frontline program, 'My Retirement Dreams', by filmmaker Marian Marzynski. An overview of each site is provided, and the sites are grouped into nine categories, including:

- ◆ General senior sites
- ◆ Surfing 101
- ◆ News
- ◆ Finance
- ◆ Legal
- ◆ Health
- ◆ Travel
- ◆ Arts & interests
- ◆ Food

For those who are new to the Internet, 'surfing 101' will connect you with several sites that will help provide the basics on web-surfing, as well as to computer training for seniors. **www.pbs.org/wgbh/pages/frontline/shows/retire/etc/links.html**

InvestorGuide.com – The Internet has revolutionized personal investing, and the days of dependence on full-service brokers are over. Now all the tools you need to handle your own personal finance and investing decisions are at your fingertips. Investorguide.com makes these tools available in one very user-friendly location for investors of all levels of experience. Personal finance is one of the site's key features, and extensive US retirement and estate-planning resources are grouped into seven areas: general resources, 401K, IRA, Roth IRA, estate planning, social security and non-profit organizations that provide information on retirement planning. **www.investorguide.com/retirement.html** For global retirement planning, you might try Eagle Star International Life, founded in London in 1807 and based on the Isle of Man, an independent territory, which offers life insurance, retirement benefits and investment services in Europe, Latin America, Middle East, Asia and Africa. **www.eaglestarintlife.com**

2 Young 2 Retire

If a life of endless leisure is not your cup of tea, join the countless others who are reinventing themselves and the possibilities of their retirement years. This inspiring site offers resources 'to help you think out of the box about the life you want.' Howard and Marika Stone have gathered sixty diverse stories from people over 50 who have reinvented their lives and careers. Each story ends with links to organizations and informational resources related to that particular story. There are also 100 excellent links on business, careers, learning, volunteering and wellness. You can subscribe to the free newsletter, and even submit your own story for possible inclusion on the site. **www.2young2retire.com**

Retirement Humor

Let's face it, we're going to need it! Thankfully, there's lots of it available online: a quick search on Yahoo.com for 'retirement +humor' delivers a cool 63,000 hits! Here are a couple of good sites:

Be Wellderly.com

Mary Ann Glasgow's Wellderly Foundation is a non-profit project of the National Heritage Foundation in the US. It promotes 'programs and services that contribute to and celebrate the Wisdom, Gifts and Happiness inherent in aging WELL.' The foundation provides 'resources to expand and subsidize a light hearted, fun and inspirational program for Wellderly groups who are eager to experience and benefit from innovation, creativity and new perspective!' Free articles and action ideas available on the site include 'Celebrate life, laughing all the way', 'Excuse me, this happens to be MY life' and 'Ways to become wellderly'. **www.wellderly.com**

What Why Web

Offers a short collection of humorous stories on retirement and aging. 'Side effects' by Steve Martin is worth the trip. The site is good for a few guffaws. **www.whatwhyweb.com/retirement/retirement_jokes.htm**

SITES FOR WOMEN

National Center for Women on Aging
Provides extensive links to quality web resources of interest to women, arranged in six categories: health, housing, care giving, financial security, aging resources and other. This national center is affiliated with the Heller School for Social Policy and Management and Brandeis University in Waltham, Massachusetts. Other resources available through the center include a wealth of reasonably priced and timely publications on relevant issues, research reports and the *Women and Aging Letter*, a newsletter for midlife and older women.
www.heller.brandeis.edu/national/ind.html

The National Center for Women and Retirement Research
Forgive me, but something seems amiss when the 'National Center for Women and Retirement Research' (in Southampton, NY) 1) is headed by a man (Christopher L. Hayes, Ph.D.) no matter how accomplished, 2) who is associated with every research study and publication listed by this non-profit, 3) who consults through this non-profit and 4) who of course has been featured in the media and on numerous talk shows. Aside from Dr Hayes' bio, the most interesting information on this site is the summary results of a variety of surveys on women and retirement. **www.agingfocus.com**

WISER – Women's' Institute for a Secure Retirement
Created in 1996 by the Heinz Family Foundation, this non-profit organization is devoted to educating women about retirement issues. This site offers excellent primers on money basics (like keeping track of spending, how to start saving, and money mistakes women in couples should avoid), investing, IRAs, pay equity, health issues, divorce and widowhood and pensions. **www.wiser.heinz.org**

LEARNING:

Elderhostel, Inc.
Longstanding, not-for-profit organization. Provides affordable educational adventures across the globe. In 2000 a quarter of a million people signed up for more than 10,000 Elderhostel programs in over 100 countries. For the 55s and over.
www.elderhostel.org

Senior Summer School

'Offers adventurous senior citizens an affordable opportunity to enhance their summer through education, leisure, and discovery, at campus locations across the U.S. and Canada.' **www.seniorsummerschool.com**

Seniornet.Org

Keep up with modern technology, chat online about hundreds of topics, join the world's premier online community and technology trainer for older adults. The Seniornet.Org has over 39,000 members; publishes a quarterly newsletter and a variety of instructional materials; has over 220 Learning Centers throughout the U.S. **www.seniornet.org**

Lifetime Education and Renewal Network (LEARN)

Part of the American Society on Aging, the largest professional membership association in the field of aging. LEARN is a national community of professionals working to promote educational opportunities for today's older adults. Members of LEARN have access to a wealth of resources in the field of aging through ASA's publications and programs. **www.asaging.org/learn.html**

AFTERWORD

We close with one final thought. It is simply this. Your career adventure lasts as long as you are prepared to let it. And that can be an entire lifetime.

If you want to, you can return to the start and begin all over again. It's up to you. It's your adventure. Enjoy.

Notes

1. *Seniors at work: What retirement?,* 23 January 2001, CNN.com
2. *Time For A New Role,* Stan Hinden Prime Times 5 January 1999.
3. *Corporate transformation without crisis,* Jonathan D. Day and Michael Jung, McKinsey Quarterly, 2000 Number 4.
4. *Working after Retirement: When it Pays Off,* APA Monitor, APA Monitor, November p.10, 1999.
5. *Hoping for a Long Life? Optimism May Help,* Toshihiko Maruta, MD, Robert C. Colligan, PhD, Michael Malinchoc, MS, and Kenneth P. Offord, MS. Mayo Clinic Proceedings, February 2000, pp. 140 – 143.
6. Employee Benefit Research Institute, (EBRI).
7. *Heart & Soul: the impact of corporate and individual values on business*, by Des Dearlove and Stephen J. Coomber.
8. Author interview.

INDEX